THE
SINKING
MIDDLE
CLASS

THE
SINKING
MIDDLE
CLASS

A Political History

Revised second edition

David Roediger

Haymarket Books
Chicago, IL

This edition published in 2022 by
Haymarket Books
P.O. Box 180165
Chicago, IL 60618
773-583-7884
www.haymarketbooks.org
info@haymarketbooks.org

ISBN: 978-1-64259-705-9

Distributed to the trade in the US through Consortium Book Sales and
Distribution (www.cbsd.com) and internationally through Ingram Publisher Services International (www.ingramcontent.com).

This book was published with the generous support of Lannan Foundation and Wallace Action Fund.

Special discounts are available for bulk purchases by organizations and
institutions. Please call 773-583-7884 or email info@haymarketbooks.
org for more information.

Cover photo of home foundations on a newly paved cul-de-sac captured
by aerial drone, © Getty images. Cover design by Eric Kerl.

Printed in Canada by union labor.

Library of Congress Cataloging-in-Publication data is available.

10 9 8 7 6 5 4 3 2 1

And then perhaps this misery of class-prejudice will fade away, and we of the sinking middle class—the private schoolmaster, the half-starved free-lance journalist, the colonel's spinster daughter . . . the jobless Cambridge graduate, the ship's officer without a ship, the clerks, the civil servants, the commercial travelers, and the thrice-bankrupt drapers in the country towns—may sink without further struggles into the working class where we belong, and probably when we get there it will not be so dreadful as we feared, for, after all, we have nothing to lose but our aitches.

—GEORGE ORWELL, journalist and socialist

CONTENTS

PREFACE

My childhood taught me that the middle class could be both a site of extreme misery and the location for labor militancy. That upbringing made it logical that I would write this book, questioning as it does the idea that the middle class ought to be saved as an unambiguously good thing in US society and proposing that the practice of separating it, as a category, from the working class should be abandoned.

My grandfather on my father's side had a "good working-class job," a concept that has decreasing meaning to young people as unions dwindle. He worked in a quarry in a strongly unionized area. Three of his sons had similar blue-collar jobs, in printing, electrical work, and pipe fitting. My dad bucked that trend. Clever and good with numbers, he took a white-collar job at the quarry after naval service in World War II. Being employed in the office meant he was not in the union. He kept the books in the company's headquarters, right next to where limestone was crushed. He shared office space with the quarry's owner and his son, the company's heir apparent. In the next room, several other clerks and technical workers toiled. The owners came and went at will; my dad clocked in and out. The owners showily kept copies of *Playboy* on their desks. My dad increasingly smuggled in whiskey bottles, having just enough unsupervised time, and for a while enough wits, to drink while doing a thankless, demanding job scrutinized by two bosses, each not ten yards away. That setup helped to kill him before age fifty. The owners dressed expensively in what would later be called business casual attire. My dad literally wore white collars, spending a fair amount to signal success. He was upwardly mobile. Nevertheless, materially, and most of the time spiritually, he fared far less well than his relatives in the skilled trades. He held a working-class job that required a middle-class costume and carried with it specific sets of sadnesses.

My mother, orphaned by age five, lost her mother after the birth of her twin brothers, and her father—together with his substantial income from a very good working-class job as a unionized railroad worker—in a work accident. Raised by a grandmother and two aunts, she came from a family that also rose to the middle class and declined materially. One aunt processed accounts for a coal company; the other was a longtime telephone operator, a job eventually unionized and waged rather than salaried, but nevertheless carrying requirements of education and diction that placed it in a contradictory and highly gendered class location. Those mentors made sure that my mom studied for two years in a teacher's college before she reached nineteen. She had taught grade school for a quarter century before she graduated from college, taking a course whenever she could. She made even less money than my dad. The professional organization that she joined saw teaching as a respectable middle-class profession. It arrayed itself against unions and strikes until nearby work stoppages by militant unions attracted raises and imitators. By mid-career—she taught forty-nine years—my mother was a local union and strike leader. It was only then that she secured something like what was considered a middle-class income.

The association of the middle-class job with misery and working-class struggles with forward motion thus came very early to me, certainly before I knew anything of the exact terminology. A particularly painful early memory was of an extended family fishing trip designed, I now realize, to remove my dad from the fact that had he not taken vacation, he would have been expected to work during a labor dispute at the quarry. Not unconnected to this mix was the direction of my own political maturation during the anti-war and Black freedom movements, during which I continually found my way to currents emphasizing the role of the labor movement in social transformations.

None of this made for sustained consideration of the middle class. I thought of college teaching as a working-class job. My university work remained insecure into my mid-thirties and low-paid enough for another decade and more that family and friends with good union jobs wondered at the folly of academic work. My own fortunes brightened as universities decided to overpay a few designated "star" faculty at the same time that they imposed neoliberal austerity, underpaying the rest of those teaching and increasing insecurity in employment. Such changes hardly altered the fact that that seeing academic labor as middle class contributed to making faculty vapid and powerless. Over the course of my long career, it became clearer to me that universities were soul-killing places to work. Moreover, my research came to focus partly on labor history and working-class studies, fields whose attention to the middle class often stops at the worried observation that far too many of us who are really working class are bamboozled into middle-class self-identification. This book comes out of reflection on such bamboozling, particularly in US politics. However, the work of researching it convinced me that middle-class consciousness among working-class people is a deeply complex matter, rooted in material experiences, including ones of extraordinary misery, as well as in getting fooled by ideologues and advertisers and bribed by petty privileges.

I became interested in the middle class in the early 1990s with the extraordinary rise of political appeals to "save the middle class," largely from the Democratic side. At the time, my writing mostly tackled the history of the "white worker," a potent pairing of words that disfigured thinking about class in the long run of US history. But as I wrote, the ascending Clinton wing of the Democratic Party released a raft of appeals to the presumptively white middle class into the hot air of presidential politics. It did so in such a way as to loosely pair emphases on the middle class with less frequent but disturbing appeals to an explicitly "white working class." The problem of placating the right-leaning "Reagan Democrat," learned about almost ethnographically from focus group interviews amplifying his worst racist impulses, became the great necessity for "progressive" electoral politics. The formula ultimately offered little to constituencies of color—a stance its advocates adopted on the grounds that to do so would risk electoral defeats caused by an alienated white middle class. This dovetailed nicely with appeals to the latter, not in terms of concrete pro-worker policies, but instead in terms of listening to racialized complaints about welfare, taxes, and crime.

I began thinking about this book project more than a dozen years ago and contracted with OR Books for it shortly thereafter. Several new books of mine have appeared since then, while this one languished. In part, this reflects the fact that I increasingly find short books harder to write. Some of my other work was tied to anniversaries—for example, the sesquicentennial of emancipation in the United States—and

I consequently gave them priority. More importantly though, the task proved difficult for me as a historian who had seldom strayed beyond 1940 and whose knowledge of the literature and sources on the middle class had to be built from the ground. Perhaps the research, and especially the writing, had to proceed slowly for autobiographical, emotional reasons gestured toward above. Over time, the research itself became fascinating in unexpected ways, especially as I began to move past recent electoral politics and to attempt a longer history of the varied middle classes. I less and less wanted it to end.

Before turning to acknowledging those who helped me to finish the project, a word is in order about the differences between this edition of *The Sinking Middle Class* and the prior 2020 one. The book originated from a particular alarm about the way in which a centrist political discourse regarding the white middle class sidelined issues of racial justice and displaced more robust discussion of class. I relied on the 2020 presidential race as a logical time to conclude its writing. Thus it is unsurprising that electoral matters loom large in both its structure and its details. There's no escaping that, nor is there a desire to do so. However, in discussing the book after its publication, during the urgency of the vote itself and the subsequent Trumpian misadventures attending the transfer of power, the context of the book threatened at times to overcome the content. This edition strives to be relevant not only in its moment but also years after. It creates space for the several insights generated by hard historical research reaching far beyond contemporary electoral politics. While still treating the middle class and elections, and specifically the remarkable role of Democratic strategist Stanley Greenberg in pulling US politics to the right, it now arrives more quickly at matters that proved harder to pull out in press interviews on the book: the compelling evidence that the United States is not now and seldom has been a middle-class nation; the pivotal contributions of the left to thinking about the middle class; and, most critically, the argument that the middle class must be understood as a site of precarity and misery, not simply of fulfillment and privilege. The new edition also spells out the connections of middle-class politics to neoliberalism that were clearer in my own mind than on the pages of the first edition.

Through long delays, my excellent editor at OR, Colin Robinson, remained encouraging while also leaving room for the time needed to rethink matters. This book would not exist without him. It benefited from editorial assistance at OR from Amanda Bartlett and Emma Ingrisani. Thanks also to Anthony Arnove at Haymarket Books for encouraging this second edition and the idea that the book might be recast for its reappearance, and to Ashley Smith for acute editorial advice.

Time to write has been generously provided by the University of Illinois's Program for Research in the Humanities Fellowship, the Center on Democracy in a Multiracial Society Fellowship at the same university, the Distinguished Visiting Fellow Award at the Center on Sustainable Futures at the University of South Carolina, and generous course releases and research funds provided in connection with the Foundation Distinguished Professorship at the University of Kansas. Shorter-term fellowships at Queen Mary University of London, Hobart and William Smith Colleges, the University of Iowa, and New York University's Department of Social and Cultural Analysis also allowed me to share and develop ideas. At the University of Illinois, the Working-Class History Group provided sustained opportunities to hear and share ideas, as has the Place, Race, and Space Seminar at the

Hall Center for the Humanities at the University of Kansas. Librarians at the University of Illinois, University of Kansas, and the Bentley Library at the University of Michigan were especially helpful.

Particularly formative discussions of my work on this book took place at the Million Artists Group in St. Paul's East Side Freedom Library; at the colloquium "Whiteness: The Meaning of a Racial, Social, and Legal Construct" at Emory University's James Weldon Johnson Institute and the Carter Presidential Library; at the John Hope Franklin Institute at Duke University; at Brown University in public conversation with the remarkable Tricia Rose; at the Kansas City Mid-America Arts Alliance; at the Du Bois Sesquicentennial Seminar at the University of Texas; at the Fairfield University American Studies Annual Lecture; at the Walter Rodney Lecture at Atlanta University; at the California American Studies Conference at Long Beach State University; at the St. Louis University American Studies Lecture; at the Swedish Association of American Studies in Stockholm; at the conferences of the Working-Class Studies Association; at the Race, Whiteness, and Indigeneity conference of the National Indigenous Research and Knowledges Network in Surfers Paradise, Queensland, Australia; at the Historical Materialism conferences in New York, Toronto, and London; and at the Rethinking White Societies Conference at the University of the Free State, Bloemfontein, South Africa.

After the completion of the book, a number of appearances on radio and television, as well as videoconferences and talks, helped me greatly in defining what I want to emphasize in this edition. Venues included the Economics Club at University of Missouri–Kansas City, the Marxist Education Project, the Department of African and African Diaspora Studies at University of Texas, the UAW Region

9 Council on Equity, Normandale Community College, the Mediatech Group in Bologna, and Yale Public Humanities. Among interlocutors were Matt Jacobson, Clarrie Pope, John Kendall Hawkins, Judy Ancel, Sasha Lilley, Ashin Rattansi, Chauncey DeVega, Douglas Storm, August Nimtz, John W. W. Zeiser, Allen Ruff, Megan Brown, George Yancy, and Kieran Knutson.

The book benefits greatly from editorial and blogger feedback from pieces appearing in the *Los Angeles Review of Books*, *Verso Blog*, *Critical Race and Whiteness Studies* (Australia), the *American Philosophical Association Newsletter on Philosophy and the Black Experience*, *CounterPunch*, *New Politics*, *Against the Current*, *Journal of American Ethnic History*, *Cultural Critique*, and *Historical Materialism*.

Among many colleagues and friends contributing ideas and critiques, special thanks go to Tim Engles, Ludwin Molina, Shawn Alexander, Roderick Ferguson, May Fu, Rebecca Hill, Robert Warrior, Andrew Zimmerman, John Abromeit, Brendan Roediger, Minkah Makalani, Donovan Roediger, Zachary Sell, Sterling Stuckey, Neil Roos, John Beck, Tom Klug, Graham Cassano, and Peter Linebaugh. Hannah Bailey and Zach Madison provided excellent research assistance. I chaired the Department of American Studies at the University of Kansas while writing and could not have so easily done both without the work of office manager Terri Rockhold. The influence of my colleague, partner, and sometimes coauthor Elizabeth Esch is present throughout.

1

LANGUAGES OF CLASS AND THE EXHAUSTION OF POLITICAL IMAGINATION

By the late 1990s, I sat through numerous sessions where well-known national pollsters instructed labor leaders to replace the words *working class* with *middle class*.

—JANE McALEVEY, organizer

A friend who drives buses tells me that in the break room where workers decompress between routes, management puts up signs naming things not to talk about: politics, vaccines, global warming, religion. However, class and union don't rise to the status of the forbidden, even as drivers talk constantly about work, shifts, pay, managers, and customers. The contemporary United States is something like that break room, both in its rising concern with issues of labor and safety, and in its lack of a strong vocabulary of class and of institutions capable of defending working-class lives. Class and inequality remain private matters, with those of us thinking we are succeeding to an unseemly extent and those sure we are succeeding too little both having reasons to fall silent. We go long stretches without hearing a politician

utter the words "working class," and the poor are seldom
with us when laws get made.

The sole exception to this American reticence to discuss
class forms the subject of this book. The "middle class" has,
since the Cold War, endlessly attracted attention as the re-
pository of US virtue and as what that nation can give to the
world. For the last thirty years, "saving the middle class"
has served as a fully bipartisan lodestar of electoral politics,
even as middle layers of income and wealth have declined
dramatically in their fortunes, especially in comparison to
those at the top.

Lacking a sophisticated language of class, the United
States sees appeals to the middle class supplant calls for
justice. The ends of election campaigns feature Democrats
making modest populist demands like the expansion of
Obamacare or rejiggering student debt in the name of the
middle class, while more extreme right-wing populist demands like Donald Trump's misnamed "middle-class tax
cuts" come from across the political aisle. We learn almost by
osmosis that moments of political frisson unfold under the
banner of saving the middle class—so much so that at times
Barack Obama toyed with connecting "middle class" and
class warfare, claiming the mantle of "warrior for the middle
class." Some Republicans responded by charging that any
talk of class, even of the middle class, pandered to dangerous
social radicalism; however, the attraction of vote-catching
among the middle proved too strong to allow much movement in this direction. In social movements, especially organized labor, appeals to the middle class so seem the only
game in town for talking about inequality and rights that we
get, for example, whole campaigns against repressive labor
laws conducted in the name of the middle class.[1]

The Sinking Middle Class argues that this tendency to read the class experience of the United States by imagining a social structure based on a romanticized middle class inflated in its numbers, homogeneity, and importance serves us poorly. The book attempts to show historically how, especially over the last one hundred years, we got into this mess in thinking about class. The chapters below elaborate on the stories of the historic trajectory of the class structure of the US; of the attempts of elites to aggrandize and flatter a middle class for plutocratic, anti-labor, and nationalist purposes; of the connections of the middle class to dominant systems of racial and gender relations; of the attempts of the left to understand the middle classes; and of the increasing vogue for "saving the middle class" as the key to electoral politics. Only at length can this material receive textured elaboration, but it is nevertheless worthwhile to offer some immediate, if brief, clarity as to the book's standpoint regarding class, even if it involves allowing generalizations to outrun evidence for the moment. Such directness is necessary in order to avoid confusion from the very outset in a book that both argues that the levels of middle-class identification in the US harmfully distill the results of defeats of working-class movements, and nevertheless holds that we cannot move forward without taking seriously those many people in various social positions who consider themselves middle class.

The cult of the middle class does provide a rare site where we hear the word "class" spoken in the United States, but it does so at the cost of occluding any rounded and useful understanding of the concept itself. In particular, the large part of life most of us spend having others control our time, motions, and (sometimes) emotions remains best accounted for by classic theories of class formation—Marxist ones, to be sure, but also those growing from the writings of Émile Durkheim and Max Weber—that emphasize relations among productive property, lack thereof, and labor. The presence of what Karl Marx called "a class which possesses nothing but the ability to work"—a working class—becomes harder to discern when most of the self-identified middle class has a car, some a house, and a few a boat. They could divest themselves of those and postpone selling labor for a time, though in many cases something as elemental as a health care would soon be at risk, and the class relation of landlord and tenant would often still apply. For most of the self-described middle class, the reality of needing a wage or salary would assert itself within months, as we see when health crises devastate families.[2]

This materialist approach to class leads to the conclusion that there is no singular middle class, but only middle *classes*. C. Wright Mills, esteemed as the greatest sociologist of the US middle class, insisted that it was the middle classes he studied. I follow him in that, if only to register that the senior partner joint-owner of a law firm and his army of paralegals cannot plausibly be placed in the same social category—he by virtue of his property, and they by virtue of their dress and intellectual labor. Projections of a middle class encompassing 90 percent and upward of population are based largely on self-identification, but even when researchers develop their own "objective" criteria for who is middle class, they throw together people experiencing wildly different social relations in their working lives. Important generalizations about middle-class voting behavior rest on slapdash categories driven by what data is most (or earliest) available—for example, those having attended college or those making over $50,000 a year.[3] Or we learn a person's class from their zip code or their shopping—Target versus Walmart.[4]

In assessing the pre-nineteenth-century United States, the analytical imprecision of leaving out the critical connection of property and labor matters less than it does for the more recent past—if only because in the earlier US centuries most white heads of household were self-employed, working farms or in craft enterprises they owned. But by the late nineteenth century, the employed white-collar middle class had begun to surpass the farmers, entrepreneurs, and free professionals. When we retroactively attach the term "middle class"—few living in the nineteenth-century US identified in that way—to both the employed and self-employed in that period, the connection between labor and productive property becomes obscured.

Insistence on seeing class as made at the point of production, and by what impels working people to that point, leads in the chapters below to sustained consideration of the shifting and situational line between the working class and the middle class. One purpose of the book is, then, to chip away at the unthinking acceptance of middle-class identity by those paid, driven, and surveilled as workers. The ways in which such identification is coerced and cajoled by elites receive emphasis. In politics, for example, the current choice is not so much between presenting demands as a middle-class subject or as a working-class one, but between being intelligible (by doing the former) and ignored (in the latter case). I identify with the lament that Jane McAlevey sighs in the chapter's epigraph; indeed, it burdens us that so many imbibe an understanding of class that leads away from identifying the causes, and the solutions, of their miseries as significantly located away from the workplace. Such an understanding leads to individual solutions to social ills and misses the collective power of workers. It would be a great and liberating thing if every social worker, every person with a good union job, every clerk, every chemist, and every teacher awoke tomorrow thinking of themselves as working-class people holding interests in common with other workers.

That said, for at least three reasons, the middle class appears in these pages both as an ideological creation and, nevertheless, as a formation worthy of serious consideration and even sympathetic attention. The first of these reasons flows from the fact that consciousness is itself important. Socialist thinkers realized, from early in their attempts to organize labor in factories and transportation—the beating heart of those they saw as key to labor's advance—that often such employees did not see themselves as a working class and certainly did not actively imagine themselves as bound to produce social transformation. The celebrated distinction between the working class as a "class in itself" (involved objectively in an exploitative relationship with capital) and a "class for itself" (acting to emancipate itself and society) came more from twentieth-century Marxist thinkers than from Marx himself. The distinction reflected an optimism that daily experiences could radicalize workers. It further articulated a knowledge that at times collective actions turned such experiences into something qualitatively greater.[5] There is little reason not to approach the white-collar worker with similar patience and confidence.

Secondly, there are considerable sectors of the labor force who, in structural terms, are entrepreneurs or otherwise self-employed and uncontroversially middle class. Still others—the plumber who sometimes works as an independent contractor with apprentices and at others for a wage; or the strata of management that is well remunerated but closely bossed and without independent decision-making power—are in what the sociologist Erik Olin Wright calls "contradictory class locations," significantly embodying some elements of a middle-class experience and some of a working-class one.[6]

Finally and most importantly, if hyper-identification with the middle class by workers has in many ways been manipulated by elites, is has also sustained itself over a long period with the active consent and participation of tens of millions of working-class people, including many who identify situationally: that is, sometimes as middle class and others as working class. While a sense of accomplishment and ascent underlies many claims to being middle class, *The Sinking Middle Class* unearths the considerable extent to which white-collar proletarians faced some class-based miseries earlier than their blue-collar counterparts, especially with regard to the management of their personalities, the extent and character of their overwork, and the depth of their consumer indebtedness. To dismiss middle class testimonies as only the products of ideology is therefore to miss class grievances. For all those reasons, the goal here is both to deconstruct middle class identities and to understand them as having material dimensions.

PEAK MIDDLE-CLASS POLITICS: THE RECENT PAST

At the intersection of Google searching, journalism, and comedy lies a new but already played-out form of social criticism. Search engines assemble sound bites in which every conservative talk show host, or everyone in the "liberal" media," or every leading Republican politician, or every prominent Democrat says more or less the same hackneyed thing. The echoing comments, put together equally well by

Sean Hannity's or Stephen Colbert's staff, both imply a conspiracy of "talking points" being foisted onto the public and an utter lack of substance and conviction in what is being parroted. No such montage would lead to more revealing and plentiful results than one constructed around a search for the phrases "defending the middle class" or "saving the middle class." Indeed, that rallying cry crosses the partisan political divide. Democrats and Republicans vie for the lead in terms of promises to stand up for the putatively noble but chronically fragile middle strata of the class structure. Both parties praise the middle class as the broken heart of the nation and hold that only they can mend it.

Such insistent appeals to a middle class so distended and ill defined that it cannot be associated with any particular set of demands have so come to dominate US politics that it is hard to imagine presidential elections without them. Nevertheless, as this book argues, "save the middle class" vagaries had a distinct origin in national politics: during Bill Clinton's 1992 presidential campaign. Though drawing on older anti-labor initiatives and popular language, especially as developed to serve Cold War aims, the cult of the middle class as election fodder is only reaching its thirtieth birthday. Even so, this means that a majority of the current electorate has cast ballots only in campaigns utterly dominated by vacuous appeals to the middle class.[7] *The Sinking Middle Class* aims to show that it is possible to imagine a politics that is not so overwhelmingly electoral, not so eager to embrace myths about the national past, not so wedded to unserious class analysis that begins from a cobbled-together middle, and not so disastrous in furthering the inequalities to which many who think of themselves as middle class fall victim.

The 2012 presidential election best captures the relentless political appeals to the supposed center of the social structure. That election serves, therefore, as a good point of departure for a book seeking to explain how we get stuck in such political monomania and what we lose in our inability to move past it. In February 2012, the political scientist Cal Jillson concluded that President Barack Obama had "settled on a message of middle-class support." Jillson correctly predicted that the Obama strategists, knowing they "were on to something," would be systematically pursuing the issue throughout the campaign. Obama, who before that point had hardly been silent regarding his love for the middle class, redoubled his commitment by declaring himself a "warrior" on its behalf in pursuing reelection. Practically the first act of his first presidential term had been to set up the Middle Class Task Force, led by Vice President Joe Biden. Charged with getting "the backbone of this country up and running again," the initiative identified a "strong middle class" with a "strong America." To speak even louder about those in the middle class in 2012, Obama insisted, was not about "class warfare." Instead, it concerned the "nation's welfare." Obama argued, first at a small high school gym in Kansas, then to the nation, that the "make or break moment for the middle class" defined the stakes of the election. By July 2012, a typical short Obama campaign speech would feature more than a dozen invocations of the glorious, precarious "middle class."[8]

The Republicans faced the difficult fact that polls showed Obama clearly besting GOP candidate Mitt Romney in terms of being trusted to look out for middle-class economic interests. Reporting on the number of Romney's lavish homes and estates did not help matters. Romney's decision was to match the Democrats' emphasis. He insisted that after almost a full term in office, with increasing misery among the middle class, the Obama administration could hardly claim to be effectively battling for forgotten Americans. Romney drew on "class" appeals similar to those of the Democrats, while he declared initiatives like the Obama task force to have been calamities that led to further erosion of middle-class standards. The two presidential campaigns even shared a definition of middle class: those whose annual income was less than $250,000—sometimes Romney mentioned $300,000—a category that applied to upward of 96 percent of the population. The 96 percent was not so much a class as it was a nation; to wage political war on its behalf seemed good patriotic politics.[9] Those hovering between partisan cheerleading and political journalism spread the word, from Lou Dobbs's slightly earlier *War on the Middle Class*, on the right, to the liberalism of Stanley Greenberg and James Carville's almost-parodic *It's the Middle Class, Stupid.*[10]

Here was a "middle" that included pretty much everybody, leaving out only a relative handful of the fabulously rich and, if taken literally, nobody in poverty. Obama deftly liquidated the issue of how a country with such astronomical rates of poverty could be almost all middle class. He defined the middle class as "not only folks who are currently [in] the middle class, but also people who aspire to be in the middle class." Thus, he continued, "[w]e're not forgetting the poor." At the same time, political rhetoric about the losses of the middle class tempted the rival camps to offer more precise, if contradictory, definitions, at least in communications within the campaigns. Indeed, Obama's chief economist held in January 2012 that the middle class was no longer a majority in the United States. It had dwindled, the adviser said, from 50 percent of the population to 42 percent over the last four decades, though some surveys placed the figure of those still self-identifying as middle class at double that. Romney's camp predictably emphasized that if there were a decline, much of it had occurred under Obama.[11] An appeal to the middle class, political scientist Mark Sweet wrote, worked because "most people describe themselves as middle class." The political wisdom that winning the middle-class vote predicted electoral victories could hardly have failed, so long as almost all the electorate could be wrangled into that group.[12]

However, the fiction that such sleight of hand constituted political analysis suffered from the fact that both parties had roughly equal access to it. This narrative contributed little to the task of assembling a coalition of voters from among the particularized factions of the 96 percent. The 2012 campaign thus captured in miniature a compelling and confounding array of contemporary realities and illusions about the middle class. The questions of whether a "class" can encompass virtually the whole of society, of whether it can persistently be described as the moral center of a society and nevertheless as hopelessly adrift, and of whether it can be defined sociologically by its own aspirations and illusions came squarely before us well before 2012, and they remain there today.

Citigroup analysts, thinking in 2011 about investments rather than elections, dismissed the idea of a middle-class society altogether. As political journalist Don Peck put it in asking, "Can the middle class be saved?," their study found that

> America was composed of two distinct groups: the rich and the rest. For the purposes of investment decisions, the second group didn't matter; tracking its spending habits or worrying over its savings rate was a waste of time. All the action in the American economy was at the top: the richest 1 percent of households earned as much each year

as the bottom 60 percent put together; they possessed as much wealth as the bottom 90 percent.

The politicians professed that the middle class was absolutely central, while the bankers found it at best marginal.[13]

Even as it registers changes, the handy-to-the-center-and-right emphasis on the middle class has persisted in politics. Ten months before the 2016 election, the labor writer and political analyst Harold Meyerson predicted that we would shortly see a presidential campaign that was not fixed upon winning the middle class. He added that this would be unprecedented—a claim that was incorrect, given that no national elections had centered the middle class prior to the 1990s. With pollsters as his sources, Meyerson held that the middle class has been so devastated under political leaders claiming to champion its interests that only a dwindling percentage of voters identified with the label. Shifts in such a direction certainly did occur just before the 2016 election, when Pew Charitable Trusts research found the difference in numbers between those choosing "middle class" and "lower class" from the menu of identities to be insignificant.[14] For a brief time in 2016, both Hillary Clinton and Donald Trump hesitated to specify the middle class as their prize constituency and guiding star.

Nevertheless, Meyerson's prediction did not materialize. Ironically, it was the avowedly socialist candidate, Bernie Sanders, who most insistently positioned himself as the candidate of, and in some measure from, the middle class. His *The Speech: On Corporate Greed and the Decline of Our Middle Class* sold briskly in his 2016 campaign. It earned so much in royalties that during the 2020 campaign he suffered attacks for being a multimillionaire with lapsed credentials to speak for the middle class.[15] Sanders followed Obama and Romney in ballparking "below $250,000" annual family income as the benchmark of middle-class membership, though mostly limiting the metric's use to details of tax policy.[16] Just as the recent campaigns against anti-union legislation in Michigan and Indiana conducted themselves as defenses of the middle class, with perhaps an added nod to defending "working families," the Democratic Party's left defended the middle class as it attempted to contest inequality. To complete the confusion, opinion polls showed more and more people identifying no longer as middle class but specifically as working class—by some accounts the greatest percentage in recent US history. This change, registering decline of "middle class" living standards and broader resentments, seemed a dream come true for radicals like myself. The problem was that those newly identifying as workers sometimes moved to the right when doing so, becoming Trump supporters and rallying to an embittered sense that immigrants, not corporations, had pushed them downward. Such developments demand a book that raises questions about listening to the white working class even as it focuses on discourses about saving the middle class.[17]

Both Clinton and Trump picked up "saving the middle class" in a more desultory way than Sanders, but they warmed significantly to it at times. The former sometimes conveyed both the grandeur and peril of middle-class life in pledging to (re)create a "healthy middle class," and it was particularly during more populist moments of her campaign that she tended to invoke the term. The fiercest assertions of a populist middle-class message in Clinton's campaign came from Sanders himself. After losing the nomination, he stumped on Clinton's behalf, including in Michigan venues her campaign ignored. "What this campaign is about," he told a crowded rally for her at the United Automobile Workers hall in Dearborn, "is the survival of the middle class." Trump campaigned on the idea of a "middle-class tax cut," while lacing the term "working families"—one that for me conjured up child labor when spoken by him—into his tax reform rhetoric. Trump's campaign was often one of awkward silences on class. While capable of uttering the phrases "middle class" and even "working class" at opportune times, he never tried to keep himself from bragging of his 1 percent status. Overemphasizing his self-made success and de-emphasizing his debts, he courted being seen as filthy rich, if also allegedly close to rough-and-tumble construction workers. Meanwhile, only rarely did Clinton rehearse economic worries she experienced growing up. Pundits nevertheless clearly saw the race as one for the votes of a declining middle class.[18]

In the early run-up to the 2020 election, Joe Biden vaulted to front-runner status by persistently recycling Obama's "warrior for the middle class" rhetoric. Elizabeth Warren's campaign trail book, *This Fight Is Our Fight: The Battle to Save America's Middle Class*, is her third book with "middle class" in either its title or subtitle. Meanwhile, Trump got to, or perhaps had to, campaign on his middle-class tax cut, however skewed to the rich it turned out to be.[19] Popular media, meanwhile, feeds obsessions with the salvation of the middle class, suggesting that women, Starbucks, and the wisdom of bowling-alone critic Robert Putnam just might get it done.[20]

A fair question remains: So what? Some will say that the United States simply is and always has been a nation filled with people unswervingly identifying as middle class, and that, even if they are wrong objectively to do so, politicians need to meet them around their senses of self. Others might allow that the middle class is poorly defined, fractured, and hyper-identified with white citizens in the public mind but hold that if appealing to it strengthens the chances even a little of electing a middle-of-the-road Democrat in the mold of Clinton or Biden over someone worse, the ambiguities are worth it. Among the young and not-so-young are many who think that the Democratic Party is about to be transformed into a vehicle for winning democratic socialism around the ideas of Sanders, a presidential candidate who championed demands that he identified with the middle class in a way that presumed too automatically that they can be made to equal approximately "universal" ones, serving those at the bottom in terms of wealth. The demand for free college for all, for example, is worthwhile in many ways, but devilish details and compromises will determine whether it funds mostly poor and working people or their better-resourced and credentialed peers. Terming it a middle-class demand will not clarify how it takes shape.[21]

Over the last thirty years, this book argues, self-serving, vague, and often empty political rhetoric regarding "saving the middle class" has provided the language for rightward political motion, finding its way even into unions. Put forward first by the Democrats, it has debased how we understand social divisions in the United States and sidelined meaningful discussions of justice in both class and racial terms. It has called up older, principally Cold War, usages of "middle class" beyond party politics, as a vehicle for national aggrandizement, casting the US as a beacon to the developing middle class globally. Such appeals falsely identify the US as always and exceptionally a middle-class nation and lead away from any discussion of social difference and oppression, from all that is miserable in middle-class life, and from the actual role of US empire in structural inequality in the world. In the last decade, the rise of an allied language tying political possibilities to the "white working class" has done much the same work in telling us why dramatic social change is impossible given the supposed, and supposedly understandable, defensiveness of a group named by a collective noun no better defined than the "middle class."

To insist on these points is not to imply some golden age that we should yearn to recapture. The languages of mainstream electoral politics have never offered more than very loosely drawn conceptions of class, and still less that is useful on race and class at their intersection. The people, the yeomen, Americans, free labor, the progressives, the forgotten men, and the Silent Majority, busily realizing Manifest Destinies, making New Deals, and traversing New Frontiers—such languages left all of these categories much unspecified in the interests of putting together wins at the polls. However, they did so in eras when electoral politics did not so thoroughly define the universe of all things political and preoccupy everyday life for so many—while fully alienating an equally massive number who often conclude that they couldn't care less about that thing called politics. Prior elections gave those in the United States a language vaguely defining and practically liquidating class every four years, not every day of the year. The story of the great modern Democratic conjuring trick of making the unspecified but clearly white middle class define the limits of possibility along austere neoliberal lines thus allows us to consider how the media and the candidates make such class terminology both a series of platitudes and a seemingly exciting insider's argot underpinning liberal warnings against going too far.

The very way that we see the working class narrows when electoral victory on a middle-class platform is the watchword. We struggle to remember those who choose not to vote, or who are prevented from doing so, as recently arrived and/or undocumented, as felons, as workers frequently moving around—that is, a substantial chunk of poor and working people in the United States—when the assumption is that politics largely equals voting and talking about elections. In that sense the very composition of the working class is obscured, not only by politicians shoehorning so many working people into a simplified middle-class category, but also because those most urgently needing to organize live outside electoral politics. We lavish attention on the split, close in the recent past, between the Republican and Democratic votes of working-class whites, searching for deep meaning in small fluctuations while a larger share of this group does not vote. In pursuing electoral analyses, even radicals follow the example of TV pundits in their reliance on the most quickly available voting data to construct simplistic definitions of class that have little to do with social relations. Thus income—above or below $50,000 a year—or education—college or not—somehow define a class relationship.[22]

Donald Trump helped assure that passionate embraces of electoral politics and its attendant drumbeat of saving the middle class seem urgent and meaningful. It has proven impossible to argue that he is just a garden-variety representative of one wing of the elite. Whether it is that he has presented a fascist threat, or that he is just a loose, racist talker emboldening other racists, a sexual predator, a packer of courts with reactionary judges, a jailer of children, and/or an authoritarian eager to suspend civil liberties, Trump so alarmed us that politics as usual on the liberal side seems compelling, even if we'd never otherwise speak of the middle class as the key to forward motion. But in many ways, *The Sinking Middle Class* argues, the Trump ascendency remains tied to the limits and failures of the Bill Clinton moment, a long, continually failing stretch of political impoverishment organized around silences enforced by a specific grammar of saving a middle class without addressing the illusions and miseries surrounding it.

THE BOOK AND ITS CHAPTERS

Appeals to saving the middle class thus serve us poorly in forwarding even reformist politics and keep us from dreaming beyond them. The book's argument to this effect lies in several parts beyond the political ones already discussed. One is that the United States is not a middle-class country, past or present, and to see it as such inexorably draws us into an "American exceptionalist" mythology—that sees the United States as both the most free country and the one best serving ordinary people. This assumption has long been dear to elites, who have helped to inflate the middle-class category. A second focus is on the content of long radical, and even liberal, traditions of critiquing the middle class as a problem and of showing that there are reasons why reactionaries often fare well in courting the middle class and the left historically does not. The book argues that we ought not throw that body of thought away lightly. Strands of it and insights from newer work move us to a third theme that portrays the middle class in the United States not simply as formed in either relative advantage or in fear of downward mobility, but as miserable even while able to claim middle-class status.

The chapters and arc of this short book are easily sketched. Four chapters and an afterword follow this introduction. The second, third, and fourth chapters modestly propose that we not save the middle class. They regard the middle class as a problem, indeed a congeries of miseries not defined by a specifiable class location. Chapter 2 contests the notion that the United States is a middle-class nation—available to be saved—either now or over long stretches of its history. The term itself found little use until the last ninety years, and not commonly until the Cold War. Electorally, an obsession with courting the middle class appeared later still, from the 1990s onward at the national level. The strata we might retrospectively call the middle class of the nineteenth century (farmers, free professionals, and shopkeepers) differed utterly from those of the twentieth (clerks, salespeople, employed professionals, and managers). The earlier un-bossed middle class seems a font of manly independence, distinctive by world historical standards. Ideologues can therefore invoke this mostly disappeared set of independent proprietors as the keys to the idea of American exceptionalism, a shining entrepreneurial example to the rest of humanity. The small sliver of entrepreneurs in the present therefore shape imaginations of the middle class, as well as policy, obscuring the reality that most of the self-identified middle class works and not at all independently. Indeed, they are the workers most overseen by supervisors and observed by customers, the employees whose personalities first became fully for sale. Moreover, by overdeveloped world standards, by no means is the present United States a relatively equal society in which a fair share of wealth and income goes to those in the middle.

Chapter 3 captures the sometimes conflicted, hamstrung, and supercilious—but also careful, impassioned, and humane—ways that the left has apprehended the middle class. The chapter makes no extravagant claims for the radical tradition's interventions regarding the middle class, except in comparison to alternative approaches. It starts from Marx's Marxism, noting his impatience with and political distrust of the middle class, except insofar as it was poised to slip into the working class and to be attracted by the labor movement's dynamism. Marx mostly had in mind a nineteenth-century middle class of small property holders and independent professionals, but in later writings he came to briefly glimpse a "new middle class" of paid functionaries of capital—managers, clerks, sales staff, accountants, and other workers around offices. His tendency to define the latter groups as doing "unproductive" work, and to use the same terms to describe them as the ones that named the propertied middle class seen as the enemy of emancipation, imparted confusion and a certain enduring brittleness to left accounts of the middle class. However, twentieth-century Marxists also inherited a fierce need to study and understand the "problem" of the middle class. Beginning from material conditions, they most clearly saw how numerous workers with white collars had become. Especially in Germany (Emil Lederer and the Frankfurt school's efforts to understand the middle class and fascism) and the United States (Lewis Corey, C. Wright Mills, Barbara Ehrenreich, and Erik Olin Wright), the left wrestled with its inherited texts and incredible real-life complexities to produce remarkable insights. In particular, the differences between the "old" self-employed middle class and the "new" salaried one received the most productive attention from radical intellectuals, who also took the study of the middle class into the realm of psychology.

The fourth chapter acknowledges that older emphases on the fall of the middle class are important but insists that it is also the daily misery, and increasingly the sheer impossibility, of middle-class life that ought to command our attention. Quotidian miseries of those surviving in the middle class greatly complicate any political appeals to be their saviors. Middle-class people stood, and stand, in various relations to the production process, and the material experiences uniting them—debt, anxiety, segregation, and personality salesmanship—are hardly worth saving. The so-called decline of the middle class includes falling, to be sure; but before falling, it also involves living in an untenable position, peculiarly alienated at work, indebted, and seeking satisfaction in joyless consumption. The great radical critics of middle-class life who wrote fiction, Herman Melville and James T. Farrell for example, likewise saw middle-class existence as a soul-killing problem and site of precarity even for those living the dream.

Chapter 5 returns to the disfiguring impact of saving-the-middle-class pieties on US politics with which the book began. Explaining the rise of obsessive commitments to saving the middle class, it introduces an unprepossessing figure who is nevertheless sometimes touted, not implausibly, as the central "progressive" figure of the last three dozen years. It sets his genius and his stark limits in the county that made him known. The man is Stanley Greenberg, a formerly left-ish academic who became a centrist Democratic pollster and consultant, especially around the 1992 election. The place is Macomb County, Michigan, a site of former strength of the most conservative region of the United Automobile Workers (UAW). That suburban Detroit county had been the most Democratic one in the nation in 1960. However, its residents had soon broken from such a tradition, acting instead on an attraction to the proto-alt-right and alt-white candidacy of George Wallace and hatred for the peace and multicultural-ist candidacy of George McGovern.

The context included a string of Republican triumphs stretching from 1968 until 1992 and broken only by the failed one-term presidency of Jimmy Carter. The historic voting rights victories of the 1960s added hugely to the potential to register Democrats, to isolate the right in the party, and to construct a Black/labor alliance. But by the early 1970s, capital, reeling from the expenses of war on Southeast Asia and on poverty, insisted on limits to spending, especially for the latter "war" and exported investment and jobs. The Democrats strove to adapt themselves to those neoliberal limits but in doing so risked disappointing workers and civil rights constituencies. Republicans, accustomed to talking about balanced budgets and the dangers of social welfare, proved the much-better neoliberal party in the medium term. Their "Southern strategy" appealed in segregated suburbs as well. Successful at attacking freedom movements by talking about ostensibly nonracial issues like crime, welfare fraud, and taxes, they placed the Democrats in a losing position but did so without direct appeals to a white "middle class."

The project of appealing to the middle class remained available to the Democrats, and specifically to Greenberg, whom the UAW helped bring to Michigan in the 1980s. Transitioning from university teaching and radical political science to consulting, he was tasked with figuring out what had gone wrong and how to bring what was being called the Reagan Democrat back into the fold. Greenberg eventually polled the nearly all-white county and returned frequently, indeed through the 2020 presidential election. He, especially after Bill Clinton discovered and embraced his work, made Macomb County, as seen from its white houses and not its factories, the charmed spot providing the key to election victories. Central to his success was ambiguity. On one hand, Macomb's voters were seen as white and workers, ennobled by their labor and rightly concerned with straitening economic circumstances. On the other, they were to be paid attention as a suburban white middle class, not as trade unionists. Given that there were few economic fixes or even meager labor law reforms on offer, the listening that

Greenberg urged seized on racially coded issues: neighborhood schools, taxes, crime, and welfare, the last two of which
the Clinton administration did deliver on with a vengeance.

The sad genius of Greenberg and Clinton was to be able
to promise to save the middle class—Greenberg's signature
book on Macomb County was *Middle Class Dreams*—by placing a specifically white space at the center of what they called
progressive politics. In order to be saved from integration
and social spending, Macomb County and its unions would
have to accept economic decline and, ultimately, the North
American Free Trade Agreement. Because keeping Macomb
County Democratic had become a top progressive priority,
Black voters would need to abjure far-reaching demands and
accept defeats. Middle-class racial appeals to white workers
became a feature of various returns to Macomb County.

An afterword locates the uncertainty of (talking electorally about) the fate of the middle class in a time of COVID,
the US defeat in Afghanistan, and continuing economic crises that call neoliberalism into question even among elites.
It argues that recent resort, among Democrats, to explaining
Trump's 2016 election as the fault of the "white working
class," the success of the right in mobilizing around American identity, and modest gains in the numbers of people
claiming working-class status portends possible change
yet again in the fortunes of appeals to a supposedly timeless middle class. The recently conjured-up entity of the
white working class bespeaks flux and even desperation. It
includes more or less the same people who had been and
continue to be hailed as the middle class when that suits
Democratic strategists—often the very experts who now ask
us to imagine not the needs of a working class but of whites
within it. Belief that our present crisis is to be remedied by
listening to white workers represents as dead an end as the

attempt to save the middle class. As much as we need to move past the use of the middle class as an empty signifier, white working-class analysis represents no advance. Rhetorically both race conscious and class conscious, it adapts in practice to an electoralism that, like Greenberg's middle-class dreams, discourages substantive policy discussion on those issues. Indeed, Greenberg himself has recently cast matters in terms of winning over a white working class, while not distinguishing it from the middle class with any consistency. So far the shift in rhetoric is fitful, but it does reflect a certain hesitation to believe that old, hollow appeals will work forever in the face of skyrocketing inequality, in the wake of fifty years of neoliberal attacks on wages and on welfare.

The afterword also considers the work of law scholar Joan C. Williams along with a number of other recent academic and political interventions concerning the white working class. It asks how their (auto-)ethnographic gaze manages to see such white workers from a distance as alternately terrifying and understandable—a close match for the expectations of their readers and a foundation for the continuation of politics as usual. The concluding pages query whether there is any "white working class," arguing instead that "white" is bound to get the emphasis when that trifecta of words gets invoked. Similarly effaced is the role of the white, suburban upper middle class as a base for both the pandering to white advantage and the class privilege that occur when progressive politics are premised on courting those referred to as "Biden Republicans."[23] The afterword also weighs whether failures in neoliberalism and a declining US empire are finally creating the conditions in which middle-class appeals will give way. To address the rightward drift of electoral politics in the last thirty years, the afterword concludes, we must break with vagaries regarding saving the middle class and/or paying attention to the white working class. Such a break also requires us to look for clarity in thinking about class beyond electioneering.

A preemptive word or two word is in order. The book argues, as strongly as I know how, that we ought neither to save the middle class nor to pay attention to the white working class. It courts iconoclasm in those regards, but it does not mean to embrace callousness. Certainly many white working people—I grew up with and go home to them—are afraid. They fear "falling" out of the middle class, falling ill in a society that sneers at safety nets, and falling behind on payments. They fear being "replaced" by immigrants and becoming "strangers in their own land," as some informants recently conveyed to the ethnographer Arlie Russell Hochschild.[24] But the land is not "their own," and neither a commitment to saving an indefensible system nor the premising of white workers' human claims on their epidermis will make any of us free, or even secure.

2

THE PRETENSES OF A
MIDDLE-CLASS UNITED STATES

Like the Holy Ghost, the Middle Class relies on faith
rather than empirical evidence of its seemingly immortal
omnipresence.

—BILL ONASCH, Kansas City labor activist

R adicals commonly lament that official society makes it
hard to identify as anything but middle class—a com-
plaint that is peculiarly rife in the United States. It is easy to
suppose that absent such notions we would be much closer
to the sober analysis necessary to define and win meaningful egalitarian goals. But while middle-class identification
might be forsaken situationally, it is far less likely to be abandoned wholesale. Almost every spring for the past thirty-five
years, for example, I have taught a survey class to hundreds
of state university students. In each case, when lecturing on
the history of the middle class, I have asked, "How many
of you are middle class?" Immediately almost every student
listening has raised a hand. Of the fifteen thousand or so
respondents over the years, perhaps fifty have answered my
further question: "So who is not middle class?" The outliers
sometimes said they were working class, more often poor.

One student held, improbably, that he was already a member of the "ruling class," causing others in the University of Minnesota auditorium to ask about his presence there.

At first I thought I could convince, or remind, lots of students that they came from working-class families and would tellingly hint that many of the upper-middle-class jobs they thought they would soon occupy were disappearing. That was mostly an idle wish given the few hours that they heard my lectures and in the context of flagship state university classrooms, themselves incubators of the idea that middle-class aspirations made student debt seem supportable. The legendary Dadaist Julien Torma once aphorized that "Hunger justifies the middle classes." We might now want to add, "So does student debt."[1] And yet among the hundreds of graduate students whom I have also taught, pursuing degrees in mostly leftish disciplines and not discernibly different from undergraduates in terms of socioeconomic background, a majority make at least some claim to working-class identities and often share a lofty disdain for the middle class. Context matters, and things change. In this chapter it is the shifting historical context that shows how poorly "middle-class nation" describes the United States.

UNDEFINABLE AND TENDING TO THE RIGHT

The vexing questions of the size and the composition of the middle class are so variously posed and answered as to make the category a blunt tool for social analysis. In the preceding chapter we encountered the discrepant figures of 42 and 96 percent of the US population fitting within the middle class. Those estimates were offered by presidential advisers paid to know. *CNN Business* recently built a series around the question "What is middle class, anyway?" It offered five headings as possible ways to figure out an answer: income, wealth, consumption, aspiration, and demographics—the last based on a complex matrix, even a flowchart, developed recently by staff at the Federal Reserve Bank of St. Louis. The text under each heading suggests several more approaches. The article counts between 20 and 60 percent of the people as middle class, avoiding the astronomical numbers more often given by not putting a figure to the "aspirations" category.[2]

Problems of definition cannot fail to appear, because the middle class is, at least as theorized to date, not really a class. The greatest US study of the middle class, C. Wright Mills's *White Collar*, tells us as much as early as its subtitle, which announces a study of the "middle classes," plural. Later in the book Mills describes the futility of expecting class-conscious mobilizations from the middle class by pointing out that the middle class is a jammed-together group, one "contradictory in its material interest" and even "dissimilar in ideological illusion." It gets created either in the imaginations of experts studying the middle class or those of men and women claiming membership in it.[3]

The foundational distinction, and confusion, in popular and scholarly attempts to define a middle class lies in whether the label is to be applied by sociologists and pollsters based on set criteria or whether it is a self-sticking one chosen by respondents based on their subjective consciousness of themselves and of the social structure. *CNN Business* had it both ways, holding that it was necessary to "read this" to learn if one is middle class, but also including a subjective category based on aspiration and presumably self-identification. Some recent schemes have identified certain quintiles, for example of income, wealth, or spending, as manifestly middle class. These tend to be the very middle, for example the quintiles straddling the median income. But others categorize wide sectors of society as poor or working class and look for the middle class nearer the top, for example between the fiftieth and ninetieth percentiles.[4]

Because such mechanisms hold the middle class as a constant percentage of the population, they have the advantage of creating easy ways to compare the resources held by those in the middle of the hierarchy of wealth over time. They therefore underpin many of the recent laments for the "shrinking," "hollowing out," "vanishing," or even "lost" middle class, although in fact if the middle class declines in prosperity, the associated quintiles do not disappear at all; only their wealth does. Another twist also sets statistical parameters for middle-class membership by proceeding from median income, but by reckoning that households making between two-thirds and twice the median income are middle class. This method allowed a splashy 2015 Pew Charitable Trusts study to declare that the middle class had reached a "tipping point" on its way to becoming a minority: it had dwindled from 61 percent in 1970 to 50 percent forty-five years later.[5]

The very studies reporting the crisis of the middle class amid growing inequality also at times endorse the idea that in the United States, "if you think you're middle class, you are." Reliance on self-identification helps to generate huge majorities in the US that are middle class—upward of 70, 80, or even 95 percent. Those percentages make the middle class seem a shiny object to political strategists, the place to seek support from voters ranging "from a single, part-time bartender scratching by on $13,000 a year to a suburban power couple pulling in $230,000, or 90 percent of US households in all."[6]

The hottest controversies over the size of the middle class have come from the left, and especially from writer-activists

in the developing field of working-class studies. In reject-
ing the idea that an overwhelming majority of Americans
are members of the middle class, Stony Brook University
economics professor Michael Zweig and labor studies edu-
cator Jack Metzgar offer critiques turning on how the size of
the "middle class" is determined. They point out that surveys in which the term "working class" is absent from the
choices offered to respondents artificially inflate the numbers choosing a middle-class self-identification. Zweig cites
cases in which, in the absence of a working-class alternative, an overwhelming majority choose middle class. With a
working-class category on offer, the proportion choosing to
identify as middle class sometimes drops to less than half.
In the recent past, such trends, documented by Zweig for
two decades, have accelerated. More recent studies show that
the middle class has not only lost wealth but faith in its own
status, and that it is opting to identify in new ways.[7]

Zweig's 2000 book, straightforwardly titled *The Working
Class Majority: America's Best-Kept Secret*, also parts company with the idea that class is simply a matter of self-identification. He argues that the relationship of most wage
earners to an employer or manager puts them objectively
in the working class, their responses to sociological surveys
notwithstanding. Zweig is cautious about determining when
declining conditions of work and pay push certain occupational groups into the working class. Only in his most recent
writings do nurses and teachers register as proletarianized.
Even reckoning so cautiously, Zweig concludes that objectively two-thirds of the labor force is working class and that
subjectively up to half or more at times claim that status.[8]

Meanwhile, the radical journalist Barbara Ehrenreich and
social policy expert John Ehrenreich argue that even members of the professional-managerial class (PMC), which they

alternately call the "professional middle class," have seen a degradation of work that has left many of them outside the middle class.[9] "PMC," like "middle class," amalgamates people in very different social relations within the process of production, indeed in different classes, though it produces some useful insights in doing so. To reify its members into one distinct class works less well now than it did at more foundational moments of its theorization. Such reification becomes particularly counterproductive when left pundits imagine the PMC as not only a class but *the* class we must most oppose in class struggle, and as the source of "identity politics" (the supposed bane of the left). Movements around race, gender, and sexuality are multi-class movements that include many labor radicals, and the disappearance of such movements would not automatically send activists flocking to the labor left.[10]

The plea here is not just for more exactitude in definitions. Real life itself is complicated and inexact. Many of us know someone who once had a good, unionized, working-class job earning thirty-five dollars an hour who now makes only eleven as a "manager" in a big-box store. Or we befriend a farm family holding on to a small amount of valuable land by undertaking waged work providing health insurance. Nevertheless, notions concerning the outsized middle class, spread by many political campaigns, journalists, and even social scientists, ought to provoke challenges. Emphases on the importance of that group help to guarantee that politics is played on a terrain far more congenial to the right (and ultra-right) than to the left. This is true no matter how much some hope that the middle-class 96 percent, posited by the Republican and Democratic Parties (and the latter in particular), will magically transform into the class-conscious 99 percent hoped for by the Occupy movement. Social divides of real importance struggle to emerge when a social category is so distended and when the metaphor comes to seem real and to imply the basic goodness of the system.

Two examples illustrate the costs of the 96 percent metaphor. Where labor rights and the minimum wage are concerned, the 96 percent includes wage workers, their managers, and their employers. Not surprisingly, the glue binding possible coalitions together leaves labor law reform and the fight for a fifteen-dollar minimum wage endlessly deferred and opens space for vaguely drawn and authoritarian appeals that link prosperity with austerity, borders, and the rallying call of national greatness. Secondly, seeing matters through the frame of a nearly universal middle class especially obscures questions of race and class. If we measure the middle class via median wealth, the problem emerges starkly. In 2013, for example, the wealth of a white family at the exact statistical middle of the US social structure was just north of $95,000, while the median Black household wealth was just over $11,000. Controlling for class by including education alongside race as a variable, the wealth differential for those with college degrees remained just short of eight to one, white over Black.[11] Many factors conspire to lead US citizens to think "white middle class" when they hear the words "middle class." Patterns of who has historically done hard manual labor and of relative access to education have left whites overrepresented in professional, white-collar, and managerial labor. One recent large-scale study of private sector employment found 12 percent of employees were Black, but just 7 percent of managers and 5 percent of senior managers. Black workers were far less likely to be salaried employees and far more likely to be paid by the hour than whites. Bureau of Labor Statistics figures from 2020 show Hispanic workers even more underrepresented in managerial and professional ranks.[12] Loose talk of saving the middle class obscures this past and present.

THE UNITED STATES AS NOT A PARTICULARLY MIDDLE-CLASS NATION

Fortune magazine weighed in on the dire fate of the middle class in a 2018 spread titled "The Shrinking Middle Class." So stark was the economic decline that being middle class had gone from seeming a rightful expectation to being a rare privilege. Yet amid the gloom, reporters for the magazine briefly reminded readers that anyone could become middle class simply by deciding to do so. Moreover, they held that "[t]he US is a middle-class nation, founded on middle-class ideals."[13] Such reassurances already sickened Mills by the 1950s, when he complained that theories regarding "white-collar people" fostered the falsity that "there are no classes in the United States" and the co-conspiring notion that "psychology is the essence of classes."[14]

The United States is *not* a middle-class nation in its present, in its recent past, or, in any compelling and coherent way, in its longer history. Since 1970, people in the center of the social structure have fared poorly. The squeeze they have experienced in an austere, neoliberal world is captured by comparing the situation in the United States with that of other nations. Broad national comparisons placed in a graph by *Fortune* illustrated stark inequality in the United States, which looked more like Putin's Russia than France or the United Kingdom. The magazine bolded a telling headline to accompany the graph: "In Awkward Global Company."[15]

CNN Money illustrated the fate of the US middle layers in 2014 with another graph that offered a tidy math lesson on the difference between two kinds of averages. The left side of the graph arranged nations by their average wealth in the form of a mean—all the wealth divided by all the households. The $301,000 average showed the great private wealth in the United States, which per capita trailed only the relatively small nations of Switzerland, Australia, and Norway. On the right side, median wealth—50 percent have less and 50 percent more—determined the ranking of nations. Here the average wealth in the United States plummeted to $45,000, and the world ranking fell to a pedestrian nineteenth, trailing France, Italy, the United Kingdom, and Japan (all in the top five) as well as Canada, Spain, Germany, and the Netherlands. When measured so as to account for great wealth at the top, the United States fared well. When measured from the middle, not so much. The article featuring the graph carried the apt title "America's Middle Class: Poorer Than You Think." Meanwhile, in another investigation of the topic, the *New York Times* ran a piece under the headline "The American Middle Class Is No Longer the World's Richest." Looking at data on raises in the United States and "other advanced countries" over the last three decades, reporters found the United States suffering by comparison.[16]

Praise songs regarding the middle class are so ubiquitous that the impassioned incoherence of recent presidential campaigns regarding class might seem timelessly commonsensical and "American." History is valuable in puncturing such balloons. When Harold Meyerson wrote of the 2016 election as possibly the "first" contest not centering on the middle class, the practice was in fact not even twenty-five years old. The specific electoral homilies regarding the middle class—as opposed to "forgotten Americans" or "silent majorities"—are relatively recent inventions in presidential politics. When Republican wunderkind Kevin Phillips wrote *The Emerging Republican Majority* in 1969, he produced what is in retrospect a kind of prequel to Stanley Greenberg's *Middle Class Dreams*, but coming from the right. Phillips urged the assembly of aggrieved ordinary Americans as Republicans united behind a disdain for elites and a desire to move away from social justice. But he used the idea and language of a "middle class" hardly at all, organizing matters instead around opportunities for the right created by regional issues in a variety of racially charged ways.[17]

Prior to Clinton's 1992 campaign, the term "middle class" had worked its magic and malevolence in conservative causes on a smaller scale. It had served to organize opposition to integrated housing and schools in the 1960s, as historian Kevin Kruse's work on Atlanta shows, and to mobilize anti-tax revolts in California in the late 1970s. Pat Caddell, who was a strategist for both Jimmy Carter and Bill Clinton, had experimented with the effectiveness of the term "forgotten middle class." The Republican New Yorker Alfonse D'Amato made the same phrase a centerpiece of his 1980 Senate campaign, claiming his mother as his inspiration.[18]

"Middle class" had at times seemed the property of white segregationist Democrats and at others of Republicans on the right, but this overwhelmingly applied to those on the local and state level, not nationally. In the 1970s, rightward-moving Democratic adviser Ben Wattenberg reckoned about three-quarters of those in the United States were middle class.[19] Democrats who embraced middle-class dreams from the 1990s forward had reason to think that they were disarming reactionary strategies. However, the "middle class" terrain on which they increasingly chose to fight remained one where the right had more savvy and practiced arguments. Clinton and Greenberg's use of the term in 1992 was something of an experiment, and Obama's success with it in 2008 and 2012 still carried a heady air of discovery.

A 2013 study by the Center on Applied Research at Georgetown University comparing language used by the last ten presidents in public statements and official communications involving social class underlined this point. Obama mentioned "middle class" in just over half such statements, taking the leading position in its use. Bill Clinton, who came in second, used it only half as much. Obama occupied last place in references to the "poor" and to "poverty," mentioning them in only 26 percent of his statements—about half the figure for the next lowest, George H. W. Bush. In contrast, Lyndon Johnson referred to "poverty" in 84 percent of such communications and used "middle class" just 1 percent of the time. No president from late 1963 until early 1981 used "middle class" in more than 3 percent of their communications regarding class. Indeed, things changed.[20]

And things stayed changed. In the heat of the 2016 campaign, Binyamin Appelbaum wrote in the *New York Times* under the headline "The Millions of Americans Donald Trump and Hillary Clinton Barely Mention." The subtitle revealed the identity of the taboo group: "The Poor." Amid all the ink spilled connecting Clinton's defeat to the "white working class," almost no curiosity surfaced regarding how much the dearth of specific discussion of the poor, across color lines, suppressed voter turnout and shaped electoral outcomes. Nor is there recognition that it was specifically the rise of the middle class in political boilerplate that coincided with elbowing the poor out of public discussion. Even in the relatively high turnout (by US standards) of the 2020 election, eighty million eligible voters abstained, their number decisively skewed toward the poor. About 20 percent of 2020 voters made under $50,000 a year, as compared to 43 percent of nonvoters.[21]

In misplaced paeans to the US middle class as distinctive, timeless, and globally pace-setting, three emblematic quotations chronically appear. For ballast within the Western tradition, and disregarding questions of translation and political economy, Aristotle frequently enounces: "A city ought to be composed, as far as possible, of equals and similars; and these are generally the middle classes. Wherefore the city which is composed of middle-class citizens is necessarily best constituted in respect of the elements of which we say the fabric of the state naturally consists." Aristotle fangirl and anti-Communist novelist Ayn Rand comes next. "A nation's productive—and moral, and intellectual—top is its middle class," she writes. "It is a country's motor and lifeblood, which feeds the rest . . . the upper classes are merely a nation's past; the middle class is its future."[22] Walt Whitman's 1858 endorsement, itself perhaps gesturing toward the praise of the "middle station" in Daniel Defoe's *Robinson Crusoe*, affirmed that "[t]he most valuable class in any community is the middle class." Bohemian, brilliant, and fully in the American grain, Whitman is invoked in order to establish a long national lineage for middle-class virtue. In fact, at the time he wrote, "middle class" was sufficiently unfamiliar as an expression in US print culture that Whitman had to immediately offer a definition: "the men of moderate means living at a rate of a thousand dollars a year or thereabouts."[23]

Through most of US history, well beyond and before Whitman, "middle class" was scarcely available as an identity to those in the United States. Ngrams—graphs generated by searches of the huge numbers of words in digitized databases to gain a sense of use of words and phrases over time—tell us that "middle class" hardly appeared at all in US publications until 1840, when it finally reached just one usage in every ten million words. Many of the nine-teenth-century US print usages described the middle class abroad, especially in Europe, where the term had far-greater currency. Usage climbed to twice 1840 levels only in 1880 and doubled again—to a rate of once in 2.5 million words—in 1920. In 1911, the *International Socialist Review*, then the most reputable US-based English-language journal of its kind, featured a long, belabored article titled "Which Class Is Your Class?" It did not even mention the middle class. Steep increases in the term's usage occurred with the crisis of capitalism in the Great Depression, when "middle class" appeared once every 1.4 million scanned words, and it rose again in the period of the Cold War, when usage of the term was part of anti-Communist arguments emphasizing the standard of life and absence of class conflict in the United States. It reached its peak in the 1960s, skyrocketing to as much as an appearance every in 800,000 words. As the Cold War declined, so too did writing about the "middle class," returning to 1930s levels, though it would find a new life in specifically electoral rhetoric during and after the 1992 presidential race.[24]

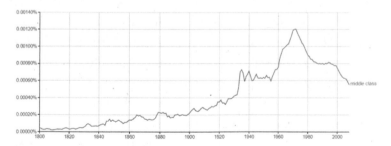

Figure 2.1: Ngram on Use of the Term "Middle Class."
Source: Google Books.

Further evidence of the late arrival of "middle class" in US discourse comes from a classic work of community sociology from the 1920s, *Middletown* by Robert S. Lynd and Helen M. Lynd. The Lynds studied Muncie, Indiana, a middle-sized and Middle American city in what remains the best sociological account of a largely white community yet produced in this country. They used "middle class" just four times in a 550-page book, and only once substantively. Though noting use by some other writers, the Lynds rejected without much apology the terms "lower," "middle," and "upper" class, favoring instead a simple dyad: "working class" and "business class." Taking a view of the upper class as more or less the 1 percent, they doubted that more than ten Muncie families would belong in it.[25] By the mid-1930s, however, when they returned to Muncie during the Great Depression, their *Middletown in Transition* reflected the uptick in awareness of a middle class that the Ngram shows us. They wrote then, with hesitant acceptance of the idea, that while data remained "tenuous," a "trend" toward the "separating out of a middle class" had begun.[26]

Works recalled today as classic renderings of the role and life of the middle class in fact got by largely without the phrase. Werner Sombart's argument in his early twentieth-century book *Why Is There No Socialism in the United States?* is remembered as hinging on the presence of a well-fed middle class, but we encounter that term in front and back matter to modern editions rather than in the text itself. Sinclair Lewis's 1922 satire of the troubled realtor George Babbitt, whom we would now regard as the very embarrassing embodiment of middle-class man and of middlebrow culture, proceeded without use of the phrase "middle class." However, when the Nobel Prize for Literature went to Lewis in 1930, the presentation speech found *Babbitt* to be the story of "the ideal of an American popular hero of the middle class."[27]

None of this means that "middle class" cannot be applied retrospectively. "Racism," usually considered by scholars to have come into common usage in reaction to systems of oppression under Nazi rule, has, for example, surely been usefully applied to social realities unfolding centuries before the term itself gained currency.[28] Similarly, the careful work on the nineteenth-century middle class by Stuart Blumin, Mary Ryan, Jeanne Boydston, Sven Beckert, Richard Sennett, Gwendolyn Wright, and others shows how new urban layers of businessmen, tradespeople, professionals, and eventually corporate-connected employees in sales, office work, accountancy, and management came together in families, churches, neighborhoods (eventually suburbs), colleges, ice cream parlors, reform politics, and elsewhere. These disparate figures forged linked identities through lived experiences, shared values, and even conflicts as the self-employed and white-collar corporate employees struggled to coexist in families. However, they only rarely knew themselves as middle class and did not produce anything like a middle-class nation.[29] As my old teacher Robert Wiebe wrote, the nineteenth-century and Progressive Era middle class "was a class only by courtesy of the historian's afterthought."[30]

MAKING THE US MIDDLE CLASS

By the 1930s, there was modestly growing good press for the idea of the United States as a middle-class nation. A boost for the idea came in part from editors and media owners with a self-interest in seeing matters that way in the age of mass industrial unionism. The Lynds had noticed as much by the time *Middletown in Transition* appeared in 1937. In it, they quoted at length from a 1936 editorial from a local newspaper, "The Middle Class Rules America." The editorial declared the United States immune from the "ferocity of the revolution in Spain" because it had never been "feudal." The United States always invested "sovereign authority [in] a great middle class," however many individuals were very rich and very poor. Although the rise of the Congress of Industrial Organizations dominated the news, the "class baiters" could never win in the middle-class nation of the United States.[31]

In February 1940, the then-stylish business magazine *Fortune* produced a breakthrough for the idea of a middle-class nation in popular media. The magazine expanded its regular "*Fortune* Survey" feature into a fat special issue developing a "self-portrait" titled "People of the U.S.A." The very first subheading affirmed a foundational fact: "The U.S. Is Middle Class." Those it identified as the "people," that collective noun so dear to the left at the time, roughly equaled the middle class. A spectacular statistic, if not fact, anchored the argument: 79.2 percent of respondents identified as members of the middle class, even as the decade of the Great Depression and mass industrial unionism ended. With recovery still far from complete, supposedly only a quarter of factory workers described themselves as "laboring" or "working" class. Among the Americans responding as middle class who offered a further adjective, most specified "middle middle." Less than 3 percent opted for "upper" or "upper-middle" class. As *Fortune* put it, there were "singularly few people," even executives, who were "willing to tag themselves as anything more than plain 'middle class.'" The most breathless article in the special issue expressed special admiration for the nation's "30,000 Managers: Earning $15,000 to $200,000 Plus, They Drive the Economic System and Coddle 56,000 Capitalists." Those in this group identified themselves as regular middle-class folks too. The "great American salesman," seen as a swashbuckling "artist bounding in and out of the halls of business," concurred. Though there had been precedents for holding that the middle class was larger than the working class, *Fortune*'s assertion that a startling four-fifths of a nation barely off the skids claimed to be middle class has meant its survey is still cited even today.[32]

The *Fortune* survey also raised questions that continue to trouble discussions of the middle class. The framing of the volume neatly illustrates that the ideal of a middle-class United States was not only embraced by many individuals but also loved by powerful elites. The ideology of a middle-class United States was and is central to the dream work of those elites and some ordinary residents. The special issue frankly strove to recapture the élan with which *Fortune* had been founded at the heady tail end of the booming 1920s. It exulted that the nation remained impervious to the formation of "any self-conscious proletariat such as a Marxist would wish for." Pollsters themselves sometimes expressed similar views. The researchers, who seem to have been even more committed to the idea of a middle-class nation than the survey's respondents, vigorously massaged data to shore up the case. Actually, only 47 percent of respondents to the survey had initially said that they were middle class—impressive but no majority. Researchers then went back to all those not offering "upper," "lower," or "middle" class as an answer—27.5 percent originally gave responses putting them in a "Don't Know" category—and asked which of those three choices they would opt for if pressed.[33] The data therefore reflected freely chosen self-descriptions in the first instance and answers to guiding questions requiring an upper/middle/lower rubric in the second. On the other hand, *Fortune*'s editors seemed at times to relish a good provocation. Just two years after the "Portrait" special issue, they featured a poll showing that one American in four favored socialism, with another 35 percent reporting having "an open mind" on the issue.[34]

The *Fortune* volume also engaged the ways in which academic researchers used "the middle class" as a term by claiming that class can be measured by self-identification. Robert S. Lynd both deployed the magazine's survey figures and derided self-identification as merely "subjective self-rating." The *Fortune* researchers could appeal to the large and enthusiastic 1935 study of the middle class by liberal writer Alfred Bingham, which held that "if the bulk of the people, in a modern capitalist country like the United States [think] of themselves as being middle class," they have established a social fact.[35] *Fortune*'s special issue reflected the knowledge that people who were objectively positioned differently in the economy chose to invent themselves as middle class. Thus, the survey remarked bemusedly on the propensity of "the prosperous" to nevertheless identify with the middle class and lingered over the fact that over 70 percent of the "poor" claimed middle-class status. In a rare nod to racial division, the researchers found that "the Negro" self-identified as middle class less than half as often as whites but also chose "upper class" far more often.[36] Such a breakdown suggests a fascinating further problem with self-reporting regarding class. Respondents doubtless drew on direct experience to position themselves—not within the nation but within the communities in which they lived, which were segregated by race and class. To report being in the middle or at the top of the hierarchy in a ghetto or in a coal-mining town did not necessarily imply any attempt to compare oneself to the US population as a whole. Thus, the very workers who organized the Congress of Industrial Organizations in auto, steel, and rubber might have been tempted to portray themselves to *Fortune* pollsters as having risen to the middle of their communities.

In the terminology of the late French theorist Louis Althusser, *Fortune* successfully "hailed" those polled as being middle class, inviting them to—again Althusser—"interpellate" into the class structure in a certain way. The cop yells into a crowd for a thief to stop, hailing him in the hope that he will indeed halt, accepting that designation describes him, and separating himself from the crowd. The process invites those called upon to identify themselves as subjects, exercising choice even as they fit themselves into systems of domination. Especially during World War II, and then during the Cold War—both featured political repression of the working class and celebration of the United States—the call hailing people to be middle class got a desired response. Recall that the postwar economic boom was concentrated in the relatively unscathed United States—conditions that made for relatively high degree of identification with the middle class. Sixty years ago, the British Marxist Andrew Grant cited a Gallup poll in his country showing self-identification as "middle class" outpaced "working class" by 49 percent to 46 percent. Grant lamented that popularity of the middle-class label but added that in the United States, middle-class identification had reached 88 percent. The Institute of Public Opinion likewise found a whopping 88 percent of those polled in the United States claiming middle-class status, bracketed by small slivers of uppers and lowers.[37]

Even so, the results remained uneven and highly dependent on the wording of the questions. In 1949, for example, a study by Richard Centers reported self-identification as "working class" outdistancing "middle class," 51 percent to 43 percent. Eight years after that, an extremely open-ended study by John Haer of the RAND Corporation found that in both Tallahassee (where only whites were surveyed) and Minneapolis, middle-class responses outpaced working-class ones handily. But in neither case was "middle" the majority response, and in Minneapolis it did not reach one-third. The "don't know" figures were astronomical and, when correlated with other data, identified those confused or reticent as also poor. Other responses underlined failures in interpellation as respondents self-identified as members of the "white class," the "friendly class," or the "religious class."[38]

THE MIDDLE-CLASS NATION AND AMERICAN EXCEPTIONALISM

There are understandable tendencies to regard today's political chatter about the middle class as mere boilerplate, or as describing a vessel into which liberal and even socialist ideas may be poured as easily as reactionary ones. Instead, such middle-class identification, still firmly tied to the "American exceptionalist" view of the United States as a blessed and exemplary place, stunts political imagination and possibility. To lots of us both American exceptionalism and the idea of a middle-class nation ring hollow, as does the promise that everyone can move up to become middle class. Nor does the exceptionalist narrative even cohere on its own terms, as it needs Americans to *already be* overwhelmingly middle class at the same time that they are constantly triumphally *becoming* middle class. Nevertheless, such ideas remain pillars of political commonsense for those thinking electorally or even just tuning into Fox News, MSNBC, or CNN. It is therefore worthwhile to attend to the history of how the middle-class nation—one that is implicitly, and in its segregated suburbs explicitly, white—and the idea of American exceptionalism came to be joined in politics, social thought, and media, and then how they became fully merged. Since the terms of that merger so privilege one tiny fraction of the middle classes— the entrepreneur—to stand in for the whole, the process carries even more importance.

If the Cold War nationalist efforts hailing almost everybody as middle class remained incomplete, they were nevertheless impressive and destructive. Joined, even during good times, by miseries that made for a sad but unifying middle-class experience (as we will see in the following chapters), such hailing frequently found response. This was especially the case when the middle class being courted was placed by politicians and pundits within the context of a never-equaled nation, an "American exceptionalist" one. It seemed to be not so much capitalism, but the specific adoption of a US model of supposed free enterprise, capable of generating a giant middle class, that would best Communism. The nationalist notion of a transcendent US model identified the US middle class as the key to everything good. For example, in the face of challenges from the New Left, Black Power, and above all the Vietnamese in 1968, the Bay Area philosopher and waterfront worker Eric Hoffer found fame as the voice of reason and order. For Hoffer, as for Ayn Rand, the middle class gave us Western Civilization, and the US example showed that such a class could become "real" internationale, rendering hopes of socialist solidarity hollow and ridiculous.[39] Politicians, as we have seen, have increasingly championed such views. Labor unions have also gravitated to a middle-class-forward approach, attracted to it not only as a present strategy, but also as something unions had supposedly supported "for generations." Kansas City activist intellectual Bill Onasch rightly connects the post–World

War II popularity of the idea of a middle-class majority with "a hardening Cold War union bureaucracy," but the end of the Cold War has not lessened commitment to it.[40]

As with trade unionism, the period of steep decline of the middle class domestically since 1970 nevertheless coincided with the United States being put forward as an exemplar of how to do things right in consolidating a middle class. Fanfare greeted the doubling of the world's middle class in twenty-five years—1.4 billion people were said to be in that class in 2014. But the new global middle class makes between four and one hundred dollars per day, with most far short of the poverty line in the United States. Optimists predicted that the US example and neoliberal policies could lead to a new dawn in which 90 percent of India would be middle class. More sober analysts suggest the actual figure today is nearer to 2 percent. In 2020, according to Pew Charitable Trusts figures, India shed 32 percent of its middle class in the face of COVID and other setbacks. The labor journalist Paul Mason argues that the example of the United States and its "rich-world counterparts" does attract followers globally but leads "steadily to stratification and more service-oriented work."[41]

The idea that the United States occupies a special, leading, and exemplary place—the world's exceptional nation because of its middle class—has existed inchoately for a long while, but the connection between exceptionalism and the middle class has tightened over time. Patriots and European travelers saw the United States as especially promising for its particular freedoms, distribution of (formerly Native) land, and absence of aristocratic and churchly restraints. Frederick Jackson Turner's writings on the frontier, like some of the work of Marx and Engels, posited that access to land set the United States apart from class-ridden Europe, with Turner adding that the frontier itself made for democratic practices. However, for Marx, Engels, and Turner, this process had an end, as frontiers ran out and troubles lay ahead.[42]

The precise term "American exceptionalism" came much later and amid rich irony. One recent account locates its origins with Stalin, who in 1929 was searching for a name for a heresy within the world Communist movement he dominated. Jay Lovestone, a US labor leader, led a tendency within the Communist Party that argued in the late '20s that new strategies were necessary because US workers were not ready for revolution. Stalin branded this deviation as "American exceptionalism," and Lovestone, arguing his corner, did use the phrase "middle class" to describe elements to be targeted in party appeals.[43]

The most famous Cold War intellectual to take up what made the United States special, Louis Hartz, argued in 1955 in his incredibly ambitious volume *The Liberal Tradition in America* that because the United States lacked a feudal order against which to rebel, it could only generate limited traditions of revolt and even of social democracy. Hartz so fully embraced the idea that the United States was hardwired against socialist movements that he is often mistakenly remembered as a champion of the glories of American exceptionalism. He is better understood as a radical writing sadly and with deep awareness of Marxism. *Liberal Tradition*'s one use of "exceptionalism"—the term "American exceptionalism" does not appear—refers to the debates among Marxists in the 1930s. Hartz does use "middle class" centrally, though far less frequently than "bourgeois," as his goal is to discuss bourgeois revolutions and their ideas, more than class structures. Far from seeking to ground exceptional national glory in the middle class, Hartz stressed the limitations of both that class and the nation. "The Americans," he lamented, "though models to all the world in the middle-class way of life, lacked the passionate middle-class consciousness which saturated the liberal thought of Europe."[44]

The "middle-class nation" and "American exceptionalism" found each other late, and under specific circumstances. As the economic indices showing stagnating wages and soaring inequality have increasingly challenged both notions since 1970, the view that the United States is the product of their marriage has only gained political currency. Especially over the past thirty years, the reflexive response to middle-class decline has been to promise more loudly to defend the middle class and, through it, the nation.[45] When Burton Bledstein began his valuable 1976 history of the middle class with the words, "From the 1840s until the present, the idea of the middle class has been central to the history of American social attitudes," Cold War politics animated the over-reading involved in his assertion. The ersatz ubiquity that Bledstein assumed across space and time—one that led the historian Loren Baritz to liken the study of the middle class to "searching for air"—fed in particular on the American exceptionalist certainties of Bledstein's next sentence: "No other national identity has been so essentially concerned with this one idea."[46] After Ronald Reagan established the potency of the direct invocation of "American exceptionalism" electorally in the 1980s and Bill Clinton demonstrated the power of direct appeals to middle-class dreams in the '90s, the two came to prosper together among politicians and pundits.[47]

In 1996, the eminent centrist political scientist Seymour Martin Lipset revisited Hartz's ideas. Forty years down the road, exceptionalism was front and center, from Lipset's title forward in his celebrated book, *American Exceptionalism: A Double-Edged Sword*. The middle class immediately made an entrance, as Lipset wrote of a nation "dominated by pure bourgeois, individualistic values" over the long haul. Although Lipset allowed that in some of the best-designed studies, more people in the United States identified as working class than middle class at the time, the emphasis on a nation exceptional because it was middle-class ran through the volume. Hartz's gloom gave way in Lipset's gleeful study.[48] Between 1980 and 2000, a recent study shows, there was "a lot of talk" about American exceptionalism—457 mentions in national publications. However, in the new century's first decade, this ballooned to 2,558 instances. The first two years of the 2010s nearly doubled that of the entire prior decade. The most over-the-top example came in 2011 with the publication of conservative congressman (and historian of sorts) Newt Gingrich's *A Nation like No Other: Why American Exceptionalism Matters.*[49]

An early campaign profile for the relatively left-of-center 2020 presidential hopeful Elizabeth Warren appeared in a Salt Lake City publication under the headline "Make the Middle Class Great Again." Her campaign must have smiled. Indeed, such commitment to saving the exceptional middle class, which seems heartfelt at times, animates campaigns across party lines. Obama, for example, faced no more reelection campaigns when he said in 2014: "I believe in American exceptionalism with every fiber of my being." However, identification with the middle class wanes situationally. Beyond elections, the liabilities of pairing the "middle-class nation" and American exceptionalist tropes are clear. In a 2017 Pew poll, a large majority of under-thirties believed that "there are other countries better than the US."[50]

In still another way, the joining of the middle-class nation with the idea of American exceptionalism encourages fighting on terrain favorable to the Trumps of the world and to capital. Who is imagined and catered to when middle-class salvation gains a hearing? Since the so-called middle class is such a hodgepodge of workers and owners involved in all sorts of different social relations, it can hardly surprise us that those writing about it consistently make one segment of it stand in for the imagined whole. To his credit, Mills titled his major book on the subject *White Collar* and, as we have seen, referred in his subtitle to the middle classes, plural. Still, his work is taken as if it apprehends the whole of an actually existing middle class. British and German writers have similarly connected the middle class to a certain kind of employment (and dress), using either "white collar" or the very cool phrase "black-coated worker."[51] John and Barbara Ehrenreich, as noted earlier, shift back and forth between calling their subject the "professional-managerial class" and the "professional middle class." The latter's singly authored book on the subject, *Fear of Falling*, nevertheless uses a subtitle identifying the whole middle class as the book's subject. Immediately after that, the introduction bemoans the inadequacy of the very term "middle class."[52]

When we connect American exceptionalism to a middle-class nation, the small numbers of entrepreneurs in the United States acquire inflated importance. To suppose that the United States has "always" been middle class requires that huge numbers of farmers and a small number of independent businesspersons and professionals of the early United States be the founding fathers of the modern middle class. Their storied (and overstated) virtues of manly independence come to be writ large onto the modern United States, which has for a long time not resembled a society of independent proprietors at all. As the historian Steve Fraser recently summarized this transformation, the (white, male) nation in 1820 was "80 percent self-employed and by 1940 80 percent worked for someone—or something—else."[53] Family farms (and their male heads of household), so important to the mythos of American exceptionalism, have long ranked among the least "American" things in the modern world. Less than one-half of 1 percent of the world's five hundred million family farms are in the United States, which trails the European nations significantly and the global South utterly in percentage of farmers.[54] Going behind such numbers, Mills wrote, "The nineteenth-century farmer and businessman were generally thought to be stalwart individuals—their own men." The white-collar man is "always somebody's man."[55] We would be tempted to add "or women," but it is not quite that easy, as the attendant ideology was and is masculine, though not always in a very self-assured way. The great dissenting US scholar G. William Domhoff, for example, introduced Richard Parker's searing book on the new middle class a half century ago by describing its subject as "a class of property paper pushers and people manipulators who must go along to get along."[56] Interestingly, it was experience in this new middle class that sometimes sharpened dreams of being self-employed. In 1905, a poll of retail clerks found that half of them had imbibed enough of what the German historian Jürgen Kocka described as "businessman as model" ideology that they not only hoped but believed that they were transitioning to self-employment. After World War II, when unionized autoworkers were often seen as ascending to middle-class status, sociologist Eli Chinoy's celebrated study of them found widespread desires to instead own a business or farm.[57]

Today, just one American in sixteen is an entrepreneur, and since about half of small businesses fail within five years, "ex-entrepreneur" is a more robust category. But the cult worship surrounding this tiny group drives rhetoric and policy.[58] Again, the appeal is bipartisan, with liberal-seeming universities competing manically to see which can most emphasize the entrepreneurial in their vision statements. The peculiar recent US idea that being a businessman or "delivering a payroll" qualifies a candidate for political office finds its roots in the aggrandizement of the entrepreneur. Not even the Trump presidency has managed to discredit it. Where I live, in Kansas, the recent past has delivered tax cuts that amount to business tax exemptions specifically favoring entrepreneurs and established big businesses, bringing public education to the brink of ruin. The highest-paid state employee, University of Kansas basketball coach Bill Self, suddenly found much of his income untaxed as it came from allegedly entrepreneurial activity, not salaried coaching.[59]

We deserve bigger and better explanations for this obsession with entrepreneurs than mis-leadership by demagogues. Philosopher Michel Foucault's theorizing of the "entrepreneurial self"—no relation to Bill Self—among those far from being self-employed offers clues. Of course, wage laborers have long had the "freedom" to choose among exploiters to whom to sell the labor that was his or her sole asset, as so brilliantly elucidated by Marx and rendered by scholar and writer Saidiya Hartman as making for "proprietorial conceptions of the self."[60] However, neoliberal calculations magnify such a sense. The desire to someday become "independent," the importance of housing market decisions (especially among whites) to personal wealth, and the self-management of retirement accounts, as well as the calibration of how and when to invest in one's own health and own re-skilling, help shape such a self.[61] Alloyed with the advantages of the dominant race, the proprietorial self became one propped up by possibilities of what American Studies scholar George Lipsitz has called the "possessive investment in whiteness," treating its bearers to possibilities—and illusions regarding possibilities—of independence.[62] The political chorus regarding an exceptional white middle-class nation, supposedly chock-full of entrepreneurs, remains with us, profoundly influencing how "saving the middle class" is heard and acted upon.

3

HOW THE LEFT HAS LIVED WITH THE PROBLEM OF THE MIDDLE CLASS

He succeeds with it; he fails with it; he dies with it. But why did he have it? Isn't it true that he had to have a false dream in our society?

—FREDRIC WERTHAM, radical psychologist, on the impoverished middle-class dream of Willy Loman in Arthur Miller's *Death of a Salesman*

Plenty of history runs through what follows in this chapter, so much so that we had best begin with what is at stake for our current moment in understanding that past. At its biggest convention to that date, the Democratic Socialists of America voted in August 2019 for Resolution 32, committing resources to its Labor Commission and to implement a "rank-and-file strategy." Having suddenly grown to fifty thousand members, DSA promised to nurture "workers' sense of being part of something bigger—not just a union, but a working class—that is capable of fighting, winning, and ultimately ruling." Such stirring pledges and hopes have from time to time—but not so much recently—found expression in US history. In their heyday, the hope was attached to

workers in heavy industry, to those on docks and in ware-
houses and mines, with images featuring male brawn and
resolve, often as against the effete world of working and
lounging without wearing blue-collars. Resolution 32 sup-
ports efforts to send radicals to jobs in "strategic sectors"
where they live, giving a single example of such a sector:
K–12 education. It mentions one publication as a model for
others forthcoming, the pamphlet *Why Socialists Should Become Teachers*.[1]

That is, hopes for the longed-for rebirth of a working-class
movement now cohere around an occupational group long
considered middle class. Indeed, even Michael Zweig—the
labor studies scholar credited earlier as most responsible for
arguing, over the last quarter century, that the working class
still outnumbers the middle class in the United States—only
very recently decided that teachers, along with nurses, had
sunk into the working class. Setbacks in working conditions
and pay, as well as losses of autonomy on the job, sent them
down. There were further ironies. The DSA resolution called
for the new initiative to use the "Troublemakers" training
program developed by activists around the publication *Labor Notes*. Some of those promoting the new DSA policy came
from the important *Labor Notes* tradition, which began in
part out of radicalized New Leftists, often college-educated
and the children of professionals, moving to Detroit and
elsewhere to be part of the struggles of industrial workers.
To their credit, some of these activists themselves helped to
write Resolution 32, with a new emphasis on leadership by
teachers. They had by then long participated in and learned
from the struggles of troublemaking teachers and nurses.[2]

Such a transformation had antecedents in a long process
leading to a realization that teachers and nurses might not
simply be in the working class, but helping to lead it. For

some time, writers on the left have connected teachers to the beginnings of new movements. In the wake of Donald Trump's election in 2016, the most dramatic labor protests saw teachers in "red states"—that is, Republican-dominated ones—mount massive strikes and marches to confront austerity directed at themselves and at those whom they taught. Mobilizations in Oklahoma and West Virginia stood out especially in suggesting that teachers within and beyond conservative areas have begun a new workers' movement. "It started in West Virginia," we are told, sometimes with the added and more questionable proviso that the electoral campaigns of Bernie Sanders coalesced the movement of teacher activists there.[3]

When the reactionary governor Scott Walker of Wisconsin launched an attack on state workers, the poor, civil liberties, and the environment, an inspiring 2011 "Wisconsin Uprising" opposed him, occupying the State House in Madison. Lots of activists backed planning for a general strike, but some also wondered if the slogan "Re-organize Wisconsin" might have legs. That is, since anti-union forces were using Wisconsin as a laboratory for their worst ideas, might not unions and the left use the state to develop their best ones by pouring in organizing resources and people while trying to make union-busting a strategy as costly as possible to Walker's corporate supporters? Although opponents tried to remind Walker that Wisconsin was a "union state," it had largely ceased to be one, particularly where private sector unionism was concerned. In choosing electoral strategies, which not only demobilized protests but also long failed to dislodge Walker, organized labor reflected its own lack of resources and a certainty that labor law was not on its side.

Lack of confidence that white-collar workers could win historic victories also shaped decisions. Worries about whether the labor movement could for a time be centrally about teachers and other public employees went beyond questions of whether private sector workers would support public employees. Given their position at the point of attack and their militancy, any rebuilding of the state's labor movement in Wisconsin would have had to empower public employees to lead. Teachers in particular would have had to be in the forefront, including in efforts to build momentum for private sector unionism. The electoral efforts that soon became the central strategy to defeat Walker achieved at best mixed results: he survived a recall effort in 2012, going on to win reelection in 2014. When I attended a postmortem on the Wisconsin Uprising in Madison in 2013, there were plenty of regrets to go around. The clearest insights, though, regarded the movement's underestimation of the social power of public employees, too often considered as limited in their range of motion by professionalism and atomization. Tellingly mentioned, for example, were workers who record deeds at the county level and the teachers who, among much else, provide childcare to much of the labor force. [4]

Within these hopeful moments, "middle-class" occupations attract our attention as near to the working class's leading edge. However, they point to a set of problems, not to any easy solution. Certainly, real life is a great teacher, and the desire to draw firm lines between blue- and white-collar labor as if they had enduring and deep meaning is on the run. As recently as two decades ago, leading labor historian Nelson Lichtenstein wrote of a "collar line" that, until conditions changed following World War II, had more resembled a chasm: "Unlike the blue-collar working class, public employees often sat behind a desk, public employees took a regular paid vacation, and kept their fingernails clean." Missing the large numbers of public workers doing blue-collar jobs (not to mention the numbers of private sector blue-collar workers with paid vacations and clean nails), Lichtenstein reflected a view that has some strong and even understandable roots within the radical tradition of thinking about the middle class. Militancy among professionals and retail clerks, and, sadly, a sharp decline in blue-collar, private sector organizing have, as Lichtenstein himself later shows, more than challenged such a view.[5]

But as important as it is to recognize that teachers, nurses, and millions of less adequately paid office and sales workers are key elements of the US working class, contradictions of everyday life won't let us rest there. What are we to do with a teacher, or nurse, or sanitation worker, or meatpacker from Green Bay who becomes a labor activist while professing to also be middle class? Must she pick? Should labor scholars decide for her? These questions are especially vexed because the working class is largely defined by a relation to capital and management, while the middle class includes a variety of such relationships and often turns significantly on personal choice.

The task of radicals hinges only partly on showing the size and breadth of the working class. Such corrections to the prevailing belief that the United States is an overwhelmingly middle-class society are helpful, but within limits. It is reassuring for those supporting labor to realize that, on some reckonings, a near majority in the United States sees itself as working class, and a whopping majority might reasonably be counted as members of such a class by social scientists. But even if Zweig's figures are correct—in my view, the "objectively" working-class population is far larger than two-thirds—the problem remains. At a minimum, one US resident in four labors in a working-class job but identifies, at least situationally, as middle class. Debunking can only move that figure so much.

This chapter discusses how recognition of the problem of the middle class, combined with appreciation of a fear of falling, helps to elaborate a powerful socialist critique of middle-class conservatism, but also of white-collar conditions of work. Radicals have had sufficient problems with timing and tone as to leave themselves open to charges that the left perpetually predicted a fall from the middle class that never arrived and ignored white-collar workers. The socialist tradition was not so much wrong in its fear of a reactionary middle class, nor even in its hope that middle class forces would be recruited as they fell into dynamic working-class protests, as it was too optimistic about the staying power of the industrial labor movement when confronted by extremely hostile state forces and corporate opposition. At times it failed to believe its own analyses regarding the working-class status of most white-collar and government employees strongly enough to imagine that the middle class could be disaggregated and won over patiently instead of in a projected cataclysm. In that sense, the left shared with many pro-capitalist thinkers and mainstream sociologists the view that people in very different social relations nevertheless occupied a middle-class position.

SOCIALISM AND THE MIDDLE CLASS: MARX'S MARXISM AND THE WEIGHT OF CLASSIC ARGUMENTS

For upward of four decades, I have written books thinking that almost no one who happened on them in a store would be interested in socialism. The changes of the recent past—polls now show that more young people in the United States have a positive view of an unspecified socialism than the capitalism they know too well—suddenly suggest an alignment of the market in books with my personal commitments. Well, one hopes.[6] In any case, a chapter on the problem of the middle class must necessarily address the story of socialism. The intimate connections of a socialism-proof American exceptionalism with ideologues busy inflating the size and trumpeting the virtues of the middle class ensure as much. The idea that the very presence of a middle class "disproves" Marxism remains ingrained and will have a further legion of publicists if socialism gains a substantial toehold in US politics. Much less familiar is the impressive tradition of thinking about the middle class by those wanting to transform society—and by those who oppose the transformation of politics in a fascist direction. Sometimes counterrevolutionary and susceptible to mobilization by the far right, the lower middle class has generated particularly urgent attention. Marxist concern with the middle class positioned socialist scholarship to shape much of the earliest and the best of all thought about the middle class. Even "falling," the keyword that structures investigations of the middle class from sociology to journalism, emerged from socialist tradition and extended into mainstream writings.

Radical thinking has long insisted that playing to an aggrieved middle class fights on terrain favorable to right-wing politics and endorses a cultural wasteland. The left feared empowering the shock troops of reaction. As recently as the Cold War, even liberals counted the middle class as the lonely crowd, the organization men, and the housewife victims of the feminine mystique. Its members did not need saving, but rather a way out. It is the ease with which some of the left campaigns for middle-class salvation that is new and untenable. The idea of "saving the middle class" is of no use in clarifying when and how white-collar and professional workers act as working-class people or in explaining materially why the term "middle class" also seems meaningful to so many in the United States.

Present at the creation of modern socialism was the problem of the middle class. The 1848 revolutions and the publication by Engels and Marx of *The Communist Manifesto* that same year heralded a movement that was beginning to seek roots in the working class, in part by critiquing the middle class. The *Manifesto* consciously tried to break from the middle class, or perhaps to acknowledge a break already made in real life, in its very title. In the preface to the 1888 English-language edition, Engels called the work the foundational text of socialist literature, (strangely) from "Siberia to California." He added that when he and Marx wrote *The Communist Manifesto*, they could not have used "socialist" in its title because socialism was then considered a middle-class movement, while "communist" signaled a working-class one. The two authors had no doubt about opting for the latter term and never "repudiated" it. Nevertheless, Engels also liked the fact that by the 1880s socialism had come to be understood as a working-class project. The *Manifesto* roundly dismissed any revolutionary potential of the middle class: "The middle class—the small manufacturer, the shopkeeper, the artisan, the peasant—all these fight against the bourgeoisie, to save from extinction their existence as fractions of the middle class." Engels and Marx concluded, "They are therefore not revolutionary, but conservative," except and until the moment of their impending transfer into the proletariat.[7]

The middle class seemed to validate such views during the 1848 revolutions. Opposition from the lower middle class, in the view of the Communists, proved decisive in the rebuff of freedom dreams. In reflecting on the 1848 revolutions, Marx rehearsed the range of the responses that would dominate his thought, and that of many socialist revolutionaries for a century to come. For Marx, the German middle class and "its professors, its capitalists, its aldermen, and its penmen" had, from 1846 onward, exhibited an "unexampled spectacle of irresolution, incapacity, and cowardice."[8] He wrote of France, a nation where class issues and workers' militancy particularly stood out in the 1848 revolts, as a place where "[n]o one had fought more fanatically in the June days for the salvation of property and the restoration of credit than the Parisian petty bourgeois. . . . The shopkeeper had pulled himself together and marched against the barricades in order to restore the traffic which leads from the streets into the shop."[9] As the Hungarian revolutionary Béla Kun wrote seventy years after their defeat, the 1848 revolutions "revealed the political bankruptcy of the revolutionary section of the bourgeoisie. That revolution laid bare not only their weakness, but also how dangerous they were to the work of the revolution." In France, he argued, the working class was "crushed" by "this very lower middle-class," not by the capitalist class.[10]

In *The Communist Manifesto*, Marx and Engels argued that capitalism itself propelled history toward a solution to the problem of the middle class. They put matters in the baldest terms possible. "The lower strata of the middle class" would simply step off the stage of history: "small tradespeople, shopkeepers, and retired tradesmen generally, the handicraftsmen and peasants—all these sink gradually into the proletariat." They would do so both because their "diminutive capital" would lose out to concentrations of industrial wealth and because new methods of production would render "specialized skill" obsolete. The bulk of the middle class would rise by falling into the working class. "The whole society more and more splits into . . . two great classes," Marx and Engels wrote even more famously, "directly opposed to one another: Bourgeoisie and Proletariat."[11]

This elegantly simple solution carried its own problems, ones that have plagued socialist approaches to the middle class since 1848 where questions of terminology, timing, and tone are concerned. The lines in the *Manifesto* regarding the middle class sinking are seldom missed by those who ridicule socialism as being in the prediction business and as dead wrong on the disappearance of the middle class. These charges usually focus on the "mistakes" of Marx and Marxists. The fact that industrial capitalism transformed the United States from a nation 80 percent self-employed to one 80 percent employed in the space of a century therefore bears emphasis in response. The fall of the old self-employed middle class, including farmers, that Marx predicted did in fact occur. His mistaking of a trend for an absolute direction frayed generalizations around the edges, and a new waged or salaried middle class produced within modern capitalism increased complications. Thus, there is plenty of socialist sloppiness and smugness to critique, and substantial critique has in fact come from within the socialist tradition. At the same time, however, the middle class and the working class have been moving targets, meaning that we are dealing with complexities in the world as much as mistakes in analysis, and the socialist "error" of misunderstanding or somehow ignoring the middle class remains largely an invention.

For Marxists, the complexity of the problems associated with the middle class made a simple opposition between workers and capitalists compelling. In what may be the most famous passage on class written in English since World War II, the British social historian E. P. Thompson asserted: "The [class] relationship must always be embodied in real people and in a real context. Moreover, we cannot have two distinct classes, each with an independent being, and bring them *into* relationship with each other. We cannot have love without lovers, nor deference without squires and labourers." Thompson continued with an equally famous sentence on class consciousness: "And class happens when some men as a result of common experiences, inherited or shared, feel and articulate the identity of their interests as against other men whose interests [differ]."[12] What then of the middle class? Who is their lover, their squire, their other? The answer must be multiple. Those in the middle can look up or down for a supposed adversary, or they can look both ways, seeing themselves as perpetually ground between those above and below. In the great European revolutions, the middle class could at first join those grown rich in the market to oppose the aristocrats above. However, when the other above those in the middle was the industrial millionaire and the other below was the working class and/or the racialized poor, political parties directed middle-class anger downward by standing more willing to hear grievances directed against those below than against those on top.

The other half of Marxist hopes for the middle class is far less visible from our vantage point. The *Manifesto* and Marx's writings on the 1848 revolutions did not just foresee the decline of the middle class, but also its mid-descent attraction to a rising working-class movement. This too began almost from the moment of the 1848 revolutions, especially in France. There, Marx reasoned, because the working-class movement had so advanced and basic liberties were sufficiently secured, the middle class would soon learn to follow the lead of working-class militants, not only out of economic desperation but also because they were impressed by the social power of labor. Glimmers of such radicalization did occur, but the picture painted by Marx illustrated problems with tone, and eventually with substance. Marx described a key moment in the French class struggles in a way appropriate to melodrama but also farce. After the middle class sold out street protests in order to restore commerce in their stores, sobering realities ensued: "[T]he workers were crushed and the shopkeepers, drunk with victory, rushed back to their shops, they found the entrance barred by a savior of property ... who presented them with threatening notices: Overdue promissory note! Overdue house rent! Overdue bond! Doomed shop! Doomed shopkeeper!"[13] To make appeals to the middle class on the basis of the desirability of that group's imminent fall could only be tricky business, as George Orwell's satire of the inability of the left to take seriously middle-class people underlined. To apprehend a class in terms of its descent offers opportunities for compassion—think, for example, of the recent and humane books on the sadnesses of middle-class life by Barbara Ehrenreich and Katherine Newman, or the tragedy of Willy Loman's fate in *Death of a Salesman*. But the words of Marxists, and sometimes of Marx himself, emphasizing an awaited tumble had to seem unfeeling to those in the middle classes striving so mightily to stay upright.[14]

As the *Communist Manifesto* had it, the "industrial middle class" suffered defeat at the hands of the "industrial millionaires, the leaders of the whole industrial armies, the modern bourgeois."[15] The damage done to the precise vocabularies of class by this dramatic rendering was profound, given the plasticity of the term "bourgeois," especially as it suffered translation. The old "industrial middle class" of small producers, plummeting already or poised to plunge, and the ruling capitalist class both counted as "bourgeois," also rendered at times as "middle class." Both terms were pressed to do far too much work. Jürgen Kocka's beautifully researched *White Collar Workers in America* included important comparative dimensions drawing on German examples. Kocka developed a long early section on problems of transnational usage, arguing that both the French *classes moyennes* and the German *Mittelstand* shifted over the time Marx wrote to exclude the more upwardly mobile bourgeoisie amid sharpening awareness of class differences between workers and a bourgeois ruling class. Kocka rightly insisted on this context in explaining the rise over time of an identification of a "lower-middle class" as a catch-all term combining "artisans, retailers, government clerks, office workers, members of the lesser professions," and others. In the United States, he held, weaker class politics saw to it that the language remained looser.[16]

But nowhere was it very tight. In *The Condition of the Working Class in England*, Engels used "middle class" (the German was *Mittelklasse*) to refer to the "English classes corresponding with the French bourgeoisie." Marx made some effort to use *petit bourgeoisie* to signal reference to the lower middle class, but by no means consistently. The language and the ethos involved, along with the anti-revolutionary actions of some of the middle class, made it possible to identify that group with opposition to labor's emancipation, at least until the instant of their falling.[17] Among later revolutionaries seeking to keep power, especially in the early Soviet Union, middle-class elements could seem again the key to every difficulty, especially when they sought to restore systems of private credit. Thus Kun rehearsed Marx's arguments on the dangerous but doomed lower middle class in a pointed 1918 birthday tribute in the official organ of the Soviet Communist Party, *Pravda:* "The [Soviet] Revolution,

when celebrating the centenary of Marx's birth, will not for-
get the sentence he passed on the lower-middle class."[18]

For Marxists, the difficulty with terminology and sometimes with politics has resided in our joining with bourgeois
social scientists in the lumping together of people in various
social positions under the singular heading "middle class."
Engels observed that popular use of the term in England was
in fact "middle classes," a considerably more precise appella-
tion.[19] The *Manifesto* nevertheless stuck to aggregating those
sliders about to fall from the perch of self-employment.
Meanwhile, an eventually far-larger "new middle class"
emerged, at first in large measure around the need to sell
and advertise products and to keep track of the circulation
of capital. Salespeople, secretaries, and bookkeepers reached
Marx's radar, but as subplot to the great drama of commodity production in industry. He wrote of them fleetingly in
works less read, less translated, and sometimes unpublished.
Whether such fragments amount, as the New Left Marxol-
ogist Martin Nicolaus argued, to a "theory of the middle
class"—elsewhere Nicolaus says of the "new middle class"—
is debatable, but it is certain that Marx did not disseminate
such a theory to socialists generally. The hints Marx provided were tantalizing, as in the insistence that there would
be a "constant increase" in "the middle classes" poised between labor and capital. Their rise, he thought, lagged behind that of the working class but was structurally necessary
to "serve" the broader interests of capitalist development, in
part by consuming the surplus bounty produced in the factories by workers. Marx also predicted that falling, and fear
of falling, would structure the existence of this growing and
important group, as they did the declining numbers in the
old middle classes. He added that what we would now call
white-collar wages would fall faster than those of "average

labor" when office labor was divided into smaller tasks requiring less skill and when more widespread education increased competition for office jobs.[20]

Marx's later work also offered a meandering discussion
of a distinction between productive and unproductive labor,
with the middle class linked to the latter. "Productive" workers directly fabricated commodities, or carted and ferried
them about. The "unproductive" elements served capital and
capitalism generally. The latter category inchoately included
office workers, service workers, accountants, and salespersons alongside a wonderful list of categories unearthed from
various sources by Nicolaus: valets of the industrial millionaires, landlords, night watchmen, civil servants, lawyers,
the kaiser, the pope, politicians generally, paupers, and "el-
egant paupers" such as churchmen, as well as criminals and
landowners. Here was Marx very much learning new things
from the new economy and challenging his own insistence
on a Manichean split between bourgeoisie and proletariat.
But he also was spinning out a more or less aimless distinction, one undermined over time by the fact that the work
of night watchmen and of caregivers, of secretarial labor, of
janitors, and of all variety of other contracted-out services
is now often itself the commodity produced in new regimes
of accumulation.[21] The idea of the "unproductive" clerk or
secretary or call center worker—increasingly the workers
called middle class—could hardly have equipped socialists
to understand white-collar and service labor as like that
of other workers. Nor did it create urgency to support their
organizing.[22]

THE POLITICAL PROBLEM OF
THE NEW MIDDLE CLASS

From a Marxist point of view—one valuing analysis of material relations over time—it would be shocking if ideas developed by socialists 175 years ago applied easily today. Back then, a huge majority of people in the United States were self-employed or enslaved; today, an equally large majority is waged or salaried. At its best, Marx's Marxism gave later thinkers a method that led them to study the changed economy and find a new, enduring, and growing strata of the middle class doing working-class jobs. However, his more famous works spoke mainly of the self-employed middle class, one existing on borrowed time, typically opposing human emancipation, and interesting mainly for its coming disappearance. Poised to enter decisively into history by accepting proletarian leadership, its members also appeared as figures of fun—feckless, fawning, and culturally philistine until being forced into glory for reasons they could not always comprehend.

A particular difficulty in the classic socialist tradition of thinking about the "middle class" lay in defining it in terms of its opposition to revolutions and organizing. The differences between those victimized by capital in factories and those suffering in offices seemed not only a matter of where and how people worked but also whether they might become active in revolutionary politics. In the case of industrial workers, Marxism had a long tradition of insisting that, even in periods of long quiescence, social relations established the presence of a working class, though one sometimes unable to speak its own name. The conservative blue-collar worker remained a worker, however misled. On the other hand, where white-collar workers were concerned, inaction and conservative political behavior led Marxists to regard them as middle class, or at least to not challenge the tendency of the larger society to regard them as such. In many ways socialist theory and practice regarding the middle class "failed" not because they wholesaled extreme ideas but because they insufficiently challenged commonplace ones. Despite all these difficulties, for most of the twentieth century, Marxists and those attracted to Marxism increasingly took the middle class seriously as a political problem and, especially in Germany and the United States, wrote the best work yet produced on the subject.

Sometimes the desire for close empirical study of economy and society and for compelling revolutionary meta-narratives clashed. The idea of a lasting "new middle class" emerging from the continuing development of capitalism—hinted at by Marx's later works—began to be explicitly theorized in the late nineteenth and early twentieth century. The setting, Germany, was significant as it was not only a center of working-class support for socialist politics, but also a place with great appetite for drawing status distinctions within the occupational structure. Salary in Germany came in monthly installments, as opposed to the weekly pay and subtraction for hours taken off in sales positions in the United States around 1900. The "new middle class" analysis emerged initially from outside the left, or from the most reformist provinces of Marxism. Both put forward the new class as proof that capitalism could create buffers that kept it from lapsing into a two-sided class war destined to be won by workers. The leading evolutionary socialist, Eduard Bernstein, held not only that white-collar workers were not being ground down toward proletarian status, but also that the self-employed would actually increase in number as capitalist development continued. Not surprisingly, many socialists opposed such theories; in doing so they sometimes minimized what was new in the world.[23]

The intellectual and political trajectory of the German Marxist economist Emil Lederer teaches much regarding how reactions to the idea of a new middle class were bound to be influenced by history and by tensions within the socialist tradition. Lederer published a spirited and complex, but sympathetic, critique of the theory of the disappearing middle class in 1912, showing the increase in new strata relative to the self-employed old middle class and to the industrial working class. He identified various strands within a new middle class. While arguing that the most immiserated white-collar employees would soon resemble the proletariat and be open to alliances with it, he also predicted that they would not readily accept working-class leadership. However, in the wake of German defeat in the First World War, the failed German Revolution, and the achievement of a brief, fragile democracy, they did just that. Membership in white-collar trade unions quadrupled from 1917 through 1923, and salaried workers both struck and met in revolutionary workers' councils with socialist and Communist blue-collar workers. Returning to the "new middle class" in 1926, now with Jacob Marschak as coauthor, Lederer lodged a devastating critique of his old position, deciding that "all gainfully employed" workers could unite, if not necessarily in "a single organization." He elaborated a host of reactionary implications of "new middle class" analysis, holding that it obscured the presence of a ready-for-radicalism "employee" sector. This mistake, according to Lederer and Marschak, encouraged an alliance between the old middle class and the new in defense of property. The authors argued explicitly against analytical focus on a new middle class and for emphasis on the "white-collar proletariat." Full of close statistical work, this research became a model for US studies of the middle class, especially after German texts were translated by the New Deal's Works Progress Administration and after Lederer himself, exiled as both Jewish and Marxist, helped to develop the New School for Social Research in New York City.[24]

If an upsurge in militancy provided seeming clarity for Lederer and Marschak in 1926, the "rumblings of fascism were already being heard," as they wrote. Indeed, the gains in white-collar organizing gave way in Germany after 1923. By the time of Nazi terror in and after the 1930s, German radical intellectuals faced a need to understand the unprecedented. They produced the most important body of antifascist scholarship to date. Grouped around the celebrated Frankfurt school, these researchers undertook detailed survey research seeking to grasp empirically the structures of belief and personality leading to acceptance of authoritarian rule. Their efforts generated models of sociological research unsurpassed anywhere, excepting the studies that W. E. B. Du Bois and others produced at Atlanta University. Their command of Marxism and psychoanalysis together produced profound insights. However, this work did little to advance the disaggregation of groups stitched together within the so-called new middle class. Some studies did tackle white-collar workers specifically, none more creatively than Siegfried Kracauer's brew of poetry and empiricism in *The Salaried Masses*. Kracauer certainly regarded his subjects as proletarianized and sometimes as even more miserable than industrial workers. But he also found them unresponsive when approached—he thought maladroitly—by the left and susceptible to Nazi appeals.[25]

The identification of the lower middle class as the social base of fascism spread widely. Leon Trotsky, the Red Army leader turned exiled revolutionary, offered an intriguing variation on this theme. Speaking about French politics, he described the petite bourgeoisie as "human dust," incapable of self-organization but ready to be swept up into fascism or, given proper leadership, someday into socialism. The middle class and its character structure become in this view the sources of fascism's "detachments," with the word resonating militarily and psychologically.[26] The French revolutionary Daniel Guérin's almost-instant 1939 history, *Fascism and Big Business*, turned out to be as much about the middle class as about corporations.[27]

Even the adventuresome and apt appeals to psychology tended to analyze a tragic lower-middle-class fascist subject. Thus, according to Frankfurt school leader Erich Fromm, "Nazism resurrected the lower-middle class psychologically while participating in the destruction of its old socioeconomic position."[28] The emphases on psychology and class developed by Fromm and others centered on *Arbeiter und Angestellten*, which could be translated as "blue- and white- collar workers" or, nodding more to the sense that white-collar workers were not quite workers, as "the working class and salaried employees." Such ambiguities reflected the problem of the placement of the "white-collar proletarian" vis-à-vis the working class and the lower middle class. When repeated in exile in the United States in the 1940s, the studies conducted by the Frankfurt school found the US middle class scoring as less authoritarian and anti-Semitic than the working class. The opposite had been true in Germany, though Fromm found considerable overlap. Amid such ambiguities authoritarian personalities were increasingly linked with mass society under capitalism, less than with specific classes.[29]

In the United States, the idea of premising analysis on the presence of a fractured "new middle class" came later than it had in Germany and was more distinctly the product of leftist intellectuals. First and foremost was the Italian immigrant Louis Fraina, who led the formation and unification of the Communist Party. Running afoul of the Communist International after a series of purported scandals, Fraina changed identities in the early '20s, working as a printer and then reinventing himself as a left-liberal business journalist under the name Lewis Corey. As labor organizing quickened in the 1930s, Corey tried, in the words of his biographer, to "write his way" back into the Communist movement. His most successful effort was the 1935 study *The Crisis of the Middle Class*. That fat, readable volume featured charts like those in Lederer and Marschak's work, and later in Mills's *White Collar*, detailing the transition to an employed and largely proletarianized new middle class. Positively reviewed in the Communist press, *The Crisis of the Middle Class* sold briskly in party bookstores, where it was distributed along with a printed critique of the book. For Corey, the "split personality" of the middle class left it pulled toward the workers' movement but also burdened with "outworn ideas" compatible with "the monster of fascism." In its own way, Corey's work matched Marx's in its certainty that the middle class rose by falling and then by *falling under* the sway of working-class leadership. When Robert S. Lynd and Helen M. Lynd published *Middletown in Transition* two years later, they premised their new openness to the idea of a middle class in Middletown squarely on their reading of Corey.[30]

In comparison to peers in Germany or France, writers like Corey in the United States experienced less of the presence of a socialist movement and less of the threat of fascism. Nevertheless, in a minor chord, class and political conflicts did shape understanding of the middle class. In no case was this clearer than that of C. Wright Mills's post–World War II writings. White-collar unions had long been relatively tiny in the

United States, where in 1935 about one white-collar worker in twenty was in a union. In Germany before the Nazis came to power, that figure reached over four in ten salaried workers. However, by the time Mills wrote enthusiastically about the middle class, proletarianization, and radicalism in his 1948 *New Men of Power*, some victories had accumulated in the US. These included new initiatives among retail workers, the impressive beginnings of organizing among foremen, a general white-collar workers union within the Congress of Industrial Organizations, and the growth of the United Public Workers, the latter two with left leadership. Indeed, as the Communist Party itself shed an emphasis on immediate revolution centered on blue-collar workers, it registered a rising interest in white-collar organizing in a lavish 1936 special issue of *New Masses*. Experience with white-collar layoffs had by then undermined the notion that salaried employees enjoyed far greater job security. In 1948, Mills's confidence rested on the power of the industrial union movement, fresh off a major strike wave, to attract white-collar workers as much as on the downward trajectory of the salaried employee. He tempered such confidence with an awareness of how much the Taft-Hartley amendments to national labor law could change everything. That body of anti-labor law did seriously hurt the general momentum of labor, the specific prospects of unionizing foremen, and the possibilities of left union leadership. In the language of socialist theorists, it was not that the proletarianization of the white-collar middle class slowed, but that the attractive force of industrial unionism suffered under withering attack.[31]

With *White Collar*, his brilliant full study of the middle classes, Mills became the intellectual known for distinguishing the old from the new within those strata. He drew on Corey, right down to the tables the two books featured.[32]

Informed too by German radical scholarship, Mills pivoted every bit as fully as Lederer had twenty-five years before. Taking stock of the dire changes in the three years since his 1948 book, *White Collar* embodies what his biographer calls a "thoroughly disillusioned radicalism," directing itself not only toward the middle class but also at the inability of the labor movement to inspire middle-class supporters. Mills privately wrote that *White Collar* aimed at "total damnation of everything in this setup."[33]

White Collar reproduced much analysis offered by the socialist tradition, including its contradictions, but without its hope. The book's sense of loss continued to be widely shared, as industrial working-class militancy ebbed and blue-collar jobs vanished. In 1935, Corey believed that an advanced capitalist society without a majority of blue-collar workers was impossible. "Salaried employees," he wrote, "have not displaced the wage workers, and they cannot." Technically, he remains correct—about 59 percent of US workers were paid in wages in 2017—but only because so many people in traditionally "middle-class" jobs such as sales are wage earners.[34] The century of glorious, flawed efforts of socialist intellectuals and socialist militants to figure out how to see and nurture radicalism among salaried workers and others termed middle class undoubtedly had its failures. It featured loose terminology, superciliousness, abrupt shifts in theoretical moorings in light of short-term setbacks and hopes, and disillusion. But it was also through immersion in social struggles, in big ideas, and even in illusions regarding the historic mission of blue-collar workers that socialists became the leading interpreters of the middle class. If new and global movements are now coalescing, it is this fierce urgency that they should inherit, not specific homilies that we can glean from a tradition that could only go so far.

Even during continuing lulls in class conflict, Marxist and ex-Marxist writers have followed up on Mills's work powerfully. Down to the present, they have continued and deepened earlier left narratives of falling—though now with little possibility of falling into something grand. Their work has thereby intersected with mainstream media interest in, and political obsessions with, the decline of the middle class. Barbara Ehrenreich's impressive career producing both serious materialist analysis of the professional-managerial class and popular journalism on its "fear of falling" stands out in this regard. Studies in the labor process established how thoroughly and easily scientific management moved from factories to offices, making management able to monitor productivity and even motions of office workers. Harry Braverman's classic *Labor and Monopoly Capital* offered the provocation that office work, rationalized, became manual labor.[35] The middle class thus fell as a whole, fell in segments, fell by occupational category, and, in the work of Ehrenreich, Newman, and countless journalists, fell poignantly as individuals.[36]

In the late 1960s, when the New Left group Students for a Democratic Society (SDS) attempted to organize a disparate "new working class," the sociologist Richard Sennett participated in meetings of "shoe salesmen, secretaries, and office clerks" and inquired into the experience of those who had "passed into" such jobs after growing up in blue-collar households. Sennett and coauthor Jonathan Cobb later described the ways in which wearing suits to commute to jobs downtown could command prestige from family and friends in the neighborhood. That success, they argued, existed alongside the fact that the jobs themselves were "exhausting and unrelieved." Cobb and Sennett took this to mean that SDS's formulation of a new working class described reality better than the sociological emphases on a "new middle class" or "new petty bourgeoisie." One famous if dubious formulation of the latter that became popular around the time they were writing implied that 70 percent of the US labor force fell into the latter category, which somehow expanded to include all white-collar workers.[37]

The most ambitious US Marxist research on the class and collar line since Mills undoubtedly came from the late sociologist Erik Olin Wright. Wright found a clever and mostly useful way to refuse a choice between, on the one hand, retaining shibboleths regarding the necessity of a growing industrial proletariat in a mature capitalist state and, on the other, the view that only a new middle class mattered. Wright is sometimes oversimplified today as a thinker forcing our confrontation with the presence of an important middle class, one that hidebound fellow Marxists allegedly refuse to acknowledge. However, from his early interventions, Wright is more convincingly read as arguing against "new class" theorists and holding that a significant working class remained. He added that even the middle class, which he regarded as roughly the same size as the working class, contained elements of working-class experience and consciousness as well as elements of capitalist logic and interest. Wright thus theorized a middle class defined by multiple "contradictory class locations"—those occupied, for example, by small businessmen working in their own enterprise and by middle managers controlling workers in firms but not empowered to make decisions about investment and production. In my view, Wright quite underrepresented the numbers employed in working-class jobs, for example by not including teachers and nurses. Nevertheless, he wrested precious insights from the data that he produced, elaborating the idea that middle-class experience included elements of working-class experience and showing why the sad, torn, and powerless middle manager so populates popular television from *The Office* to *The Chair*.[38]

No significant part of the socialist tradition, from its most dismissive to its most humanely sympathetic treatments of the middle class, was naive enough to maintain that simply "saving" that class was either possible or desirable. The following chapter argues that we can go further in seeing the ways that middle-class and working-class consciousness overlapped when we realize, with the Frankfurt school theorists, that middle-class life had its own gathering of miseries. Indeed, it was and is constituted by them. If we see the middle class as a plight as well as a perch, we can understand something of why many workers regard themselves simultaneously as middle class, working class, and living impossible lives.

4

FALLING, MISERY, AND THE IMPOSSIBILITIES OF MIDDLE-CLASS LIFE

The wedding is the chief ceremony of the middle-class mythology, and it functions as the official entrée of the spouses to their middle-class status. This is the real meaning of saving up to get married. The young couple struggles to set up an image of comfortable life which they will be forced to live up to in the years that follow.

—GERMAINE GREER, feminist writer and scholar

In a recent article that somehow manages to live up to its wonderful title, Columbia University epidemiologist Seth Prins and others associate the middle class and sadness in a way that complicates yet again the idea that there's something here to be saved. The title of their contribution to the journal *Sociology of Health and Illness* asks and answers questions: "Anxious? Depressed? You Might Be Suffering from Capitalism." The researchers specifically design strategies to assess the incidence of depression and anxiety in middle managers, the heart of the "professional managerial class." They adopt the sociologist Erik Olin Wright's ideas regarding "contradictory class locations" within the middle class to describe a torn and torn-up group, sharing some of the authority and compensation upper management enjoys but little of the decision-making power held by their bosses. They suffer, the article argues, with contradictions that follow them off the job, much as Herbert Marcuse maintained that production in advanced capitalism generated not only "socially needed occupations, skills, and attitudes but also individual needs and aspirations."[1] The results include higher rates of anxiety and depression. In raising questions of middle-class pain, Prins and his associates follow a path Mills also took in *White Collar*, where he wrote, "The misery of twentieth-century man is psychological even more than it is material, at least here in America." The Prins article so struck a nerve that it was widely reposted and became the grist for journalistic spin-offs.[2] To separate the material and psychological, or for that matter work and leisure, will not prove easy in a system that inflicts daily and prospective pain on many who could plausibly claim a position in the middle class. But surely Mills and Prins pointed us in the right direction with a focus on misery.

In *Cubed*, Nikil Saval's stylish study of the "secret history" of the office, we learn the transnational story of the cubicle, the tomb where a majority of office workers spend much of their lives. Ninety-three percent dislike it. Born as reform-minded design by a visionary 1960s architect, the cubicle was debased enough by the 1970s that its originator lamented its existence. Tied to cost savings, valued for its ease of dismantling during downsizings, and smaller as decades progressed, the cubicle illustrates how hard it is, in thinking about the tragedy of the middle class, to separate the fear of falling from the grind of daily misery. Saval captures well what many of us know from experience or relatives. "The surest sign of trouble," he tells us, came when an employee "lost his office." We meet a Kodak worker who knew something had changed when consigned to a cubicle after commanding a large office with a secretary. It is equally harrowing to be doubled up in cubicles, as the next shoe to drop can be loss of a job altogether. The fears of falling into and out of a cubicle compound the miseries of actually working in one.[3]

The towering, if abject, figures within nineteenth- and twentieth-century literary portrayals of white-collar and sales work likewise point us to a combination of misery in the worker's present and fears for the future. Both the title character in Herman Melville's dark nineteenth-century short story "Bartleby, the Scrivener" and Willy Loman in Arthur Miller's twentieth-century play *Death of a Salesman* fall tragically. The white-collar workplace from which Bartleby falls into incarceration in New York City's infamous Tombs and then to his own tomb is itself a site of poverty and illness. All the adult workers suffer from what we would now call occupational diseases. Layoffs and threats of cutting hours of workers already managing only the barest of lives are the companions of the employer's faux compassion. The child laborer in the office brings in the cheap ginger nut wafers for which he is nicknamed, and which allow the labor force to subsist. The most plausible reading of the story finds Bartleby *choosing* to fall further from an already-unbearable situation.[4]

Similarly, Loman's fall and death—a suicide after a series of failed attempts—come not at once but over a lifetime of misery: of having to smile while in mortal fear of being laughed at, of uncertainty in a job where confidence was a necessity. He experienced first what the cultural historian Daniel Clark has called the "crisis of the clerk" and then the particular crisis of "the clerk who isn't young."[5] In

White Collar, when Mills constructed composite ideal types of workers in "the great salesroom," one was "the charmer," who "focuse[d] less upon her stock of goods than upon herself." Charmers had, if they stayed on even as little as a decade, to think about a transition to the often disgruntled and nostalgic ranks of "the old timer" category. Loman followed a male version of that declining path.[6]

This chapter grapples with why countless Willy Lomans in working-class jobs have long seen themselves as middle class. It tries to regard their choices, however tragic, as more than the result of being bamboozled by elites. It argues that the middle class occupies a place of misery even before it falls. That misery is itself part of what binds together those disparate elements who consider themselves middle class, with more than a few blue-collar workers included.

Common sense does not completely mislead us when we regard prosperity and homeownership as the keys to making wage workers feel middle class, but such traces of embourgeoisement only take us so far in accounting for a material basis of buying into the middle class. Miseries, shared at times by industrial workers with white-collars workers, salespeople, technicians, lower and middle management, and professionals—likewise matter. They include debt, alienated labor in which personalities as well as production are for sale, and cycles of overwork and overconsumption. The spread of these miseries to larger strata of the population became in many ways the story of how the modern United States generated a middle class that was distended by world standards but bound together by its very sadness. Such glum solidarity, even bitterness, makes the idea of "saving" the middle class from falling at best a partial fix for a larger emptiness. Because being middle class involves a set of unrealistic expectations—of improvement of living standards across generations, of putting kids through college without debt, of a dignified retirement, of balancing labor and leisure—life in the middle has come to seem less desirable and less possible.

WHEN THE MIDDLE FALLS

Much of the misery of the middle class fits well within narratives of sudden descent in material terms, but much also involves psychic pain. This is true in good times as well as bad. Of course, if we accept the Obama / Romney / H. R. Clinton / Trump definition of the middle class as the bottom 96 percent of the US income earners, it includes the poorest of the poor and all manner of misery. But even above those mired below the poverty line, the reach of "truly" middle-class desperation surfaces regularly in the news. The "middle-class homeless," we learn, include teachers, nurses, and chefs, camped in their cars to survive in areas of California that provide work but also feature exorbitant housing costs. They are often elderly and/or disabled people reeling from medical setbacks, but they are also working families unable to make ends meet. Or they are the seemingly prosperous early retirees from the early 2000s, who, bent on enjoying bouts of travel in their RVs, were then wiped out by the Great Recession. Many now use those same RVs as their sole domiciles, following Amazon jobs and living on Walmart parking lots.[7] Others living in vehicles or couch-surfing are homeless PhDs, young and old, teaching as adjuncts in colleges and universities as what the journalist Jim Hightower calls "the highly educated working poor."[8]

Middle-class hunger touches those who have lost and those who have kept their homes. In fact, it can flow from scrimping to avoid foreclosure and then finding that "you cannot eat a house," the structure borrowers have overextended themselves to acquire. *National Geographic* writes of the "new face of hunger" as that of middle-class people who manage to keep up appearances while being unable to eat adequately. The college student, perhaps best symbolizing the intersection of the aspirant and the solidly established middle class, hungers for more than knowledge. Very conservative estimates of food insecurity within higher education have it afflicting 11 percent of four-year college and 17 percent of community college students, almost exactly the same figures as those for college student housing insecurity, whether couch-surfing, car-living, or on the street. Other studies place the incidence of college-student food insecurity above 40 percent.[9]

Neal Gabler's 2016 reporting on the "secret shame" of the middle class in *The Atlantic* touched a nerve. Gabler showed from Federal Reserve Board data that about half the middle class—himself included, he confessed, even after solid and enduring success as a writer—cannot imagine raising $400 in the face of an emergency without selling off assets or borrowing.[10] After thirty-five years of politicians declaring the need to save the middle class, the middle class has precious little accessible savings.

FROM CONTRADICTION TO IMPOSSIBILITY

According to a Commerce Department study done in 2010 for the task force on the middle class led by then vice president Joe Biden, being middle class has revolved around a series of basic goals: striving "to own a home," "to save for retirement," "to provide [their children] with a college education," to "protect their own and their children's health," to "have a car" for each adult, and to manage "a family vacation each year." These goals, an uncharacteristically tart Brookings report on the middle class recently observed, far exceed the capacity of a single parent with two kids and making the median income of $25,000 per year.[11] However, it is not only having to forego this or that particular expectation or aspiration that has begun to erode identification with the middle class. Rather, it is an increasing sense that the whole project of middle-class life is impossible.

The difficulties typically come in pairs and as contradictions. The Irish writer Terry Eagleton captured the main such contradiction and the impossible psychic demands structuring it. "Capitalism needs a human being who has never yet existed," Eagleton wrote, "one who is prudently restrained in the office and wildly anarchic in the shopping mall." Mills had gestured at the same point half a century before, lamenting the accelerating treadmill that had so much of the middle class "selling little pieces of themselves" at work and then "trying to buy them back each night and weekend with the coin of 'fun.'"[12]

I thought of Eagleton's remark in a loud restaurant bar in Minneapolis recently, on seeing advertisements on the wall for Red Bull and vodka, sold under the name of Liquid Cocaine. The wall menu sat next to cardboard cutouts advertising various brands of beer, each image a monument to hedonism (and often sexism), but also urging, in far smaller type, moderation in drinking. The larger tableau and the particular mixture of hyper-caffeination and hard liquor in Liquid Cocaine catch perfectly US society's double addiction to honing concentration, especially at work, and to forfeiting restraint, judgment, and even consciousness, especially after work. The results are so familiar that we do not much linger over their strange combinations of asceticism and abandon—for example, hearing multiple public figures claim to have tried pot but not inhaled, and being at the top of the table among nations when it comes to the consumption of both porn and church. When I raise the contradictions pointed out by Eagleton to audiences, both in and out of classrooms, they can fill in the blanks with symbols of the twinned needs for productivity and restraint, on the one hand, and for profligacy and immediate gratification, on the other. These include the casino ads with phone numbers for gambling-addiction counselors, the cycles of credit card debt followed by the taking on of a second or third job, and even addictions to work.[13]

A more familiar way to see the impossibilities of middle-class life would put matters in terms of overwork on the one hand and of debt on the other. Here, the neglected research of the historically minded economist Juliet Schor captures better than any other scholarship how worker/spenders who had "never existed" historically came to be the US ideal and our problem. Indeed, when business news talks about "positive economic indicators," it cites increased "consumer confidence" and rising hours of labor and labor force participation—that is, overspending and overwork. Schor's books show the problems with the idea that these are considered measures of what make economies and personal lives work. Her first book on these subjects is called *The Overworked American*, the second *The Overspent American*. Together, the pair chart much of what we need to know on both subjects. Because they're covered in separate books, readers might easily imagine one group in the United States afflicted with the first problem and another group plagued by the second— that the overworkers stayed out of debt via high income and that the indebted needed to knuckle down and get out of the hole they'd dug. However, Schor shows that middle- to upper-income families are much plagued by debt. Indeed, the two books challenge the widely held view that getting and spending are separate spheres. Schor shows how alienated labor contributes to sad attempts at psychically compensatory spending, developing the idea of "work and spend" cycles.[14] The very richness of statistical evidence in the books has made them seem dated rather too quickly, but the imbricated tragedies that they identify very much abide with us. Schor's more recent work in these areas, identifying the ecological consequences of overwork and overconsumption, makes her ideas more relevant than ever.[15]

This mix of overwork, hyper-management, desperate searching for satisfaction in consumption, and consequent debt spreads so widely that the resulting combination of anxiety and alienation sometimes seems a condition of mass society within advanced capitalism as a whole. However, it was the conventionally defined middle class—salaried and suburban—that first experienced a particular modern malaise born of overspending and overwork. When they were joined in their miseries by others paid by the hour, often neighbors and family members, all identified as middle class as much out of shared pain and a common sense of impossibility as from a sense of triumph.

THE TRAFFIC IN PERSONALITIES

Success writer Dale Carnegie avoided both the Missouri farm life into which he was born and the new middle-class life of selling other people's products, a career that he tried out in his twenties. Instead, he sold his own line of courses and books designed to teach others how to speak publicly, be happy, and win. Changing his name as a young adult from Carnagey to Carnegie, which he thought would bring to mind the steel magnate Andrew Carnegie, he owned

educational ventures with hundreds of thousands of gradu-
ates and earned extravagant royalties from books. His writing career culminated with the 1936 publication of *How to
Win Friends and Influence People*. Endlessly reprinted, it sold
five million copies before his death in 1955. Carnegie's marketing prominently featured speaking in public and gaining
friends, but his biggest selling point was getting ahead at
work. For instance, Carnegie appealed to fellow salespersons
by promising to help them identify what closed the deal.[16]
Perhaps no US historical figure has more perfectly embodied
the wisdom of Joe Strummer, front man of The Clash, who
reminded us that "selling is what selling sells."[17]

Carnegie's further genius was to know that the modern
middle class, especially the employed new middle class, was
on display at work, where the marketability of their very
personalities mattered to their bosses and their careers.
He tapped complacently into a truth that C. Wright Mills
would deliver a generation later as an indictment. According
to Mills, "Salesmanship seems a frenzied affair of flexibil-
ity and pep, the managerial demiurge, a cold machinery of
calculation and planning." However, he added, "the conflict
between them is only on the surface; in the new society,
salesmanship is much too important to be left to pep alone
or to the personal flair of the detached salesman."[18] Carnegie worked this intersection of sales and management cheer-
fully, prospecting also in the byways of the office worker, the
bookkeeper, the professional for hire, and the small businessman. "Dealing with people is probably the biggest problem
you face," Carnegie wrote, "especially if you are a businessman. Yes, and that is true also if you are an accountant, an
architect, or an engineer."[19] He promised, "People who smile
tend to manage, teach, and sell more effectively," adding as
a near afterthought that they also "raise happier children."

The novelist Sinclair Lewis's bitter critique of Carnegie as an advocate of "yessing the boss" pinpointed both the content of Carnegie's guide to the pursuit of happiness and the place to pursue it.[20]

Philosopher Michel Foucault applied his pronouncements on the transformation of the modern subject into an "entrepreneur of himself" and indeed "his own producer" to the era of neoliberalism, but it had long and disturbing roots in how the salaried middle class was managed, and self-managed, dating back at least to Carnegie.[21] Crafted and marketed selves were what the buyer wanted. Management thought shining images reflected well on the general state of things in the firm. To learn the secrets of the workplace, Carnegie studied Hollywood actors—their smiles and images—which he identified with the successful marketing of sincerity. He emphasized that all of us "are evaluated and classified by four things: by what we do, by how we look, by what we say, and how we say it." Fourfold too was the solution. Success required "tact, praise, modesty, and a little hypocrisy."[22] Feigning interest in others was a Carnegie job skill long before it became a speed-dating one.

So was smiling, everywhere a concern of the success industry. Carnegie, for example, reckoned the steel magnate Charles Schwab's smile was "worth a million dollars." Correspondents told Carnegie of the fortunes their smiles earned, and guidebooks tutored customers on the use of mirrors to perfect smiles that were sincere, practiced, and winning.[23] *How to Win Friends and Influence People* was such a sensation that a book-length parody, Irving Tressler's *How to Lose Friends and Alienate People*, itself became a best seller in 1937. Tressler's hero hated all things about the mass-produced personalities influenced by Carnegie and overrunning the business world. Each said that the narrator looked half his age and had a surpassingly cool middle name. "All," he continued, "sit on the edge of their chairs breathless for my next word, and with a smile on their faces that looks as though it was painted there." They clearly needed to put in more hours with the mirror. The deftest parody came from the great Armenian American writer William Saroyan, whose short story "The Dale Carnegie Friend" complained that conversation could only begin after the Carnegie convert "smiled the way that was supposed to be sincere" and found his "voice that was intended to be winning." Saroyan's narrator reckoned that three Carnegie protégés showed up at every party he attended.[24] Appropriately enough, the most penetrating scholarly writing on Carnegie comes from the expert on the sociology and history of management, Reinhard Bendix. In Bendix's massive 1956 classic *Work and Authority in Industry*, Dale Carnegie assumes more prominence than Andrew Carnegie. The former claimed to have perfected, according to Bendix, "personality salesmanship" in workplaces in which "[h]ow [the worker] looked or what he said . . . was of great importance for the salaried employee."[25]

The sale of one's personality hardly came into being with the ascendance of the new middle class. It was a stratagem of sales work even when that work was un-bossed. Music critic Greil Marcus's recent introduction to a reissue of Constance Rourke's classic study of humor and the US national character captures well Rourke's description of the solitary, itinerant "Yankee peddler." Marcus writes that if that salesman "has a true face, not even the mirror ever sees it."[26] Melville's Bartleby, the most famous white-collar worker in American literature, copied documents by hand a century and a half ago under the watchful eye and the abruptly shifting judgments of the lawyer who employed him and who narrated his story. (The employee and lawyer would, by the inflated modern standards, both be middle class.) Bartleby's character, appearance, dress, and personality are judged according to whether they please both the lawyer who hired him and potential clients. All the personal judgments delivered by the narrator focus on the workers, not the horrific workplace itself. Even the vantages of observation shift in Melville's tale, as a screen supplementing "ground glass folding doors" comes and goes according to when the narrator wants to see Bartleby and others and when he does not.[27] Over time, salespeople and clerical workers have hugely increased in numbers, and the bureaucratic minutiae of judgment have matured without losing their potential for arbitrary managerial opinion.

In the middle of the twentieth century, the practice of personality salesmanship expanded still further, enthralling many workers doing manual labor at the same time that they were beginning to be hailed as middle class. Earlier in the century, as Bendix concluded, "how [the manual laborer] looked or what he said had little importance." Frederick Winslow Taylor, as the leading theorist of the management of manual labor at the time, cared about whether or not a worker could move forty-seven tons of pig iron in a day. He liked temperance and energy among workers and loathed sociability during the working day. But everything he encouraged or decried came directly in the service of increasing production. Experiments in management at the Hawthorne Works Western Electric plant outside of Chicago in the 1920s and '30s began a shift in management strategies. These experiments produced some evidence of what was later called the "Hawthorne effect," in which the mere observation by and interaction with a management researcher seemed to spark positive changes in an employee's behavior. The first lesson drawn from the study emphasized the personality of the manager—the bigger the better.[28] Over time, especially after World War II, judgments regarding the personalities of all workers—including their positivity, enthusiasm, and commitment to team building and rules—became systematized. New and growing companies like IBM and Polaroid led this trend, which later spread into heavy industry and even fast food. Whether in a customer-facing job or in the back, a McDonald's worker, for example, is judged as productive based on his or her personality in the face of the pressures of frantically paced work.[29]

As such changes took place, a line between what was called the middle class and the working class blurred in an overarching emphasis on liberal and bureaucratic modes of management. Elites clearly believed in these modes, which were introduced when retention of trained workers was a priority but survived when it was not. As late as 1965, the sociologist Richard Sennett calculates, a white-collar career included on average four or five job changes. Now, more than a dozen job changes are typical, but bureaucratized judgments on the personalities of those who will be leaving still seem as important to employers. As Edgar Cabanas and Eva Illouz's study of the "science and industry of happiness" argues, for just about all of the employed, "happiness is required to succeed." Management increasingly casts deficiencies in enthusiasm—that is, deficiencies in the performance of enthusiasm—as disloyalty. But there is scant evidence that the bureaucratic rubrics measuring "positivity at work" are less arbitrary than the whim of a foreman in an earlier industrial workplace. Nor of course does the nurturing of positivity supplant speedups of production.[30]

Our bone-deep understanding of the civilized horror of modern workplaces ought to help us understand that the middle class has historically labored in systems that place their personalities as well as their labor power on the market. The generalization of such a regime of control can hardly count as an advance. If it contributes to more workers seeing their jobs as middle class, they do so out of shared misery as much as from registering a rise in status. It is easy enough to critique the increasingly alienating and sped-up office as "factory-like," but offices, burger joints, and universities also feature soul-killing management strategies that have bled over into factory management.[31]

The tremendous emphasis on bought and sold performances of personality so overlapped with the performance of gender that white-collar alienation in early twentieth-century fiction was best conveyed through the plight of women, often young. Secretarial work abruptly switched from the male preserve depicted in "Bartleby" to a majority-female labor force after 1920. If a "woman's place was at the typewriter," men still overwhelmingly supervised. At times they sought sexualization of the office, and at others (or simultaneously) they wanted a second domestic sphere in which women served coffee and emotional support while also producing relentlessly. However, personality saleswoman-ship in such workplaces also offered opportunities for women workers to exercise agency. Managerial desires proved subject to manipulation, with the office sometimes seeming an overwhelmingly feminine space culturally, although not in terms of power.[32] Such agency had limits. Mills planned an extensive treatment of what would now be called sexism and sexual harassment in *White Collar*, collecting upward of a hundred interviews on those subjects. However, he ended up jettisoning the projected chapter titled "Sexual Exploitation in White-Collar Employment." He did say that in offices and sales, "younger women tend to be subordinated to older men." When Evelyn Nakano Glenn and Roslyn Feldberg revisited the "proletarianization" of clerical work in a 1979 sociological study, they concluded that management used "sex as a basis for control."[33]

Department store sales work provided even more dramatic examples of women creating solidarities and women's spaces amid rivalry, harassment, and surveillance. Women workers there forged ties not only with each other but also with middle-class female customers in ways that could be used against management. Thus, a desire to appeal to elite and middle-class customers made it even more important that they present themselves as both attractive and proper.[34] Theodore Dreiser's novel *Sister Carrie* became the best window into what Richard Sennett called the "tawdry respectability of native-born lower-middle-class Americans." Especially in the 1920s, the "white-collar girl" figured prominently in American literature. Christopher Morley's novel of the cosmetics industry, *Kitty Foyle*, perhaps most captured the ways that bodily and emotional appearances mattered as it described autonomy and glamour but also peril.[35] The title character in Booth Tarkington's *Alice Adams* learned in youth that her "delicate and fine" hands were her best "possession;" they surpassed her "mind and character," it was implied. She set out therefore to live a "life of gestures," in part to draw attention to those hands, her passport to avoiding business college through marriage into greater wealth. The most apt portrayal of a male office worker in the same era, James T. Farrell's short, powerful "A Jazz Age Clerk," portrays a lonely desire to emulate one's betters in swagger and fashion while desperately hoping there's more to life than what the office has offered.[36]

INCREASING HOURS, CRUSHING DEBTS, AND IMPOSSIBLE LIVES

Were life lived at a certain deliberate speed, in good faith, and on an endlessly renewable planet, there could be ways to mediate the claims of the workplace and the mall. In a crude way, the hegemonic system often described as reigning for most of the twentieth century, "Fordism," pointed toward a temporary peace settlement. At least the original "Fordist bargain," offered to workers at Henry Ford's sped-up Highland Park factory just before World War I, laid out possibilities. The unfamiliar assembly-line production and its pace ran through workers quickly, causing massive problems with turnover. The bargain required workers to accept the attendant alienation in return for a greater ability to consume—the much-publicized "five-dollar day." Less remembered is the fact that Ford's original plan also cut the working day by as much as 20 percent.[37] That reform was part of a general move to the eight-hour day in industry and offices between the Civil War and World War II—a dramatic advance from almost no leisure to what workers announced as "Eight hours for work, eight hours for rest, eight hours for what we will." Almost everything conspired to suggest that more was coming. The great mainstream economist John Maynard Keynes predicted a fifteen-hour working week, and Congress nearly made the thirty-hour week the law of the land during the Great Depression. The industrial unions that finally triumphed in the 1930s and '40s seemed bent on winning more leisure. Then, just as quickly, a long historical trend reversed—in the United States especially, but also throughout the advanced capitalist world. The acceptance of what would have seemed in 1900 extraordinarily overtaxing labor survived, and real wage increases lasted for a while, but the part of the Fordist bargain that directly lessened overwork by cutting hours passed from the scene.[38]

Several of us wrote about the stall of progress in shortening the workweek and the virtual blackout of talk about such a move at about the time that Schor did, but her contribution stood out. Moving beyond description and lament, she identified for a popular audience several key ways that lives became impossible. The first is that the crisis of overwork reached beyond being a seeming glitch in history's longer trend toward more leisure. As overwork increased, it could no longer be argued that workers, feeling deprivations born of the Depression and war, naturally preferred buying things to more time off. She showed a continuing trend not only toward flat lines charting the workweek but to increases in overwork, long after the 1950s had passed. In particular, she compared 1969 and 1987 figures in a way that forced consideration of gender and of particular ways that overwork reached into life off the job.[39]

Schor found that average males fully participating in the labor force worked 2,054 hours in 1969. The average crept up 98 hours by 1987, about 2 more per week. Women's annual paid working hours increased from 1,406 in 1969 to 1,711 in 1987, about 6 more each week. When Schor added the labor necessary to maintain households and raise children, a fascinating symmetry, not to be mistaken for equality, emerged. In 1969, women, working far less in marketed labor than men, labored on unpaid tasks of social reproduction about 13 more hours per week. As women's paid hours jumped, their hours devoted to unpaid household labor declined by about 3 per week, and male housework rose by a little over an hour. Remarkably, in both years the total number of paid plus unpaid hours of labor was virtually identical for men and women, though women still did the

lion's share of housework and therefore suffered compara-
tively in terms of income. The average number of unpaid
hours—male and female together—likewise remained constant. What changed was the number of hours worked for
pay. On average, more than three hours of free time per person disappeared each week into marketed work. Schor called
the change, when measured over the course of a year, the
"extra month of work."[40]

The speedup of work became a source of tension within
families. Strains on gender roles intensified, as did increases
in divorces and single parenting. The very healthy conversation and contestation for which the women's movement
called regarding the valuation and apportionment of household work took place under dire conditions of fatigue and
stress, compounded by debt. Families suffered under, in
Schor's terms, a "time squeeze at home." Overwork became
not only an enemy of time to sleep but also, in an insight expanded by recent scholarship, to the calm necessary for rest.[41]

In several ways, overwork on and off the job impacted
the middle class in particular. First, as salaried employees,
a large share of middle-class workers were exempt at times
from federal labor law provisions regulating overtime. Their
overwork therefore sometimes remained uncompensated,
even unrecorded. During the COVID pandemic, those in
white-collar and professional-managerial jobs have often
been able to work from home with relative ease, but for
very long hours, especially if we include online check-ins.
Goldman Sachs has sometimes kept junior staff at it eight-
een hours a day. Overwork has afflicted middle-class families disproportionately. "Middle income" men are somewhat
overrepresented among those working fifty or more hours
a week, and professionals are dramatically overrepresented.
Among women, the crisis of overwork has had ideological

as well as practical dimensions. The Cold War middle-class ideal insistently preached the value of stay-at-home mothers running child-centered households, havens separated from the world of work and somehow emblematic of the superiority of free enterprise. In reality, however, middle-class and professional women became both relatively and absolutely unlikely to be stay-at-home married mothers. Already by 1977, just 35 percent of women in middle-income families made that choice, while the proportion of women in low-income families who chose to stay home was 55 percent. Within a decade, things shifted further in the same direction, so that mothers in the middle-income and professional brackets were almost three times more likely to work outside the home than lower-income-family mothers.[42]

Elaine Tyler May, a historian of gender and the Cold War, identified what was then particularly praised by US champions of free enterprise as being "located in suburbia and epitomized by white middle-class nuclear families." Of course, those same families provided the tragic raw material for Betty Friedan's *The Feminine Mystique*, a searching examination of the effects of isolating women from the world of work and power, and a critique adopted by much of the second wave of US feminism. In making bold claims to employment, women thus did more than break with an old way of life and define a new middle-class one. They also loosened connections with nationalist mythologies and moved toward alliances with other women similarly plagued by overwork.[43]

The ways in which suburban women entered the labor force guaranteed that overwork comingled with emancipation; squeezed for time, working women had unprecedented opportunities to change household arrangements and leave dangerous domestic situations. By the time Schor was writing, the militant phase of women's liberation had ended, and *The Overworked American* registered her fears that private solutions, available only to women with resources, would supplant public ones. Sadly, she was right, and we do live in a time of unpaid family leave and expensive childcare. Books like *Overwhelmed: Work, Love, and Play When No One Has the Time* and *Glass Ceilings* and *100-Hour Couples: What the Opt-Out Phenomenon Can Teach Us about Work and Family* give us a harrowing sense of the problems, but little in the way of policy solutions to overwork and the time squeeze at home.[44] Senator Elizabeth Warren's cowritten 2004 combination of encouragement and policy prescription, *The Two-Income Trap: Why Middle-Class Mothers and Fathers Are Going Broke*, likewise suffers from solutions incommensurate with the gendered middle-class plight that it describes.[45]

From the vantage of the present, three decades after Schor's indictment of overwork in the '80s, the crisis she describes looks both familiar and, at times, like the good old days. Measurement of working hours is vexed by trends toward holding more than one job. Schor's brief discussion of "moonlighting" assumed the addition of a sideline to a full-time regular job. Since she researched and wrote, virtually every president has bragged of being a record-breaking job creator. Just as routinely, the opposition has countered by quoting workers who say, "We know; we have three of them." (The three jobs themselves may be in three nominally different class locations: managing a small night shift at Arby's, keeping the books for a megachurch, and selling franchised sex toys at parties in the homes of friends.) The data make it hard to say with confidence whether the United States is absolutely the "most overworked developed nation," as even career-advice websites sometimes claim. It surely ranks near the top in overwork, in lack of public policy protections against it, and in hostility toward vacationing.[46]

Mills described a perpetual middle-class struggle to fashion a "holiday" personality, one set against the alienation at work. But contemporary figures showing a fifth of US workers laboring sixty or more hours a week, and twice that many workers at fifty or more, indicate they have given up on the struggle to construct a coequal leisured self and instead embrace a "workaholic" addiction—or hardheaded bow to necessity—centering life on the job. The trends in overwork suggest what an uphill battle the struggle for free time has become. From 1980 until 2015, a Pew Charitable Trusts study reports, the average working year increased by 173 hours—another month of extra work per year.[47] Gender differences continue to apply, with slightly more paid working time for men, and about six more hours per week of household labor of employed women compared to employed men. This continuing gap has remained so stubborn as to attract attention from the business press—as a drain on workplace productivity![48]

IMPOSSIBLY INDEBTED

Where debt is concerned, the story is much the same. This is true in terms of the extent of the misery involved, its tendency to worsen, and its specific impact on how the self-identified middle class lives and worries. Thirty years ago, Schor wondered in *The Overspent American* "why we want what we don't need." Her answer hinged on the "work and spend" cycle, beginning with alienated overwork and spiraling into compensatory consumption, followed by the need for longer hours and still more work. She pinpointed four sad, exhilarating moments on the spending side—"seeing, wanting, borrowing, buying."[49] The irrational self- and family-de-structiveness of staggering on an ever steeper and acceler-ating treadmill registers clearly, but the remorseless logic of hurtful choices also emerges. Completion of one half of the "work and spend" cycle requires that we balance our psy-chological and fiscal checkbooks through frantic activity on the other. Falling into that cycle implies less a personal dys-function than irrationality at the level of the system itself. That system needs such divided selves. Good economic citi-zenship requires debt, figured as "consumer confidence," as well as overwork. The opioid and methamphetamine crises, to take up two illegal addictions among a host of legal ones, seem the epitome of wildly selfish pleasures. But the connec-tion of the former to dragging oneself to work when injured, and the latter to efforts by working parents to have it all, could not be more stark. One recent investigation identified meth's allure as the supposed "perfect drug for the suburban woman." Similarly, porn addiction invades workplaces, with specific connections to the choice not to work, so much so that we now read of "procrasturbation" as either a threat to productivity or a seizure of lonely pleasure amid stress.[50]

Schor began with the acknowledgment that the overspent on whom she concentrated come overwhelmingly from what she calls the middle class. At about the same time, Eliza-beth Warren, then a legal scholar researching bankruptcy, reached just the same conclusion. Her coauthored book about "Americans in debt," *The Fragile Middle Class*, de-scribed the victims of bankruptcy—whose numbers had in-creased by 400 percent from 1979 to 1997—as either "solidly middle class" or "once middle class." The record debts of the 1990s that Schor described came not mainly from the poor but especially from the layer making between $50,000 and $100,000 a year—those considered solidly upper middle class in that decade. They consumed, she argued, less often with eyes on the keeping up with Joneses, and more often on keeping going as individuals with impossible jobs and schedules. However, status anxiety still lurked, not insignificantly because looks and auras of success remained central to the marketing of personality on the job. Competing demands for stimulation, emotional compensation, relaxation, and family happiness secured by money rather than time meant that even very highly compensated workers suffered both from debt and from the sense that they could not buy what they needed. Between 1987 and 1996, survey responses to the question of how much income it took to live a good life rose from an average of $50,000 to $90,000. In 1995, 30 percent of those making between $25,000 and $35,000 annually reckoned that they could not afford the things that they "really need"; but so did about two-fifths of those earning between $75,000 and $100,000, and well over a quarter of those making over the latter figure. Mounting debt and a continuing sense of deprivation stood as middle-class facts of life even during good times and among the prosperous.[51]

Schor argued that from the late 1980s to the late '90s, the cycle of working and spending intensified. But the dynamics that she describes as middle-class miseries had a significant history and have in the decades since proven that they are not waning. The self-employed and those saving to be so in the nineteenth century rarely borrowed for personal and family pleasures—plantation owners being a spectacular exception. As Marx described the dominant ethos of his time: "Self-renunciation . . . is its principal thesis. The less you eat, drink and buy books; the less you go to the theatre, the dance hall, the public house; the less you think, love, theorize, sing, paint, fence, etc., the more you *save*— the *greater* becomes your treasure which neither moths nor rust will devour—your capital."[52] One historian of debt in the United States has observed that the "Victorian money management ethic" left room for only "productive" debt as not in conflict with Puritan homilies regarding thrift and restraint.[53] Personal fulfillment and family ambition connected far more with renunciation than with spending. Sizing up of "character"—so important to business and family reputation—followed from this choice.[54]

Another historian of US borrowing periodizes the age when "personal debt was really business debt" as unfolding between 2000 BC and 1920. Changes during the two decades before and after 1920 shaped the new history of debt. By 1920 the intensifications of labor associated with scientific management and Fordism had solidified, altering the first step of the work and spend cycle dramatically, in offices as well as factories. Indeed, some white-collar workplaces had by then glimpsed the limits of the management of time and motion and moved toward efforts to manage personalities systematically.[55] The sharp post–World War I depression provided a reminder of Marx's little-developed point that the layers of the population who consumed the surplus bounty of industrial production but did not directly produce it had their uses in addressing downturns in the economy. The uneven but tremendous growth of the economy in the 1920s fueled the switch from a regard for personal debt as suspect to its positive perception as a marker of confidence. To the extent that national economies in the industrialized world had entered what the late historian Martin Sklar called a "disaccumulating" period, with more emphasis on spending surpluses and less on scrimping to save capital, indebted consumption could challenge the hold of the earlier ideals of renunciation.[56] The middle-class debtor appeared right on time as both an exemplar of the new order and a cog in it.

In 1910, installment debt, largely for household and family matters, stood at half a billion dollars. In 1930, it reached about seven billion.[57]

The '20s forged a connection of debt and social position that would grow stronger in the next decade, when those who successfully struggled to regain a credit line during the Depression were often called middle class. In 1920, the credit theorist and advocate William Post suggested how the middle class could cohere as an indebted class by redefining respectability rather than renouncing it. Post's *Character: The Basic Rock Foundation of the Four Big C's in the Extension of Credit* registered the possibility of the "deserving indebted," able to borrow because of their virtues. In terms of ideology, rising levels of debt did not endorse profligacy. Credit-buying for large household items, and of course mortgages for houses themselves, could suggest discipline—the focused and timed commitment to sacrifice for a limited number of satisfying things rather than the frittering away of paychecks.[58] For some households, the extras bought on credit were appliances making housework easier, and the small but growing number of working wives in the '20s sometimes sacrificed time for just those purchases. A growing share of "middle income" families were also ones with multiple earners.[59] Coinciding with the great Cold War expansion of the middle class, and of talk about it, was a subsequent wave of borrowing that addressed demands pent up during depression and war, as well as real shortages of housing. The golden age of the middle-class suburban family starred, according to the acerbic liberal scholar David Riesman, "the debtor class." Already in 1958, the hot-selling economist and social critic John Kenneth Galbraith was asking, "Can the bill collector or the bankruptcy lawyer really be the central figure in the good society?"[60] Credit provided enervating enjoyment. Before his demise, middle-class antihero Willy Loman lamented on stage, "Once in my life I would like to own something outright before it was broken." For the strongly unionized autoworkers in Detroit in the '50s, not only high wages but also high debt and high anxiety made it plausible to call their lives middle class. As Daniel Clark's important new account of the travails of such workers shows, fluctuations in demand and model changes made employment in auto plants episodic, often necessitating second jobs. Home foreclosures and evictions were regular threats.[61]

As is the case with working hours, the crisis that Schor described can hardly be said to have eased; in 1995, non-mortgage debt in the United States stood at about $1.2 trillion. At the end of the second quarter of 2019, the figure approached $4.5 trillion. Mortgage debt was at a record high, registering gains for the twentieth straight quarter. Total household debt and credit set records too, touching on the $14 trillion mark; as late as 1997, Schor totaled such debt at about $5.5 trillion.[62] Credit card debt, meanwhile, approached its Great Recession peak by the middle of 2019, standing at $868 billion, roughly double its 1999 amount.[63] The skyrocketing category of student debt was just short of $1.5 trillion, over a fifth of which had not been serviced for three months or more. Such figures dwarf those in the alarmed account provided by Elizabeth Warren in her 2004 call to arms against such debt.[64]

According to a 2015 Inequality.org study based on figures from the *Credit Suisse Global Wealth Databook*, nearly 50 million of the 243 million adults then in the United States ranked in the poorest one-tenth of the world's population. (This social fact pairs with figures showing that US adults are even more overrepresented in the top 10 percent of world wealth, underlining again how little the United States is a nation dominated by its middle layers). There is much more at play here than a nation's amassment of great wealth while tolerating dire poverty. The lower 50 million includes some who have no property and no jobs. They are conjured into the middle class by politicians who portray them as presumptively aspirant members with poverty-level incomes. Others qualify for a place at the world's bottom based on steep debt. Of course, to overextend so massively requires credentials and credit. They stave off loss of an already re-mortgaged house with credit cards, until they can't. They are both fallen and in fear of falling. They deserve far more than restoration of an earlier era in which they also were not saved.[65]

The numbers illuminate as well as obscure. Those state actors who measure, report, and analyze trends do so mainly with a view to assessing the health and prospects of the US economy, mostly in terms of its potential for growth. Even very high levels of personal and national debt seem compatible with such growth, except, as happened in the recent Great Recession, when they aren't. Individuals and families—both those going under and those staying afloat—cannot be quite so cheery. They know they can scarcely work more to square things. Often they must give up parts of middle-class dreams, declaring them impossibilities—foregoing paying for the college education of children, travel for vacation, and a dignified retirement. One result is that debt and overwork become even more central to the definition of the middle class, while what is positive recedes.

The personal here is also political. Sociologist and philosopher Maurizio Lazzaroto's 2012 *The Making of Indebted Man* makes this point well. While hoping that common indebtedness can unite the many, Lazzaroto argues that the processing of the miseries and impossibilities of chronic debt can lead as easily to a politics of hopelessness as to a politics of resistance. From "learning how to live with debt" in K–12 curricula onward, what he calls the "debt economy" in the United States teaches worry, guilt, and supplication. The latter is true vis-à-vis the state (especially in the unforgiving brutalities of student loan debt collection), and with regard to private lenders and their contracted-out collection bureaucracies. The aggression of the University of Virginia's hospital system against those whom they treated—leading to a 2019 scandal in which it was revealed management had sued thousands over medical bills, garnishing wages and placing liens on homes—exemplifies how hard it can be to untangle the public and private. Neoliberal regimes of debt, Lazzaroto argues, so debase the very word "confidence" as to connect it to an inability to act, and in particular to act collectively. The notion that this is an "entrepreneurial" society arises not so much because productive property is widely shared nor even because there are small armies of those who day-trade stocks or dream of owning a car wash franchise. Rather, it is due to the widespread management of one's own debt and attempts to make overwork or retraining address it.[66]

Starting in the 1950s, the psychological research on young people performed by Walter Mischel achieved great stature within the imaginations of the most thoroughly hegemonized parts of the upper middle class and within the educational establishment in the United States. In his well-known "marshmallow test," Mischel offered his preschool subjects a choice between having a relatively small marshmallow now or delaying gratification until later, when, he promised, a bigger one would be on offer. The "high delayers," allegedly possessed of more self-control and emotional maturity, were said to be bound for success, and the "low delayers" for troubles. In one interpretation, his data is celebrated as showing how easy it is to succeed within the current contradictions of capitalism by adopting middle-class values and virtues. In fact, however, it shows the difficulty of doing so, from youth onward. One of his critics, cultural historian Michael Staub, addresses these matters in a marvelous book, demonstrating how racial and class assumptions helped popularize the marshmallow test. We might wonder if the high delayers have learned judgment, trust, and the virtues of accumulation, or if instead they have divined at a scarily early age how to present, in the presence of authority, a disciplined self rather than a shopping mall, holiday self. We might also wonder how it is possible to impart consistent messages in child-rearing when parents are expected to produce both the shopping mall (now increasingly home shopping) "anarchist" and the prudent mid-management worker, putting off pleasure. Perhaps the perfect response to the impossible position of the middle class would be to refuse the small marshmallow and then to put a dozen large ones on a maxed-out credit card. Also apposite would be to order online—yes, they really exist—a (hopefully ironic) "DON'T EAT THE MARSHMALLOW" coffee mug.[67]

MIDDLE-CLASS VOTES

Stanley Greenberg, Democratic Neoliberalism, and the Rightward Drift of US Politics

> Is it possible politicians are turning to pollsters, consultants, and spin doctors not to better align themselves with shifting public sentiment but to . . . manage it?
>
> —STANLEY GREENBERG, pollster

There is no dearth of long-ago political events and movements characterized by scholars as middle class, even though the term remained largely unavailable to their participants. Popularly we can read, for example, of artisans providing the "middle-class muscle" for the American Revolution.[1] Sometimes the retrospective characterization of social motion as produced by a middle class, or the ascription to it of the kindred term "bourgeois," generates useful debate. Within the radical tradition, thinking about the American Revolution as bourgeois has slighted the heroism of waterfront workers and the specific leadership of slave owners but led to important debates as to the character of the movement. So has thinking about the Civil War as a second

US bourgeois revolution.[2] The movements to abolish slavery, or at least to prevent its spread, have attracted the specific label "middle class" regularly, with the implication sometimes being that they validated wage labor by excoriating slavery. Such an analysis provoked a salutary response challenging how it missed the extent to which emancipation was the project of Black workers, enslaved and free, and oversimplified the social bases of white participation in antislavery agitation.[3]

Among the attempts to retrospectively analyze a political mobilization as middle class, most revealing for our purposes is that of progressivism. That bipartisan early twentieth-century reform movement opposed urban disorder, waste, and immigrant autonomy in the name of expertise, scientific management, bureaucratic norms, and communication across levels of hierarchy. Not hostile to those hierarchies themselves, progressives attacked monopolies episodically without arraying themselves against corporate power. A figure like Henry Ford so embodied devotion to productivity and procedure that he became an attractive political figure for both Democratic and Republican progressives. So did Herbert Hoover, reputedly the nation's highest-paid manager, before he settled into a Republican affiliation.[4]

The intellectual energy, leadership, and votes for progressives came from many sources. To declare oneself against progress had limited appeal, and on some accounts even the Ku Klux Klan made "progressive" appeals. A strong "labor progressive" tendency also emerged by the early 1920s, with even Communists maintaining a presence—at times constructive and at others disruptive—in the Conference for Progressive Political Action. But insofar as its values, timing, and limits cohere in class terms, progressivism's fortunes rose with those of the new middle class as the latter matured inside of corporations and within newly organized national associations of professionals.[5]

It is thus possible to misread US political history as continuously about appeals to the middle class and to find other continuities with the middle-class-oriented progressives of a century ago. Also consistent across the decades were progressive hesitancies to support working-class demands, whether in terms of wages and hours or of the rights of immigrant and Black labor.[6] That the very word "progressive" so persists as a badge of honor among liberal Democrats, and even those further to the left, also leads to thinking in terms of continuities.[7]

More impressive though is the specific and strikingly belated emergence of concerted and open campaigning for middle-class votes in US national elections. This chapter shows that such a development took place only in the last thirty years, underlining from a new angle how little the United States has been a middle-class nation. The chapter places the dramatic change within a specific moment of neoliberal political economic history and traces its origins to a wing of the Democratic Party. It emphasizes the mostly below-the-radar work of Stanley Greenberg, the somewhat-unprepossessing consultant whose genius was to recognize such a moment and to address it. However, this chapter and the afterword that follows also emphasize that Greenberg's ideologically driven arguments for the white middle class as a key constituency for "progressives" have not solved the dire problems in the US or the global economy. Nor have they delivered on the constantly deferred promise to rout the Republican opposition by acting on unifying economic issues while soft-pedaling allegedly divisive efforts toward racial justice. On balance, such an approach has only helped shift politics still further to the right.

REPUBLICAN ASCENDANCY, BLACK FREEDOM, AND NEOLIBERALISM

In the 1964 election, the Republican candidate, Barry Goldwater, won just 38 percent of the popular vote and a tenth of the electoral one. Lyndon Johnson's overwhelming victory ensured that the Democrats would occupy the White House again, as they had done for twenty-eight of the thirty-six years before 1968. During the next twenty-four years, however, the Democrats would hold the executive branch of government for just one term, following the impeachment of Richard Nixon. A low point came with the 1984 election that returned Ronald Reagan to the White House; Walter Mondale's Democratic candidacy won only his home state of Minnesota. The staggering defeat sent Democrats in desperate search of new strategies, ultimately leading, in 1992, to their direct appeals to the middle class. The turn had been a very long time coming. It may even have had to wait for the end of the Cold War; after all, worship of the middle class was until then a much-practiced national virtue, and anti-Sovietism had made partisan and populist rhetoric around it a tricky, potentially divisive proposition.

The addition in 1965 of millions of potential African American Democratic voters as a result of the Voting Rights Act makes the dominance of the Republicans seem more counterintuitive. However, even as early as the 1964 election, Johnson's anxieties that being seen as the party of civil rights in a white supremacist context also cost votes received some validation. Goldwater's meager results included victories in Louisiana, Mississippi, Alabama, Georgia, and South Carolina, predicting Republican victories for decades in the formerly solid Democratic South. Moreover, Goldwater's 1964 campaign, as abolitionist scholar Dylan Rodríguez has brilliantly shown, already incorporated many of the code words, or "dog whistles," that would expand Republican success. These made it possible to appeal to a white vote inside and outside the South without indulging in openly racist appeals. (However, Goldwater's journals from the time did contain straightforward laments regarding "the louder voices of . . . minorities," which he abhorred as much as "the power of unions.") Issues like crime, taxes, and welfare would acquire deep racial inflections. By the time that Kevin Phillips published *The Emerging Republican Majority*, the Bible of developing Republican strategy in 1969, he was as much summarizing as inventing a "Southern strategy," one with appeals to whites in other regions. From Nixon's dismantling of the Office of Economic Opportunity, to Reagan's crafted routines on "welfare queens," to George H. W. Bush's contriving to run less against his Democratic opponent than against a Black prisoner who re-offended while on furlough, the strategy cultivated a white audience—without, however, using the term middle class.[8]

The victories of the social movements of the 1960s made for a welfare state in which equality ruled by statute and social movements advocated for the racialized poor; therefore, it attracted increasing opposition. When the socialist and feminist historian Linda Gordon tackled the fascinating issue of "how 'welfare' became a bad word," she traced a long twentieth-century history of discrimination in provision of social benefits that amounted to a politics of "racial attack." That attack took on new forms after the '60s and opened possibilities to direct the "middle class" to look downward toward the Black poor in explaining their own miseries. Women of color, who long had been seen as undeserving, and apt to share benefits with still more undeserving men, increasingly were cast as the *cause*, via taxes, of white malaise. These developments disadvantaged Democrats, who were trying to build new bases of strength among Black voters and to hold on to white homeowners, many of them working-class people who situationally identified as middle class.[9]

But the Republicans' advantage grew further as a result of what was happening at the top of society. Defeat in a pricey war in Southeast Asia and the impact of Chile's electoral fall into socialist hands in the early 1970s contributed to a sense of ruling-class dread—one that, for a time, did not know how to proceed as an empire but was able to decide that the War on Poverty and US global hegemony could not coexist. As the economy lapsed into bouts of "stagflation," in which lack of growth combined with inflation of prices, important sectors of capital called for reigning in taxes and regulations on businesses, and for letting global markets determine the fortunes of poor and working people. The post–World War II solution of the warfare/welfare state as a mechanism of economic planning gave way to the idea, pioneered by John F. Kennedy but increasingly Republican property, that tax cuts for business could stimulate the economy. Neoliberal elites also searched for ways to reign in the labor movements arguing that competitive—read lower—wages positioned the US best in a global economy.[10]

One feature of neoliberalism was that, in the wake of defeat in Southeast Asia, US hegemony would rely less on extended, massive military adventures and more on weapons systems, bombing, and quick strikes. The US state's more fragile leadership of the world economy in a new moment of globalization rested far more on its ability to maintain the dollar as the currency-anchoring system, making inflation—and therefore social spending and high wages—a particular threat at home and everywhere. With its private investments themselves becoming much more multinational and more rooted in finance, the United States could play a major role

in insisting that the free movement of capital provided ef-
ficiencies that national economies could not. It thus set the
stage for more capital flight, while tipping power even more
toward finance capital and away from industries that stayed
in the US.[11]

As a party, the Democrats did not oppose neoliberalism,
however long it took them to learn to operate effectively
within it. The dwindling trade union wing of the party
did not occupy a position, ideologically or politically, from
which it could challenge that reality. The broad change was
from a world system in which the global South's nations and
colonies sent materials to developed core countries for man-
ufacture, to one with expansion of industrial production in
the periphery and semi-periphery.[12] As the great labor historian Kim Moody has recently shown, this shift did not mark
the end of the working class, much less, as was sometimes
claimed, the end of history. Value added by manufacturing
continued to increase. So did the world's absolute numbers
of industrial and transportation workers. In the US, manufacturing also remains a significant sector of the labor force
with great power to change society, especially when combined with those doing the economically critical work of
goods distribution.[13]

However, in the US capital flight diminished trade union power and numbers greatly, decimating strikes. As employers successfully demanded givebacks, opportunities for
forward motion seemed foreclosed to much of the labor leadership, which interpreted stinging defeats as the wave of the
future and, it must said, did not support rank-and-file militancy in periods like 1967 to 1972 when conditions established room for aggressive bargaining.[14] Politically, the labor
movement commanded less influence based on its votes and
attempted to make recompense by being especially loyal and

generous to the Democratic leadership, which accepted and by the early 1990s forwarded trade deals bound to move still more jobs abroad. The nosedive in both membership in unions and numbers of good jobs occurred mainly in the more blue-collar private sector. Given this reality, a reckoning with the emerging weight of government workers in the labor movement might have challenged presumptions that capacity for organization and militancy lay overwhelmingly in the industrial working class and not among white-collar government employees. However, labor acted far less on the more hopeful lessons of the Great Postal Strike of 1970 than on the gloom surrounding the inability to protect strikers when the Professional Air Traffic Controllers walked out in 1981. The latter, interestingly a conflict involving white-collar, professional, and government workers, has come to be seen by many as the key to the unraveling of the unions and of the security of the middle class.[15]

Neoliberalism pressured both political parties to address what political economist James O'Connor analyzed at the time as the "fiscal crisis of the state"; they did so contradictorily and in ways that again initially favored the Republicans. As the geographer Ruth Wilson Gilmore puts it, the goal often amounted to an "anti-state state"—replete with fierce rhetoric against overspending on social goods but committed to statist policies of repression, surveillance, incarceration, and sustained war spending even after the United States at long last gave up on winning in Vietnam. Anti-state statists arrested the wilting of the Republican Party and then nurtured its growth. Initially, the long-standing Republican commitment to "balanced budgets" appeared to be something like neoliberal austerity, at least until huge deficits to reduce business taxes proved to be permissible. Republican dog whistles on race were more pitch perfect, and the coincidence of elite anti-tax policies and tax revolts by homeowners created a seeming common ground.[16] Although neoliberalism was bipartisan from the start, the Democrats had considerable losing and learning to do if they were to succeed within a political logic that encouraged distancing from the demands of both African Americans and the unions, two of their core constituencies. How they learned to split victories with the right is in large measure the story of Stanley Greenberg and of direct political and racial appeals to those who were courted as a white middle class.

CLASS, RACE, AND MEMORY IN THE MAKING OF A STANLEY GREENBERG

Stanley Greenberg towers modestly as our era's emblematic, unprepossessing progressive, typifying a time of diminished political possibilities. His life and the rise of middle-class politics so intertwine that it behooves us to attend closely to both. The Greenberg moment ripened in the post–civil rights era when, radicals had long assumed, all sorts of political possibilities would open up based on African American votes and the defeat of that bulwark of reaction, the white Southern Democrat. Greenberg occupies a position as a leading progressive by claiming mastery over understanding the categories of race and labor. His story gives us unique access to the hollowing out of left liberalism in the United States.

Greenberg theorized a middle class roughly interchangeable with an alleged white working class—their votes available for the mining in countless electoral campaigns. In the process, he made a suburban, almost entirely white Michigan county seem to be the key to all "progressive" possibility. His work in Macomb County turned on the evocation of an ignored middle class, assumptively white, when the need was to pretend that center-right Democratic appeals transcended identity politics. He identified a "white working class" more rarely, when the desire was to talk about class without wrestling with what would concretely unite workers across color lines. So successful were Greenberg and other Democratic centrists that we have hardly appreciated the amount of ideological work that has gone into disciplining both the civil rights and labor movements to accept austerity and increased inequality—all while Democrats have continued to campaign on the basis of racial justice and concern for a middle or white working class.

George Stephanopoulos, who as communications director shared with Greenberg the "war room" in Bill Clinton's 1992 presidential campaign, later praised his fellow warrior in these words: "No single strategist has done more to lay the foundation for modern progressive politics." Others echo such hosannas, and the detailed oral histories Greenberg has given describe a life spent preparing to grasp the "leading progressive" mantle.[17] Greenberg's story is overwhelmingly of his own invention. It is told especially in two wide-ranging, strategically self-deprecating, and wildly self-congratulatory histories produced for the Presidential Oral Histories Program of the University of Virginia's Miller Center. Small, frothy interviews and articles such as "Why Are You So Smart, Stan Greenberg?," along with his books, add spice.[18]

Greenberg's memories of his early years position him to accept that the Black freedom struggle held the moral high ground in US politics and to perfect the idea that appeals to presumptively center-right white working-class voters nevertheless keyed Democratic Party success. So much is that the case for his recollections of his pre-college years that we might wonder if the child was the father of the man or vice versa. Greenberg grew up, he insisted, "in the city," and specifically in "a relatively poor neighborhood, an all-black neighborhood" in Washington, DC, where, nonetheless, his Orthodox Jewish extended family could easily walk to the synagogue.[19] Raised in a strong and somewhat isolated religious community, he recalled being mostly indifferent to K–12 education.

Greenberg recalled making grade school friends across the color line. "All of my friends were Black," he maintained. This was somehow true despite so much of his family's social life centering on the synagogue, despite local public education being segregated in his primary school years, and despite his family quickly moving to a DC area he remembers as "mostly Jewish." After the *Brown v. Board of Education* desegregation decision, he joined white classmates who took public transportation to a junior high that nominally "integrated" but kept whole classrooms Black and others white. He remembered white school crossing guards being menaced by Black young people but being himself protected from trouble by African American friends from the old neighborhood. His family soon removed to nearby Silver Spring, Maryland, where his dad worked as an engineer at the American Instrument Company. According to his oral history, a high school American studies class then quickened his interest in both school and injustice. A school trip through the Jim Crow South deepened these impulses. Greenberg was also in the orbit of a Jewish social justice group for a time until his family forbade it, fearing possible Communist presence might run afoul of requirements relating to government contracts on which his father worked. Greenberg expressed sympathy for a union at the firm where his dad worked and where he had a summer job, again meeting decisive family disapproval. According to his oral reminiscences, he went back into the city to help organize the great 1963 pro–civil rights March on Washington.[20]

There is every reason to approach Greenberg's recollections with caution in terms of fact and spin. My colleagues who lived in African American Washington, DC, when Greenberg did, or who have studied that city's history, raise red flags about many of the details, from "all-Black neighborhood" forward. Moreover, as they point out, the tale of interracial adventure he offers obscures a much more standard story: his family lived in the city while schools were segregated, relocated within the city, and then suburbanized. The Greenbergs' intense commitment to Orthodox Jewish faith added complexity, but not necessarily in the direction of rich integrated experience. Silver Spring is today an exciting, diverse community. It wasn't then. The unincorporated suburb expanded in the 1920s and after with housing based on racially restrictive covenants, some of which used language preventing transfer of property to races "whose death rate is higher than that of the white race." As the historian of race and space David Rotenstein has written, "Silver Spring was a strictly segregated Southern town that vigorously resisted integration well into the 1960s."[21] Greenberg reminisced ambiguously that he "was very much in a racial culture" growing up, but the one concrete example of white racism that he mustered concerned working-class whites at the factory where he had a summer job—"people from Appalachia," specifically West Virginia.[22]

Likewise spun is the class position of Greenberg's own family. They are variously placed among DC's "poor" residents, as belonging in the "working class," and as members of the "lower middle class" Jewish community to which both the mother and the father provided religious leadership. Partly this reflects that the father's job lay in what the late Marxist sociologist Erik Olin Wright called "contradictory locations within class relations."[23] Not a college graduate but with

post–high school education in engineering, the father combined ability, white advantage, and experience as a worker
at Westinghouse to find a good professional job at American Instrument after failing as a small businessman. The
Greenbergs both were and weren't like the Macomb County,
Michigan, residents whom Stanley would later bring into the
national spotlight. His family lived seemingly outside of US
racial structures, finding their politics in synagogues rather
than polling places or social movements.[24] Sympathy with
Macomb County's suburban workers was nominally available as a result of his own suburban upbringing, but his claim
to understanding them hinged more on academic study and
political experience than acknowledged personal affinity.
His focus on historical materialist ideas about class might
have led to a more precise understanding of his family, but,
though it provided progressive credentials and ties to labor
organizations that made his work in Macomb County possible, his interest in Marxism was not sustained.

THE YOUNG PROGRESSIVE AND
HIS CONSERVATIVE MENTORS

Due regards to high school American studies, but credit for
the flowering of Stanley Greenberg as an intellectual and
a political actor belongs to Ohio's Miami University. Credit
also goes to Yale and Harvard, where he encountered both
conservative mentors and a left insisting on a frank confrontation with class in ways that would later allow him to make
sweeping claims to know just what white workers were (in)
capable of. He followed his more athletic, charismatic, scholarly, and tall older brother, Edward, to Miami. Both found
their ways to political science, first as undergraduates, then
as doctoral students, then professors.[25] Although he would

later credit Robert F. Kennedy's hopes for interracial organization of the poor as decisive in his political evolution, at
other junctures he referred to an earlier attraction of John
F. Kennedy. In any case, Greenberg was a Young Democrat
from his undergraduate days at Miami, where he was also
a leader in student government. As the anti-war movement
grew, he concentrated his campus politics on questions of
the university's assumption of parental responsibilities in
dictating student housing choices, especially by keeping
women students out of off-campus apartment housing. His
political science internships focused on the Democratic Party
and electoral campaigns. In 1964, as a Democratic intern, he
wrote a memo supporting the war on Vietnam, though he
eventually came to question that support.[26]

Insofar as Greenberg arrived at his doctoral program at
Harvard as a self-described "mainstream Democrat," it is
noteworthy that he came, over the next twenty years, to
produce significant radical political science scholarship. He
moved in this direction in nothing like a straight line. In
1964, with friend-of-friend access to Lyndon Johnson's family, he attended the Democrats' national convention as a most
enthusiastic Johnson supporter. He remembers sympathies
with the Mississippi Freedom Democratic Party delegation's
picket of the convention over Jim Crow voting and becoming
a protester who nevertheless then went inside to enthuse over
Johnson. The same willingness to split differences cheer-
fully characterized his graduate student experience. Moving
left, including on the war, and taken especially with Bobby
Kennedy's vision of what Greenberg thought of as Black
and "ethnic Catholic" unity, he nonetheless worked at Harvard with James Q. Wilson as his doctoral supervisor. The
arch-conservative Edward C. Banfield, Wilson's own men-
tor, helped round out the dissertation committee. Wilson was

for the moment still a Democrat, and his work on amateur versus professional political participation made him a logical adviser for Greenberg. The latter had secured a paid consultancy evaluating the effect of the Great Society's Office of Economic Opportunity (OEO) anti-poverty programs—his qualification being that he conducted a modest mail survey as part of his senior thesis at Miami. The research examined political participation by the poor in a hundred cities. Greenberg drew on the data in his doctoral dissertation.[27]

By 1974, Greenberg's doctoral work had become his first book, *Politics and Poverty: Modernization and Response in Five Poor Neighborhoods*. He was a young faculty member at Yale; OEO wobbled on its last legs with Banfield serving as consultant to the Nixon administration during the dismantling of the agency; James Q. Wilson had joined Banfield as an intellectual darling of the right. Banfield's excruciating earlier book, *The Moral Basis of a Backward Society*, encapsulated its pessimistic and victim-blaming argument in its very title. By the mid-'70s, Wilson had concluded that policing and prison, not welfare, were what the state most urgently needed to provide to the poor. Indeed, Wilson is credited with inspiring "broken windows policing." He produced the huge and extravagantly subtitled *Crime and Human Nature: The Definitive Study of the Causes of Crime* in 1985 in concert with the white supremacist psychologist Richard Herrnstein. Not surprisingly, the left sharply attacked both of Greenberg's mentors.[28]

Politics and Poverty effectively established limited distance between Greenberg's views and those of his powerful teachers, who were increasingly infamous in left and liberal circles. He proceeded with great empirical detail, fashioning limited alternatives to the grim views of the poor as the ineffectual, apolitical, and dysfunctional people who populated the works of Wilson and Banfield. Developing and using extensive data, especially on attitudinal matters, he argued for there not being any one story but lots of particular and local ones. Not only his own mentors, but, more famously, Daniel Patrick Moynihan's influential and controversial 1965 report on the African American family had argued that oppression and deprivation left the poor unable to act on their own behalf. Greenberg concluded that this was sometimes more true—"hillbillies" were portrayed as bereft of cultural resources for problem-solving—and sometimes less true. Banfield had grouped all of humanity termed "not lower class" as "normal," with the poor so in search of speedy gratification as to be "pathological." For his part, Greenberg countered that only some of the poor fit that description.[29]

In most of the places studied, Greenberg found political networks operating. Goals continued to be articulated, even amid misery, and an orientation toward the future survived. Mexicans, he thought, kept hope alive on far different grounds than an "alienated" and in some places violence-accepting Blacks, such as those on the east side of Detroit. Where women and family were concerned, Greenberg was far more reticent; incredibly, he eschewed discussion of Moynihan's contention that a "tangle of pathology" characterized Black family life. Greenberg later regarded such a view as not wrong but one sided. It failed to balance "culture" with "economics" as factors with "equal power."[30]

Greenberg's limited challenge to received wisdom left much of the approach of his mentors intact. Those strands were taken up at later junctures, especially in commentaries that entertained as reasonable Macomb County residents' pathologization of nearby Black Detroit. Indeed, even at the level of defense of anti-poverty initiatives, *Politics and Poverty* proved agnostic, not least when it quoted community

organizer Saul Alinsky's not-quite-clear but apparently ir-
resistible remark on the "pornography" of anti-poverty initiatives.[31] The book's five case studies promised rich local
texture based in part on political economy, and its report on
the San Jose Chicano community delivered on that promise.
But the examples are so plainly focused on a narrow study of
"racial" cases (Appalachian white, Northern African American, Southern African American, and Chicano) that reduc-
tive readings proved unavoidable.[32]

In a recent review essay, Greenberg put on display some of
Politics and Poverty's enduring problems. The essay took on
venture capitalist J. D. Vance's blockbuster exercise in victim
blaming, *Hillbilly Elegy*. Greenberg quickly conceded that
Vance was right about the pathologies of the "hillbillies,"
citing his own, now very old, book. The Appalachian mi-
grant community that Greenberg had studied in Hamilton,
Ohio, suffered from "fatalism, personal impotence, limited
time perspective, disorganization and apathy that combine
to suppress any collective political urge." Their beliefs and
participation did not rise above a "politics of resignation"—
an indictment Greenberg leveled against "hillbillies" across
time and space. Vance's disdain for Appalachian culture
was "painfully accurate," his review essay maintained. But,
Greenberg added, there was no reason to use that dysfunc-
tion to cast suspicion regarding similar failings on the whole
"white working class," seen by Greenberg to be proud, political, and planful, at least until jobs are lost. Greenberg's recent recollections of *Politics and Poverty* themselves describe
not so much a rich variety of different cities but a handful of
racial/regional types of responses, which distinctly can be
ranked in terms of efficacy and modernity.[33]

At the beginning and end of *Politics and Poverty*, strangely,
a very different book tries to get out. The start features the

possibility of the rise of "radical political man," acting to
respond to the indignities of dispossession and exploitation.
The language is often stirring, though the hardest-hitting
passages are in the voice of a vaguely identified someone who
"expects, or at least hopes for, a radical response to oppression," rather than squarely in Greenberg's voice. "Radical
political man" is only momentarily imagined as a rational
and modern political actor in the book. The radical is "apt
to endorse bizarre forms of political expression, such as sit-
ins or marches." In less than a page, radical political man
is ushered offstage, and "liberal political man" takes over.
The latter knows misery but responds "pragmatically," taking what is on offer from the political system. He—I follow
Greenberg's relentlessly gendered language here—"views the
ballot box with some reverence" and deplores those seen as
"disruptive." Radical political man is absent for upward of
two hundred pages. However, in spots there are brief evoca-
tions of radical ideas, or at least quotations from Marx on
alienation and class consciousness. Such passages sit oddly
against the book's decidedly non-Marxist reliance on the
category of the "lower class" to structure its arguments.[34]

Such brief Marxist quotations surely do not prepare the
reader for the book's astounding, almost ultra-left conclusion, in which Greenberg confesses a desire to have been able
to write a volume discovering radical political men. The brief
conclusion to the book begins by offering a Goldilocks problem to the reader. For the migrating "lower" classes that the
book studies, three twentieth-century "scenarios" were possible. They could have remained "indifferent and uninvolved"
where politics was concerned; they could have "become power
brokers ... tinkering and bargaining for their share;" or, they
could have refused to "tinker" and instead entered a radical
"confrontation with history."[35] Most, according to Greenberg,

picked the middle alternative, neither too hot nor too cold. Though posed as a continuum of possibilities, Greenberg really offered in these scenarios a pair of Manichean choices. In a way that structured the very design of the book, he pitted the feckless mass mired in a culture of poverty against the liberal political man. Arguing for differences among groups and for an exceptional, dysfunctional case among Appalachian whites, Greenberg hesitantly portrayed the poor as rational and modern political actors.

Early and late in the book, however, he adds brief material on a second stark opposition, between the liberal poor whom he documented and the radical poor whom he alternately caricatured and longed for. By the last two pages, the longing becomes overwhelming. Greenberg worries there that the "limits of explanation" in his project might outstrip its accomplishments. "Our work has not been trivial [nor] without possible consequence," he wrote with sudden modesty, but it left much "unexplained," especially regarding the disparities between communities and the under-theorized connection between belief and action. Tied to electoral politics, his own investigations had been insufficiently "demanding of history" because they were too tethered to an examination of options reflecting the thin possibilities on offer in US politics and in US political science. Perhaps, Greenberg mused, the poor were favorably disposed toward the "formation of cabals, correspondence societies [and] conspiracies" and supported the seizure of factories—or would have been if not for the "failure of revolutionary politics." He concluded that the problem lay in his studying places and times in which the range of political differences that his surveys captured was so small. That range, he reckoned, stretched from one to three instead of—as he wished—from one to ten.[36] In New Haven, Connecticut, and then in South Africa, he would soon find expanded ranges of possibility. Greenberg held on to those dreams of possibility briefly before leaving academic Marxism for political consulting. In that new role the range of possibility was again narrow and, by the time the road reached Macomb County, Michigan, dropped down into negative numbers.

Whether writing a liberal book within a conservative framework or adding a minor revolutionary chord wishing that infinitely more were possible, Greenberg produced a strikingly judgmental book, even when absolving some of the communities studied. In comparing Black sites of research, the question of willingness to use "violence" is especially crudely drawn. This imperial and empirical tone, suggesting a secret knowledge among liberals of the limits of what was feasible, would prove a great asset in his work for the Democratic Party in Macomb. By then this self-assurance had bonded with confidence born of a brush with left political forces committed to a belief that they could know "the left wing of the possible."[37]

ANOTHER PROGRESSIVISM: ACADEMIC MARXISM, THE SOUTH AFRICAN REVOLUTION, AND THE DEMOCRATIC PARTY

Greenberg sped through his doctoral research at Harvard. As the '70s began, his first wife, their twins, and he moved to New Haven, where he took up a tenure-track job at Yale. The city and the campus were intensely politicized spaces. Nineteen seventy saw the trial and fiercely fought defense campaign of Black Panthers charged with the murder of a suspected police informer. In 1972, Greenberg coordinated New Haven activities in George McGovern's spectacularly unsuccessful left-liberal Democratic presidential campaign. Attempting to negotiate the "high barrier between academia and politics," he seemed to be on a trajectory leading to increasingly radical political conclusions that might have ended in advocacy of socialism, especially in his work in South Africa.[38] It took him instead to center-right Democratic Party politics and the discovery of the (white) middle class in Macomb County. Insofar as we can briefly suspend our knowledge of that destination, we might more fully appreciate Greenberg's journey, which was by no means his alone.

New Haven hosted a strong labor movement centered on strikes and organizing on the Yale campus and beyond. So much was labor part of local life and politics that when the legendary local organizer Vincent Sirabella ran an insurgent campaign for mayor in the early '70s—Greenberg later called it, with some overstatement, a "Labor Socialist challenge to the machine"—Yale law student Bill Clinton headed Sirabella's voter-registration committee. A small Communist party remained active in the city's Democratic Party politics and in labor struggles under a "progressive" banner. Also active in the Sirabella campaign was Rosa DeLauro, who would soon become both Greenberg's second wife and the longtime Democratic US congressperson for New Haven and its surrounding areas. Through DeLauro and on his own, Greenberg became active in labor causes, befriending the dynamic young radical hotel and restaurant organizer John Wilhelm, with whom he co-taught classes at Yale. The organizing campaign for Local 34 at Yale was run in part out of the basement of Greenberg's house.[39]

Greenberg's fellowship in South Africa in 1973 coincided with major strikes, especially while he was based in Durban. His second book project—a broad comparative study of race, class, and politics in the United States, Northern Ireland, Israel, and South Africa—was taken over in its largest and best sections by the South African story. The Marxist analysis that would frame *Race and State in Capitalist Development: Comparative Perspectives*, published in 1980, reflected close contact with and deep admiration for the Congress of South African Trade Unions, radical pro-labor intellectuals, and movements in which Communists played pivotal roles. The book exemplified a mature grasp of political economy based on a sharp understanding of land and power. It quoted Marx and Marxist classics—by Vladimir Lenin and, especially, the Italian Communist Antonio Gramsci—both to settle questions and to talk back to the texts. Of particular value was his engagement with challenges regarding how to think through categories of class and the state alongside those of race. "The problem of persistent racial conflict and domination," the earliest pages averred, "is at the center of this research." Back at Yale, Greenberg began offering classes with names like "Marxian Political Economy and the Social Sciences" and "Race and Ethnic Conflict in Southern Africa." Looking back three decades later, Greenberg derided *Race and State in Capitalist Development*, by far his best book, for its "inelegant" title and "indecipherable" content. How he got to that judgment and how he embraced Macomb County are halves of the same walnut.[40]

Two setbacks in life sped Greenberg's move to a far more centrist course. The first came when the "high barrier" separating academia from politics "took a knock." First Yale denied him tenure. His later interviews claim that he was "pretty indifferent" to the decision. However, they also betray how much trouble Greenberg has had letting go of the topic, and justifiably so. The decision came from the newly appointed Yale president, A. Bartlett Giamatti, who proved over time to be an adversary of both Local 34 and of divestment of Yale from investments in South Africa. Greenberg's recollections emphasize the technical violations in the tenure process, errors which he thought laid the basis for a lawsuit even as he moved in a different direction, arranging to head a Rockefeller Foundation initiative on human rights in South Africa. However, while Greenberg celebrated the publication of *Race and State in Capitalist Development* in a private home there, spies overheard him saying that international investment did not mitigate the evils of apartheid. The South African state blocked his Rockefeller work and attacked his Ford Foundation relationships. After negotiations, Greenberg was able to stay on at Yale for another decade in a variety of Ford Foundation–funded research on South Africa and in adjunct positions in American Studies and African American Studies. But for a critical time in 1980, Yale and apartheid had each in its own way assured that he would have time on his hands and reason to think of a new career. [41]

As Greenberg faced these two career difficulties, DeLauro was aiding the campaign of Christopher Dodd, the mainstream Democratic congressman seeking a Connecticut US Senate seat. Greenberg wrote a memo that impressed Dodd, who fired his existing pollster. Dodd preferred Greenberg, who came with the added benefit that he worked "for free." Recalling that he'd "never done any polling in a political campaign," Greenberg backhandedly credited his apartheid victimizers for his new career, soon to be centered on saving the middle class. "But for the intelligence service for the South African government who bugged my presentation," Greenberg wrote, he might have remained an activist academic researcher.[42] He did for a time remain one, but in South Africa, where the Black trade union movement continued to inspire him, where he had a role in fighting for curbs on US corporate investments in the apartheid state, and where he continued to defend a broadly Marxist analysis.

As late as 1987, when he published *Legitimating the Illegitimate: State, Markets, and Resistance in South Africa*, he issued a rousing call for a new society grounded in the activities and imaginations of those in the townships.[43] In the United States, however, Greenberg had by then succeeded mightily as a pollster and consultant. Joseph Lieberman, running for the US Senate from Connecticut from the right of his Republican opponent, would soon be his most famous client. Greenberg's changing fortunes stemmed very much from his discovery of Macomb County, Michigan, in 1985.[44]

GREENBERG, MACOMB COUNTY, AND THE MIDDLE-CLASS ERASURE OF RACIAL JUSTICE

According to his own reminiscences, Stanley Greenberg went to Macomb County after the comprehensive Republican victories in the 1984 presidential election. He discovered the wayward Republican-voting Reagan Democrat and listened to him. Over fierce opposition, he persuaded the Democrats to adopt a strategy to attract the Reagan Democrat back into the progressive fold by 1992. Collected in his 1995 book *Middle Class Dreams* (*MCD*), his section on Bill Clinton in *Dispatches from the War Room*, and in passages from the documentary film *The War Room*, Greenberg's stories of Macomb County mix personal triumph and national salvation promiscuously.[45] However, read with a healthy dose of skepticism, the stories compel in a different way. They illuminate how issues of race, class, and power came to be effaced even by those who claimed most credit for discussing them as part of "middle-class" politics in the neoliberal United States.

Greenberg did not by himself discover the Democratic strategy that made Macomb County the dead center of how the party could enduringly finesse race and class issues—just as Herbert Hoover and Henry Ford did not invent the combination of technical knowledge, claims to expertise in management of colonized and racialized workers, and infusions of wealth that made them famous progressives. Like so many geniuses, Greenberg reassembled and marketed. For example, he did not coin the term "Reagan Democrat"—it had been used in the 1970s—but did popularize it as the descriptor of the working-class, trade union, white, beleaguered, ignored, presumptively male figure who turned from New Deal loyalties to vote for Ronald Reagan in the 1980 and 1984 elections. Writers had come to address working-class conservatism long before Greenberg. Pete Hamill, the talented journalist of the underdog, had been warning of the volatility and alienation of the "white lower middle class," as the title of his most famous article on the subject put it in 1969. (The cover of the issue of *New York* containing the piece portentously changed its title to "Rising Anger of the White Working Class.") The George Wallace candidacies of 1964, 1968, and 1972 surfaced the volatility in working-class whites' voting patterns, seen in the returns themselves and inflated in the oversimplifications of commentators.[46]

Nor were changes in Macomb County flying under the radar before Greenberg's arrival. In the 1972 Democratic primary, Wallace won there, the same year McGovern was trounced in the general election in the county by a margin of almost two to one. Both elections occurred during a bitter period of organized and disorganized racism in response to busing designed to integrate schools.[47] By 1980, the left newsmagazine *In These Times* had received articles from their political reporter regarding the conservatism of Macomb County workers. When Michigan overwhelmingly voted for Reagan again in 1984, both the United Automobile

Workers (UAW) regional leadership and the head of the state Democratic Party regarded Macomb County as diagnostic of their crisis. It was for that very reason that union leadership agreed to join a Democratic Party request to invite and fund a Greenberg visit in 1985 to figure out what had gone so very wrong.[48] Also already in place, though often now associated with Greenberg's rise, was the technique of the "focus group" poll, which gathers groups of people associated demographically and often interviews them collectively for an extended period—an expensive practice that had previously been used more by Republicans.[49]

The most tantalizing phrase in *MCD*, Greenberg's best-known writing on Macomb County, describes the county as "an exaggeration, a caricature of America." The phrasing offered a clever hedge in that it made the location seem hyper-representative of the nation and fully strange at the same time. To credential the county in that way relied on the view that it "so thoroughly identified with the currents that swept the nation . . . following the Second World War." That is, its residents were "just working Americans who made their way to the suburbs," a migration apparently all about American Dreaming and not race. In reality, Macomb County was not representative of much. It was too Catholic and too unionized to be typical as a suburb, and at that time too prosperous to stand in for the whole working class. Despite the accelerating decline of the auto industry, its average income exceeded by half again the average for the nation. It also had too many boat owners, a category in which it was said to have led the nation. The county's population moved from about 406,000 in 1960 to over 717,000 in 1990. This boom reflected the emptying out of white Detroit as a result of the 1967 rebellion, of integration of schools, of fear of crime, and of Black political power, not to mention the relocation of jobs. Thus, Greenberg misleads his readers when he asserts that Macomb County went from being the most Democratic suburban county in the 1960s to one of the least Democratic in the 1980s as inhabitants shifted views in light of the Democrats' racial liberalism and tax policies. After all, many of Macomb's families in the 1980s were not there in the 1960s. Macomb's overwhelming whiteness made it unrepresentative of the United States and still less of the Democratic electorate, regardless of how many times Greenberg stated that "these were America's workers."[50]

To cast Macomb County as an exaggeratedly "American" place involved impressive ideological work, based on the assumption that white identity politics in the United States need not speak its name. Such manipulation effaces both race and class. The land and history of Macomb County itself carried profound racial baggage. Home to the Ojibwe long before colonial settlement, the county took its name from that of the scion of the largest slaveholding family in Michigan and one instrumental in maneuvering much Detroit land from Indigenous control.[51] The term "middle class" served to allow an overwhelmingly white county to stand in for all counties, even in a period during which Jesse Jackson's Rainbow Coalition challenge to party leadership was the most noteworthy Democratic development. Consigned to a footnote in *MCD* is the fact that, according to what Greenberg considered the best study at the time, about 45 percent of the United States regarded itself as middle class, and the same percentage claimed working-class status. The book's title, Greenberg explained, focused on the former term because more of those polled in Macomb County chose it. Moreover, according to Greenberg, the term "middle class" ought to extend to include those who called themselves working class, because being middle class was an aspiration even for those of modest means. It is worth recalling that the title of Greenberg's book gives us "middle class" as a collective adjective, not a collective noun, so that the dreams matter more than actual class position. In the long main chapter on Macomb County in *MCD*, "middle class" recurs upward of three dozen times, while "working class" surfaces not at all, though "blue collar" substitutes a handful of times.[52]

At the time of his 1985 Macomb County Studies, Greenberg regarded himself as uncommonly able and willing to address both class and race, and those studies are now recalled as milestones in studying "white working-class" voters. His mission, or selling point, focused on educating Democratic leaders who supposedly could talk easily about race but not class. The class dimension seemed a fit one for someone who was still active on the left in South Africa and who termed himself as coming to his study of Macomb "from the left in my own thinking." As late as 2009, Greenberg described the initiative he and Clinton undertook as "thinking through how [to] reconnect with the working class." His brief in addressing Democratic officials was to say that without a viable (white) working-class base, no effective Democratic Party was possible. He also prided himself on being a fearless reporter of the depth of racism in Macomb County. One informant there told a focus group that had been given quotations from Robert Kennedy that Kennedy's liberalism made his assassination less than regrettable: "No wonder they killed him." But so committed was Greenberg to "listening to Macomb" that there was little counsel beyond registering such views, which he both branded as "venomous" and regarded as worth heeding. Indeed, the whole section in *MCD* titled "White Victims, Black Privilege" made it hard to determine where reportage ended and endorsement began. Here was a case where Greenberg's left-liberal credentials helped to reassure others, and perhaps himself, that no malice could be meant.[53]

Accounts of Greenberg's arrival in Macomb stress the drama of the coming of an unconventional figure, making for an odd encounter between pollster and polled. He was a "short, dark-haired Ivy League professor," Jewish, liberal, and in some accounts Marxist as well. They were white, allegedly bigger than average due to hard blue-collar work, Catholic, high-school educated, and conservative, if complicated. His advantage in securing trust, he recalled, lay in a willingness to listen to them and an unwillingness to condescend. He would hear their truth, though one that was inevitably and designedly partial, and at times prefabricated. The very invitation for him to study Macomb County grew out of a sense that Democrats needed to shift away from racial justice and feminist issues. The UAW hosts were the leaders of Region One, a bastion of conservative Democratic politics and of opposition to reforms within the union.[54]

Left- then right-wing journalist Christopher Hitchens's scorching and superb 1999 account of (Bill) Clintonism, *No One Left to Lie To*, offered the provocation that "[t]he polling business gives the patricians an idea of what the mob is thinking and of how that thinking might be 'shaped.'" It designed "capsules of 'message,'" prescribed to different constituencies. Residents of Macomb County contributed to their own capsules through focus group answers. But the contents of the capsules were compounded by Greenberg himself, especially in his constitution of the groups, selection of the settings in which they met, and decisions regarding what responses to ignore. The original forty subjects—those to whom the Democratic Party most urgently had to listen—were 75 percent male and the rest "housewives." They were all white and all Reagan voters in 1984.

The focus groups met in private rooms in Macomb County, mostly in sex-segregated groups of ten for about two hours. No one in the initial four groups was younger than thirty years old. Within these chosen settings—and among the residents of Macomb generally, Greenberg implied—great admiration for Reagan as a man who stood up for himself and for the "average American white guy" outweighed economic grievances. Nearby Detroit stood in for all that threatened good lives. In a fascinating formulation, Greenberg distilled the views of the focus group as defining class through race: "Not being black was what constituted being middle class; not living with blacks was what made a neighborhood a decent place to live." Integrated and historically class-conscious workplace and trade union settings did not figure in the study.[55]

The report's conclusions regarding the unvarnished racism of "blue collar" and unionized workers overshot the evidence by far. Indeed, as political scientist Michael Rogin showed, similarly glib analyses of the George Wallace vote had set the pattern of accenting the racism of his blue-collar supporters while missing that of white suburban businessmen and professionals. The so-called Southern strategy of both Democrats and Republicans was never purely about courting the white vote across class lines in the rural South; it also set up shop in suburbs of the North, South, and West, offering whites reassurance that they were not under threat. The symbol of metropolitan racism became the white working man needing to be soothed. In fact, even in Macomb County, the working class and self-identified middle classes were increasingly white-collar workers and skilled tradespeople in the auto industry. Half or more of the voters were women. A 40 percent "union household" rate meant significantly less than that in terms of union density on a per capita basis. From 1979 to 1989, the more unionized manufacturing sector in Macomb lost nearly one job in ten, while service, health care, and retail jobs all increased astronomically. Macomb County voters were brought together as whites and reduced to the skewed samples Greenberg polled to get the unrelieved picture that he discovered and solicited.[56]

Nothing in the setup of the research, and little in *MCD* itself, reflected the integrated workplaces and unions in which many in Macomb also existed. Nothing interrupted the free exchanges of whitelore that the settings fostered. The UAW auspices under which the initial polling proceeded generated little for unions policy wise. Some union leaders had reason to fear "McGoverniks" in politics, and Black caucuses and other leftist and pro-democracy challenges in their organizations, more than they valued state action to improve labor's position. Labor law reform and broader questions about what it would have taken to revitalize unions received scant attention. The major class issue hesitantly discussed, especially in the years after 1985, was the relationship between trade and jobs. However, support for the North American Free Trade Agreement and other neoliberal trade deals emerged as settled Democratic policy, largely impervious to results from focus group polling. Any listening to the "white working class" necessarily attended to their laments as whites, not as working-class people, which in any case would have required tough give-and-take across color lines. The choice of "middle class," and not "white working class," in the title of *MCD* perhaps made the absence of the unionized worker and his or her class interests a little less jarring.[57]

The line between a middle-class focus group and a whites-only encounter group proved very thin. Listening to Macomb County had to be severely attenuated when it came to issues on which the Democrats would be hurt or divided by a full airing. Inattention to labor law was only one such spectacular instance. In Greenberg's writing on Macomb County for public consumption, abortion featured hardly at all, although it was a big part of the area's politics and did figure in Greenberg's 1985 unpublished reports on the county. So did the deep gendered crises of time and money in a county that lost a sixth of its family income from 1960 to 1990, even as three times as many women entered the labor force as wage workers. Such matters largely vanished in Greenberg's published writings, where race crowded them out. His most famous polling, for Bill Clinton in 1992, came when it was possible to debate the possibility of a "peace dividend" following the fall of the Soviet Union. However much Greenberg strained to listen to "blue collar" grievances on taxes, and despite doing some polling on military issues, he left little space for informants to connect spending on war to their tax burdens, as they might have in an integrated, union-based focus group or in a county in which tank production figured less in patterns of working-class employment than it did in Macomb.[58]

Twenty years after the initial polling in Macomb County, its role in Greenberg's rise still seemed so profound that he remembered that period using present-tense verbs in rapid-fire reminiscences. From 1985 through 1994, he later recalled, "I have this odd politics because I come from the Left in my own thinking." The phrasing captures much. We are invited to either render "thinking" as meaning in his political analysis or in his self-imagining. Both were true, especially if we consider that he was still a political presence in revolutionary South Africa in the mid-'80s, where the political spectrum stretched much further. In the United States, the oddness of his position rested on the fact that he mainly worked for the Democratic Leadership Council

(DLC), which expressed a rightward pull and rapidly became what he called "the main intellectual and political
force for changing the Democratic Party." Although he and
his co-thinkers would mostly come to claim that the pull
was toward the "new" and not to the right or even to the
center, Greenberg said of a potentially uneasy relationship
with the DLC that they were "comfortable with that because
we have a similar kind of interest in trying to reach the same
kind of voters."[59]

In his own telling, Greenberg had few other choices but
the DLC. The Michigan Democrats quickly arranged for him
to present his Macomb County research conclusions to a national meeting of state party chairs, where he found the audience cold, especially to the fact that he "focused very much
on the race issues and values in that discussion" and risked
raising painful differences with the anti-racist Rainbow Coalition. The DLC's interest in Greenberg climbed after he
showed results in Lieberman's right-of-the-Republican Senate campaign. Indeed, it was Lieberman's national center-
right appeal that made Greenberg a figure in presidential
politics, long before he was in the Clinton campaign's "war
room" in 1992. In the 1988 presidential election, the issue
of race remained Greenberg's wheelhouse. The George H. W.
Bush campaign mounted racist attack ads, successfully appealing to white fears of crime. Leaders called upon Greenberg as they devised a strategy to disarm the "race issue."[60]
Rising to the challenge, he broadened his portfolio in 1990
by urging the need for Democrats to undertake a "middle
class" or "working middle class" initiative.[61]

The Macomb County Studies did not circulate publicly,
save for material Greenberg published in *The American Prospect* in 1991 that drew on them and summaries included in
MCD in 1995. Instead, he anonymized the county's identity,

calling it Greene County, and then sent reports to those whom he hoped might find them, and him, useful. He functioned, he later told interviewers, as a "pamphleteer" to a target audience. The psychoanalytic reading of the renaming—Greenberg was claiming the county as his own—is appealing. But it is also worth mentioning that Greene County, Alabama, had twenty years before been central to the story of how and where the electric words "Black Power" entered the US political lexicon. Perhaps it is no coincidence that Greenberg's "Greene County" announced, near the peak of Jesse Jackson's political appeal, how little the Democratic Party could afford to respond to Black demands.[62]

The full 1985 reports generated by Greenberg and his analysis group in Macomb County remain hard to get. In particular, Greenberg, very prone to post his own work on the internet, seems not to have shared *Report on Democratic Defectors* and *Recapturing Democratic Majorities: Housewives and Their Men*; however, they reside in the University of Michigan's Bentley Library. The former distills many quotations from informants in focus groups into a position paper. The second, zeroing in on "housewives" at the very time working wives and mothers became increasingly important, is even more leading, featuring quotations that help to argue that relative openness to women's demands for justice on the job among the middle class presents opportunities for Democrats.

A brief comparison of the two reports to *Middle Class Dreams* is valuable. Notably, these original reports nicely establish how organically the term "middle class poor" emerged in the focus groups, a pattern noted only briefly in *MCD*. The unapologetic racism of focus group participants that made its way into *MCD* receives even more expression in the original reports. They also present even more starkly the problem of how to read the reportage of such vitriol. The

"Whites as Victims" section in *Report on Democratic Defectors* very much leaves open the question of whether it means to be reporting knowledge based on experience, one truth among many, or rather a position to be combated. A respect for white identity politics simmers, one in which what counts is the "feeling" of those claiming grievance when they display "vulnerability." At one point, informants comfortably suggest the abolition of affirmative action for Blacks, but its continuation for women, all of whom seem to be white given their unchallenged view.[63]

More unexpected is the rich, lengthy material in the original reports emerging from focus groups that included trade union members. They urge a return to shop floor militancy and union power, hearkening back to the time, twenty-plus years before, of interracial wildcat strikes in the plants. Sober in their reflections on how capital flight, automation, and trade policy made militancy difficult, they nevertheless blame the Democrats and union leaders, not just structural forces in the economy. Reflecting "on a weak and divided labor movement and a self-confident management," one informant observed that ideally "[t]he Democrats are the union and the Republicans are management." The report read such a remark as evidence that the Democrats needed more "John Wayne" leadership, not that they needed to support union power. Whether in deference to the union leadership, the Democratic leadership, or tensions between union and nonunion members of the middle class, such material was sidelined when *MCD* appeared a decade later.[64]

When Greenberg recollects that he "came from the left," it is tempting to reply that he then headed elsewhere. Such repartee oversimplifies and misses the realities conditioning the stance of austerity-minded neoliberal Democrats. The emphasis of much of liberalism on what the labor writer

Harold Meyerson called (in a review essay partly on Greenberg's *MCD*) "deracialized, more class-based" issues resonated with the least supple of Marxisms, with the white populism of the best-selling journalist Michael Lind, and, Greenberg hoped, with the voters of Macomb County. Meanwhile, Greenberg and the DLC retained spiffy "progressive" credentials. The think tank founded by the DLC in 1989 took the name Progressive Policy Institute. Two years later, Representative DeLauro, Greenberg's wife, became an early and leading figure in the Progressive Caucus in Congress. Greenberg's conclusion to *The New Majority*, a 1997 collection coedited with political scientist Theda Skocpol, appeared under the title "Popularizing Progressive Politics." The trajectory of a "more class-based liberalism" has had little place for unions except in electoral campaigns. Greenberg wrote in 2009 of his lack of enthusiasm for unions' ability to play a transformational role in the United States as based in part on his experiences with brave and radical unions of South African workers, whose demands he would soon seek to curb.[65]

Clinton, James Carville, Greenberg—even amid disagreements, all continued to know each other and themselves as seekers of the left wing of the possible near the middle of the road. They could dismiss critics righteously. In particular, the Macomb County Studies concocted a middle class that everyone knew was white, a group that they also (more rarely) termed an angry working class, specifically identified as white. These loose and racially saturated "class" definitions obviated the need for far-reaching visions of change. Health care reform perhaps took the Clinton forces closest to a class-based appeal, but the failed plan remained "moderate" and "market oriented," as Greenberg himself later allowed. Polling mattered, not the hard work of thinking through and organizing around what would bring working people, oppressed differently, together. For those other target audiences of the Democrats' Southern/suburban strategies—the often white, well-to-do voters—there was little need to examine their own race and class advantage, and still less to critique the system structuring advantage and disadvantage.

When Bill Clinton announced his longshot candidacy in 1992 as a crusade for the "hard-working forgotten middle class," Greenberg and his ideas worked hard in the campaign. In the election, the amalgam of middle and working class, both reading white, delivered a much closer loss in Macomb County than McGovern or Walter Mondale had suffered. In June 1992, in what a *Chicago Tribune* columnist referred to as the "most important moment" in the campaign, Clinton visited a meeting of Jackson's Rainbow Coalition to pick a public fight. He attacked the rapper Sister Souljah for her expressed lack of surprise that whites would be victims of violence in the Los Angeles rebellions against police violence. Jackson had invited Souljah to perform, and this licensed Clinton to go after both of them. Clinton accused her of somehow being just like the white nationalist David Duke, reversed. Jackson responded, vigorously defending Souljah and wryly adding that he thought Clinton must have being speaking to an audience not in the room. That audience lived in Macomb County. In fact, Greenberg himself had suggested the confrontation with Jackson.[66]

In terms of the math Greenberg used to conclude *Politics and Poverty* just a decade earlier, his Macomb County Studies fashioned a political menu in which the choices ranged not from 1 to 10 but from 1.0 to 1.2—or more exactly, given the penchant for negativity, from −1 to 1. The Macomb County Studies defined what could not be fully heard by Democrats. That included the message of Jackson and the

Rainbow Coalition, to the extent that they were pushing toward more forthright positions on racial justice and sometimes on class and trade issues as well. Positing and polling a (white) middle class whose racial interests need not be named and a white working class in need of recognition but not consistent mention would have a great future in tailoring electoral appeals geared toward acceptance of austerity and capital flight. At a moment when maintenance of a coalition would have required, for example, vigorous support for affirmative action to be paired with reforms targeted at all working people, Macomb County perfectly explained why it was best to do neither.[67]

THE DRIFT OF STANLEY GREENBERG AND LEFT LIBERALISM

Macomb County and the obsession with working-class whites at their worst wrenched the Democrats further to the right. Greenberg himself moved even faster in that direction. Increasingly his progressive reputation has become so fragile as to seem fanciful. The changes in how he is viewed by some liberals and the left have two causes. One is the rightward motion of Greenberg himself. The other is a possible change of political moments that requires more substance regarding both race and class demands by those wishing to stay in the admittedly capacious confines of progressive politics.

The clearest threats to Greenberg's reputation as a person of the left and liberalism stem from his business activities and his political drift. They center especially on his corporate and political consulting activities, both internationally and at home. For almost forty years, Greenberg has worked as a consultant, beginning in a basement room with a phone bank and horizons that rarely reached past Connecticut.

Subsequent polling and image consulting partnerships proved to be much more lucrative and polished, culminating with Greenberg cofounding Greenberg Quinlan Rosner (GQR) Research, Inc., for which he served as CEO. The nonprofit status of Democracy Corps, a venture he started with James Carville, allows for consulting activities to be framed as providing free services to worthy centrist and progressive Democrats. The paid portion of his political consulting is substantial. In the 2018 elections, for example, GQR received $6.75 million in consulting and polling fees, with the Democratic Congressional Campaign Committee paying the largest share.[68] Greenberg's activities and the status of his wife as one of the wealthiest members of the US Congress make for a large family fortune. Scandals attending the discovery that Greenberg and DeLauro provided Rahm Emanuel with free housing over a period of years achieved traction in part because Emanuel was in powerful positions from which to help Greenberg secure Democratic polling jobs.[69]

Greenberg's consulting businesses soon reached in two directions, reflecting the pull of neoliberalism toward both deregulation and globalization. Both lent credence to charges that he had moved to the right. The first was corporate consulting, which often involved clients against whom social movements battled. These included Monsanto, British Petroleum (later BP), Boeing, and United Healthcare—firms known for a laundry list of environmental catastrophes, anti-labor practices, consumer complaints, and health and safety violations. The most damaging of his consultancies engineered the greenwashing of BP as a friend of the environment following the deadly Gulf of Mexico *Deepwater Horizon* oil spill of 2010. Another instance came at the end of the twentieth century when a bill seen by opponents of genetically modified seeds as very favorable to Monsanto was introduced by Representative DeLauro. Critics jumped on the possible connection of Greenberg's consultancy with the bill's content, but Greenberg's supporters objected that his contract work with Monsanto was limited and lapsed.[70] Such reassurances sometimes prevailed, but they glossed over the role that informal ties among big businesses, political parties, and the state play as movers and shakers change roles. Greenberg increasingly functioned as what historian Thomas McCormick has brilliantly called an "in-and-outer," collapsing and transgressing boundaries between political power and corporate power. His role in this regard becomes clearer still when we consider secondly his paid work for politicians beyond the United States.[71] That work too has increased doubts about Greenberg's continuing role as a progressive.

At first, Greenberg's international activities burnished his reputation as a progressive. His radical academic work on South Africa registered little but led, by 1994, to his advising Nelson Mandela during the defeat of apartheid and the beginnings of African National Congress (ANC) rule in South Africa. His later reflections rightly regarded that experience as his greatest moment.[72] Other Greenberg consultancies conferred less moral authority but would at first have seemed laudable among left liberals. Tony Blair was hopefully poised to rescue Britain from the conservative clutches of Thatcherism and her Conservative successors. Support for the Partido Revolucionario Institucional (PRI) in Mexico in 2000 aligned Greenberg with the continuation of a corrupt regime and the continuation of one-party rule. However, such work supported those making a failed pledge to keep a kind of Mexican Thatcherism at bay. Greenberg's 2001 intervention in Austrian politics opposed a far-right anti-Semite.[73] Those who were progressive-except-for-Palestine and those hoping

for a little progressivism within Israel might also have ap-
plauded Greenberg's contribution of expertise to Israeli Labor
candidate Ehud Barak's 1999 electoral victory, in what the
New Yorker called a "stunning upset."[74]

As the 2000s wore on, it became far harder to regard
Greenberg's international activities as progressive. Campaigning for Barak, he remembered in 2009, had "allowed
[me] to develop an instinctive identification with Israel."
He soon polled not only for a center-left candidate in Israel but—via the Israel Project and under the slogan "We're
fighting to win"—for Zionism itself.[75] His consulting in the
2002 Bolivian election opposed the Indigenous leader and
left icon Evo Morales. Portrayed in the film *Our Brand Is
Crisis*, the activities of Carville and Greenberg came to sym-
bolize the export southward of "dirty tricks" campaigning.[76] Greenberg opposed the leftward motion associated
with Latin America's "pink tide," especially in Venezuela,
where GQR faced charges of cooperation in the manipulation of polling data in order to deepen gloom among Hugo
Chávez supporters.[77]

In South Africa Greenberg has more recently supported
the Democratic Alliance (DA), into which the main party
of apartheid moved. Whatever sharp questions must be
raised regarding ANC politics, this striking embrace of pa-
rochialism and reaction again called Greenberg's progressive
credentials into question. The political activist and writer
Melissa Levin, an admiring colleague of his in ANC campaigning, was so insistently a protégé of Greenberg in 2004
that she was called by her friends "Little Stan Greenberg."
In 2013, she reacted to his changed allegiances in an article
titled "Little Stan Greenberg Is Dead."[78]

Greenberg's political-entrepreneurial peregrinations show
how easy it is for centrist "save the middle class" election

strategies without firm commitments regarding race and labor to drift to the right. At the same time, his constant focus
on Macomb County becomes less compelling as the electorate,
and more importantly the society, changes. We might usefully
begin with a recent remark from someone distinctly in Greenberg's world, the editor and pundit John Judis. Responding in
a recent roundtable on the "white working class" in the *Democratic Strategist* to Greenberg's lead article, Judis first paid
tribute to Greenberg's accomplishments in Macomb County
in assessing what was now being called the "white working
class's voting patterns." He then worried that continued emphasis on the county risks "becoming a cul-de-sac [that] may
provide less insight about the present or the future than they
have in the past."[79]

The wide distance Greenberg has kept between himself
and Democratic socialists risks putting him in a position of
finally seeming beyond the confines of even the meager connection to liberal policies that modern progressivism sometimes connotes. He courts being bypassed by the leftward
movement, even if slight, around him. If that continues,
some will process his isolation as comeuppance for an oppor-
tunist. A more useful stance would see Greenberg as trapped
in bigger dramas and larger illusions regarding "saving the
middle class" without challenging corporate rule or frankly
discussing how to generate multiracial opposition.[80]

DOUBLY STUCK

The Middle Class, the White Working Class, and the Crisis of US Neoliberalism

One of the many disturbing consequences of the Trump/Brexit tragedy has been the sudden widespread reference to the White Working Class in popular and academic debate. . . . The focus of much deliberation has become the question of how politicians can better attend to the interests of working-class whites. For many of those who grew up with a working-class consciousness this is beyond chilling.

—LISA TILLEY, geographer

In the wake of a chaotic US withdrawal from Afghanistan in August 2021, *The Economist* asked the celebrated political scientist Francis Fukayama for his thoughts. Fukayama's intellectual stardom rests mainly on the professional optimism expressed in his 1992 book *The End of History and the Last Man*, which extolled the virtues of the liberal state and free market capital as both the best we can hope for and potentially everlasting. The 2021 piece made news when it announced the end of US hegemony within the political economy of the world. Not only was there something new under the sun, he told readers, but it had been a long time coming. It reflected not so much a loss of dominant authority in a world system—one meaning of hegemony—as a loss of an ability to contain domestic political contention within boundaries that allowed orderly rule, a second meaning. Or at least the failures at home—the breakdown in the face of the pandemic is a good Fukayama example—conditioned the loss of world dominance. His recent article, like the big book, shows an uncanny ability to be neither correct nor consistent but nevertheless revealing, especially for our purposes.[1]

Fukayama's work shows the perils of prediction and prompts the reminder that this afterword remains one of history, more interested in what our moment tells us about the past that got us here than in speculation about where things will go. Such an emphasis is also wise because it is so especially hard at this particular moment to make predictions, both internationally and domestically. The larger context within which Bill Clinton prevailed on a middle-class platform in 1992—just in time for the end of history—featured challenges to US hegemony in the world. An accompanying economic malaise led elites to enjoin at home an austerity that Democrats struggled to package within an electoral strategy. The current US crisis involves defeat in Afghanistan, to be sure, but also far broader problems. These stem immediately from the weakness born of economic tremors begun in 2008 in the US housing sector, and the shallow nature of recovery from them. But the problems with a long-term profit squeeze are far more enduring and reach beyond US borders, featuring as they do sharp doubts globally about the market's production of the desired profits, while attracting attention to more statist strategies associated with China's rise.

The quandaries in addressing those problems remind us why periods of sustained hegemony by a single power are so rare in the history of the world.[2] To lead requires taking national interests, or at least those of the ruling class at home, into account while also being responsive—via conciliation as well as coercion—to the rest of the world. The neoliberal moment dissolved that problem by supposing that the United States could lead a liberalization benefiting investors everywhere and transcending national parochialisms. However, the absence of such strategies at the scale of the nation-state now seems to many planners and investors to be part of the crisis, with some clamoring to acknowledge that development and investment opportunities require spending, infrastructure, and inside deals.[3]

For left-liberal policy influencers—think, in the United States, of Paul Krugman—Keynesian policies involving social spending that at least slightly risk inflation are on the table, and the Biden administration seems willing to go further down this road than Trump's initial forays allowed. At least rhetorically, both administrations have pledged a renewal of the manufacturing sector in the US in ways that would have to move beyond global free trade. Given how meager the growth of manufacturing jobs has remained as compared to the advertisements for such growth, the extent of the reach of these policies must remain uncertain. Moreover, Keynesian stimulus packages are insistently paired with the word "COVID" as their justification. Nor do they in the main build social property—take, for example, the preference for green cars over public transport, and the defiant rejection of socialized medicine—in the way that Keynes's Keynesianism projected. Where labor and capital flight are concerned, there will be a great pull to avoid giving up the advantages the neoliberal period brought to management.

Perhaps more dramatically at issue if these nation-based, but global-capitalism-inflected strategies do become the order of the day is what the hegemonic role of the United States in the world could be, predicated as it has been on the promise of creating a global middle class. In the time of a united Europe and rise of the BRICS (Brazil, Russia, India, China, South Africa) economies, how does the necessity to defend a world economy based in some part on US debt and still more on the US dollar comport with a perception of the US as anything more than another advocate of its special interests?[4]

These weighty issues are beyond the scope of this book, but they can be briefly brought into focus to make concrete how the possibility of fundamental world shifts shows up in the identity appeals made within US politics. One contender emerging in the recent past that could supplant "middle class" as the locus of electoral sloganeering is "American," a term that has perhaps flown under that radar as being so ubiquitous as to resemble the flag pins in every presidential debate, inconsequential except when absent. And yet, Trump's "Make America great again" and the millions of MAGA hats it launched represent an effective and timely, if under-theorized, call out to voters. At least eighty years old, the slogan, sometimes with a "Let's" in front, originated with the Wisconsin politician Alexander Wiley just before World War II. The isolationism of Wiley's appeals echoed the soft-on-Hitler politics of the America First movement, whose slogan/name Trump also repurposed. Far-right campaigns like those of Barry Goldwater and Ronald Reagan featured the "Let's MAGA" tagline, but the Democrats liked it too. Bill Clinton used it in his presidential campaigns and in ads supporting Hillary Clinton in 2008's Democratic primaries. As Toni Morrison observed in 1992, the word "American" implies "white American" unless caveats appear, much as "middle class" does. Therefore, big opportunities for coded racial appeals apply, with the added bonus of not burning bridges with voters of color who so identify. *Wikipedia* seems to regard the MAGA slogan as having been benign until 2015, when Trump supercharged it with racial appeals. However, that is doubtful, given its capacity to invoke nostalgias of race and empire across time. Trump's strategy centered, with laser-like focus, on efforts to connect it to white nationalist appeals surrounding the border wall and "our jobs," to cancel H-1B skilled worker visas, and to champion Islamophobic restrictions on migration. Within this framework, grievances around trade deals and foreign aid could also gather as powerfully "American" ones.[5]

At the least, "American" has become a modifier when the middle class, or even the worker, gets a shout out. Erstwhile Trump loyalist Anthony Scaramucci celebrated the 2016 election with a hasty book whose contents often lost track of the far-fetched thesis its title proclaimed: *Trump, the Blue-Collar President.* It does however capture a Trump strategy able to court voters with "middle-class tax cuts" in service of a larger goal of seizing the word "American" for reaction. Scaramucci placed "MAGA" within a long history of betrayals on trade and aid, going back to the post–World War II Marshall Plan to redevelop Europe, which he imagined as having "had devastating consequences on the American worker."[6]

Ominously enough, given the possibilities for terrible outcomes of US demands for what won't be acknowledged as debt relief from China, this line of thought will not be confined to the Republican Party. Joe Biden and his advisers thus call for a "foreign policy for the middle class" in which a confrontation with China largely structures the priorities, vague as they admittedly are. "Main Street," one enthusiast proclaims, "meets foreign policy."[7] Clearly, how these appeals develop will reflect whether the globalizing neoliberal sureties of the previous fifty years survive in new forms or whether national solutions permit "American" to be uttered more and more breathlessly—perhaps modifying "middle class." There is much we cannot know, but also much we can, about the ways in which middle-class appeals coexist now with some open overtures to the "white working class." It is with that distressing dynamic that we conclude.

UNCERTAIN CHALLENGES TO MIDDLE-CLASS POLITICS

As the historic failed attempt to organize Amazon workers in Bessemer, Alabama, reached the voting stage in spring of 2021, Senator Bernie Sanders addressed a small Birmingham crowd in what was intended to be a mass rally showing union strength. Sanders's talk followed that of the rapper Killer Mike, who delivered a raw account of class and race relations during slavery and sharecropping, and of their lingering impacts. Speaking to a struggle at a workplace where 80 percent of the workers are Black, Killer Mike forcefully argued for multiracial working-class unity. Sanders studded his talk with references to "starvation wages." He spoke of workers and their exploitation at the hands of the rich—in Amazon's case by the richest capitalist in the history of the world. He then rang out a conclusion that incongruously named what he saw as at stake in union struggles: the expansion of the "middle class."[8] Within the logic of his own electoral career, and even within his prior campaigning regarding Amazon, Sanders's phrasing is perhaps less than surprising. The author of the hot-selling 2011 manifesto *The Speech: A Historic Filibuster on Corporate Greed and the Decline of Our Middle Class*, Sanders had praised Amazon's 2018 announcement of fifteen-dollar-an-hour minimum wage for its employees as a victory for that same middle class. Talk of the middle class has a hold on us.[9]

However logical in terms of reigning political discourses, Sanders's invocation of the middle class at such a point in a union election was unwise. Amid an organizing campaign during which COVID curtailed worker-to-worker meetings and with the voting itself to be done by mail, the middle-class framing invited fears of falling and discouraged collective solutions. In those ways, it mirrored company propaganda that sought to ennoble what employees might achieve on the basis of what Amazon "provided," potentially raised the specter of the precarity of life without an Amazon job, and elbowed aside framings based on common workplace grievances.

Political appeals to the middle class are so much a part of the repertoire of almost all US politicians that the intervention of Sanders might have seemed more verbal tic than rousing crescendo. We are, for now, stuck with them. But with them, if the arguments in this book are correct, comes a deeply misremembered and problematic past as well as a distorting impact on how we see things today. As we have seen, the cult of the United States as a middle-class country has corresponded to little of its actual history. It has contributed to pretenses of an exceptional nation, especially in the context of the Cold War. It has elevated entrepreneurs over workers as a national priority and divided workers in offices from workers in factories. In the most recent past, it has contributed to the hollowness of US political debate over both racial justice and class difference, while contributing to confused and confusing ideas of what class is. Nor does the current, ostensibly pro-middle-class way of speaking politically work even on its own terms. During the three decades during which the salvation of the middle class has dominated national political debate, the middle layers of the US structure of wealth and income have fared abysmally. There is ample reason, then, both to ask after the prospects of getting past the quest to save the middle class, and to appreciate the difficulties facing us in doing so—especially insofar as the vocabularies in electoral politics structure a choice between "middle class" and the even more destructive choices of "American" or "white working class" as loci of appeals to win office.

Politicians help make the middle class an empty signifier. In the run-up to the 2020 election, Joe Biden's campaign took to reminding voters that everybody called him "Middle Class Joe." This came before he got traction among party leaders and liberal media as the singular hope of defeating first Sanders in the primaries and then Trump in the general election. Reporters had fun with Biden's claim, pointing out that they could not, in fact, find people who did call him that.[10] When Biden emerged as such a hope, the rebrand focused on the rather different nickname "Amtrak Joe." That tag carried more of a material basis in that he was a longtime Delaware-to-DC rider of the train, originally to provide care after work for his surviving children after an accident took the lives of his wife and an infant daughter in 1972. *Marie Claire* held, implausibly, that Biden rode that train "every day for 36 years."[11] "Middle class" was perhaps not worth insisting on when more plausible adjectives and nouns like "Amtrak" and "Scranton" (where he lived until age ten) could connect Biden to ordinary folks, hard times, and hard coal. The infrastructure proposals that were the troubled centerpiece of Biden's first year in office impressed *Nation* writer Joan Walsh as a "Scranton-inflected agenda for racial and economic justice." Biden's plans amounted, in his words, to a "blue-collar blueprint" for building the "middle class." He earned (Walsh's words) the nickname "Scranton Joe."[12]

As fanciful as much of this shape-shifting of images sounds, their variety does count as a part of a growing trend that heralds, in a small way, a decline in head-on appeals to the middle class. Some indications suggest that the cult of salvation of the middle class is under threat at age thirty. At moments when elites speak to each other, the dismissal of the idea of a middle-class society has taken bold forms. A 2011 study by investment analysts at Citigroup reached the conclusion that for financial purposes all the action concentrated at the top, with the top 1 percent controlling the lion's share of US wealth. "Plutonomy," the term they coined to describe the pattern they documented, left little to discuss in terms of a middle class.[13] Even in politics, similar judgments have matured, as in the reckoning by Barack Obama's chief economist in the run-up to the 2012 election that the middle class included just 42 percent of the population. (The Obama campaign nonetheless launched appeals at just that moment to a middle class said to include 96 percent of the population). As standards of living worsened and inequalities soared, labor journalist Harold Meyerson's predictions in 2016 of an election without echoing appeals to the middle class rested on significant, though contradictory, polling that showed a dis-identification with self-labeling as middle-class.[14]

In some cases, those polls registering dis-identification with the middle class showed increasing openness toward working-class self-identification.[15] Such clarity proves volatile from poll to poll not only because of varied methodologies of those gathering data but also because the identity taken on is itself likely to be contradictory and situational. As this book has argued, respondents have deep miseries on the job as well as ones regarding debt and consumption off the job that have often been packaged as middle-class grievances. Indeed, even specific problems regarding how management

of personalities deepens alienation at work might be regarded as originally middle-class ones, emerging as they did
so early and pointedly in white-collar and pink-collar work.
The hope that the exploited and miserable suddenly realize
that they are working class thus requires tempering. The notion that increasing misery—sinking—will propel such motion becomes complicated by the fact that much in popular
and political culture leads to the processing of the maladies
themselves as middle-class ones.

In any case, the hope that real life will send the middle layers toward working-class identities never historically constituted more than half of the reason for radical optimism about
its trajectory. The other half stressed the attractive power of a
working class in motion. Unions remain at a low ebb, whether
measured in numbers of members or, some recent good news
notwithstanding, numbers of strikers. Occasional upticks
will hopefully turn into a trend, but when they do those of us
hoping to see the spread of working-class identities will still
face the problem that the labor leadership itself participates
in the exaltation of the middle class. As Wade Rathke's justifi-
bly mordant reflections after the death of longtime AFL-CIO
head Richard Trumka emphasized, "We have not organized a
single private sector mass employer. Not Walmart. Not Amazon. Not McDonald's." He continued, "It won't be the AFL-
CIO that answers these questions [regarding organizing], and
as union density decreases and with it the resources to ... organize the unorganized it may be impossible for any union
to solve this riddle on its own."[16] Restiveness by labor has
spiked modestly in the recent past, but the increase in strikes
came on top of a very low base, with big jumps at the end
of the 2010s reaching only levels a quarter of those common
in the much-smaller economy of the 1970s. This combative-
ness, more than the record of the labor leadership, permits

some confidence that we could see the kind of organizing that would lead to a massive embrace of working-class identities. However, it is a fragile trend interrupting a very long decline and scarcely showing up in organizing successes.[17] The temptation to find an easier route toward engendering a new or renewed language of class thus looms large.

Given its power and the current assumption that politics means electoral politics, the Democratic Party is best poised to provide such a seeming shortcut. Indeed, elements within it have showed signs of offering one, with their sudden embrace of the idea that appealing to a "white working class" somehow promises progressive gains. Here, this afterword argues, the cure damages quite as much as the disease. Moreover, the new grammar of class does not do much to address the problem of empty uses of "middle class." Instead, recent calls to pay attention to the white working class offer a supplement, served up by more or less the same strategists, to be deployed *alongside* rhetoric urging saving the middle class. Middle-class and white working-class appeals function much more as an ensemble than as opposing positions.

MANUFACTURING THE "WHITE WORKING CLASS"

Seeking "white working class" support is different from casting about for middle-class votes in one critical way. Membership in the middle class has functioned as an identity applied to and embraced by many in the United States at least since the 1930s. That variously defined middle-class identity, massaged over time for anti-labor, Cold War, and partisan political purposes, rather easily became the basis for forms of identity politics appealing to voters imagined as white but not named that way. The history of the white working class in the

US lacks anything like such reach. Figure 2 plots the relative use of the two terms, showing the contrast. The graph effectively captures the trajectory of patterns of published uses of "middle class" over time. However, uses of "white working class" so pale in comparison that its trajectory simply hugs the bottom line, conveying nothing. In order to see some shape for the latter we must, in figure 3, adjust the graph by magnifying usages a hundredfold. The rhetoric of saving the middle class deserves to be considered a kind of white identity politics—bereft of meaningful policy goals—that does not speak its name. "White working class," on the other hand, has very modestly entered the scene as a newly manufactured identity politics based on almost no one's actual identity.

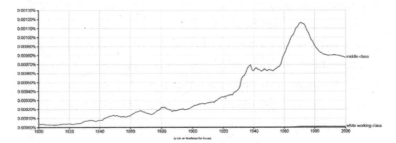

Figure 2: Ngrams Plotting "Middle Class" versus "White Working Class." *Source: Google Books.*

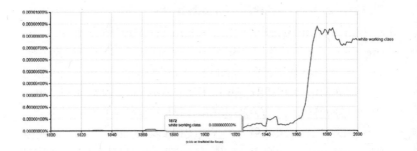

Figure 3: Ngrams Plotting "White Working Class," Axis Modified. *Source: Google Books.*

The lack of use of "white working class" has reflected two significant handicaps facing the term. The first was the Cold War, which made it hard to sustain any use of "working class," whatever the adjective added. The term suggested Marxism, militancy, and ties to a world labor movement. Eventually, even union leaders opted for "middle class" because it mainstreamed labor's cause, promised to make alliances with Cold War liberal groups easier, and opposed the language still used by oppositional left and pro-democracy groups in the unions. So potent was the censorship and self-censorship regarding the language of class that, more than thirty years after the fall of the Soviet Union, there is still sufficient frisson at seeing "working class" in print that a writer in the leading socialist publication *Jacobin* recently leaned on Stanley Greenberg's emphases on the "white working class" as if they represented a class struggle tendency inside the Democratic Party.[18]

If "working class" proved a hard sell, so did "white." As sociologists Michael Omi and Howard Winant have argued, the moral grandeur of the civil rights movement happily made open appeals to white interests and white supremacy—so regular a feature of earlier US politics—harder to utter in its wake. If the new order seemed to require color blindness, with the center right of the Democratic Party its champion, open appeals to "white" interests carried liabilities that "middle class" did not. Labor radicals, still the most likely group to use "working class," have had sufficient sense to know that adding "white" undermines labor unity and confuses locations of advantage with those of exploitation.[19]

The rising usage of "white working class," meager as it still was, coincided with the triumphs of the civil rights movement and backlash against it. Usage peaked during the triumph of Reaganism's coded pro-white appeals, which tracked the awful zenith of the career of California fascist and former Klansman Tom Metzger. Organizing around what he imagined to be the concerns of the white working class, Metzger professed to be inspired by the militancy of the Industrial Workers of the World, minus that union's interracialism. In 1980, Metzger won over forty-six thousand votes as the Democratic candidate for Congress in a San Diego–area district. He received a further seventy-six thousand votes in a California US Senate primary in 1982 before presiding over the creation of the murderous White Aryan Resistance organization.[20]

Mainstream Democratic Party strategists kept the term "white working class" a little alive as a way to couch political appeals. As chapter 5 showed, Greenberg promised to teach Democratic politicians how to appeal to white workers while deciding to name his research subjects as "middle class." He twice used "white working class" in his *Middle Class Dreams* work on Macomb County. One version of naming the new Democratic base wooed in the Greenberg-piloted Clinton campaign in 1992 split the difference, seeking votes from the "hard-working forgotten middle class." Others did opt for using "white working class" at about the time that Greenberg's star rose, but again without arguing that they were proposing an alternative to talk of saving the middle class. The most intelligent contribution was a 1991 meditation on what would later be widely called "dog whistle politics," initiatives that made racial appeals to whites without using the word "race." It came from Mary and Thomas Edsall, who repeatedly invoked the "white working class" in discussion of such appeals while sometimes adding "and lower-middle class." Their *Chain Reaction: The Impact of Race, Rights, and Taxes on American Politics*, published the following year, used "white working class" as a collective noun just once, generally opting for "lower middle class."[21]

"Middle-class" and "white working-class" appeals thus came from the keyboards of the same strategists and commentators, but with "middle class" holding more attractions and carrying less baggage. "Middle class" dominated, with "white working class" occasionally present as an added friendly amendment. The two terms performed similar functions in defining a group key in all elections, one that required constrained demands for racial justice if it was to be won.[22]

In the early twenty-first century, a small knot of books, articles, and authors continued to make the white working class the key to their work. Ruy Teixeira and Joel Rogers's *America's Forgotten Majority: Why the White Working Class Still Matters*, a 2000 book in which avowedly left authors emphasized that a specifically *white* working class counted as the nation's largest neglected group, exhibited a stridency on that terminological point that remained an outlying position. They, and very few others, argued for the white working class's centrality because of its size and its tendency to swing from one party to another.[23]

The two strands of political language of race and class became more distinct—and usages of "white working class" again slightly increased—as Democrats jockeyed for position around the 2012 election. The crescendo of the use of "white working class" after 2016 as a way to respond to Trump's electoral triumphs has obscured the ways in which the new vogue for the term emerged somewhat earlier—not in a fight between Democrats and Republicans, but in wars of position among competing Democrats.

During and after the Obama years, fears that the Democrats were abandoning white workers grew as it became clear that white workers were fast becoming—Rogers and Texeira's title to the contrary—a forgotten *minority*, their ranks dwindling. Obama's overheard and widely reported 2008 remarks charging whites in declining industrial regions with "clinging" to their guns, Bibles, opposition to immigration, and— less remembered—hatred of trade agreements made him vulnerable to charges of lack of empathy with white workers.[24] His insistence on saying "middle class" at all possible moments seemed to doubters to leave workers out. Those who felt themselves to be outside Democratic inner circles had no hope of capturing the "warrior for the middle class" label from him but had some prospects as champions of a white working class. Nor did Obama's victory in 2012 assuage critics, who pointed to Democratic failures in so many other races. Thomas Edsall, who frequently breaks out of the limitations of the "white working-class" paradigm that he helped to create, warned that some journalism on the 2012 vote so insistently foregrounded the "white working class" that it pushed both voters of color and the racial views of whites in other classes to the margins.[25]

In the run-up to the 2014 congressional elections, political analyst Andrew Levison defined the Democrats' greatest challenge as the "white working-class problem."[26] Greenberg himself then published "Why the White Working Class Matters." He helped energize the White Working Class Roundtable, which met often and produced streams of articles and "white papers" under the auspices of the *Democratic Strategist* group. The second of the group's major roundtables centered on responses to Greenberg's contribution, "The Battle for the White Working Class Is Just Beginning."[27] What journalist Susan Glasser has called the "Democratic Civil War" heated up during the 2016 election, with the critics of Hillary Clinton's perceived orientation to women and

minorities—those making the complaints included Greenberg and those around him, Joe Biden, and on some accounts
Bill Clinton—taking up the white working-class banner.[28]
The candidate Clinton, who had so excoriated Obama for his
gaffe regarding those in the de-industrial heartland clinging
to Bibles, offered her own free gift to Republicans in 2016
when she tossed many Trump supporters into a "basket of
deplorables" as racists, sexists, homophobes, Islamophobes,
and more—a statement that was read as belittling the white
working class.[29]

While it is true that a Clinton victory in 2016 would have
disarmed many of the "nasty" postelection conflicts that
Glasser has described, the achievements of the "white working class" thinkers in the Democratic Party before Trump
were significant and divisive. They insisted on invoking
both the middle class and the white working class to counter the identity-politics wing that they believed had become
dominant in the Democratic Party by emphasizing race and
gender. Without any clear program to address the pressing
needs of working people, they seldom allowed that the main
roadblock to doing so was not identity politics but limits set
by what change was permissible to capital and Democratic
leaders. Nor could they make a popular breakthrough.

Happily, no large group of people has signed up for the
"white working class" label, however much they have identified as whites and as workers. In trying to convey a sense
of "white working class" to readers, Katherine Connor Martin, head of US dictionaries for the *Oxford English Diction-
ary*, has recently observed that "[o]verwhelmingly when
people are using the phrase 'white working class' it seems to
be in the context of electoral politics."[30] The Trump victory
seemed to offer the chance for Democrats advocating for
a white working-class strategy—again, one in which they

simultaneously invoked the middle class—to wield greater influence.

By the beginnings of the 2016 campaign, loud solicitations of an alleged white working class also came from the Trump campaign. These overtures perfectly illustrated the dangers of reinjecting the pursuit of "white" interests into US politics. The celebrated political scientist Walter Dean Burnham pointed to June 2015 as the origin of such concerted efforts from Trump forces, regarding them as squarely focused on recruiting "the less-educated lower-middle/white working class, major victims of policies pursued by established elites of both parties."[31] Trump himself mostly remained content with making vague allusions to his supposed affinities to those who built his hotels and casinos, but his white nationalist strategist Steve Bannon—*Vanity Fair* called him Trump's "new CEO"—trumpeted the campaign's race/class appeals constantly. The phrase "white working class" inevitably accents its first word and undermines its last; Bannon forwarded that dynamic with a particularly extravagant and wicked élan. Staid conservative enterprises like the Coalition for a Prosperous America suddenly moonlighted as advocates for Bannon's white "working-class revolt." [32]

REACTIONS: THE WHITE WORKING-CLASS MOMENT AND PERSISTENT MIDDLE-CLASS APPEALS

Almost no pro-Democratic strategists and journalists anticipated Clinton's defeat in 2016, but it turned out that they were ready with a narrative explaining Trump's victory. The white working class starred in that drama. The day after the election, based on unreliable exit polls, the *New York Times'* front page piloted the idea the election was "a decisive demonstration of power by a largely overlooked coalition of mostly blue-collar white and working-class voters." The broad and insistent consensus around this interpretation included liberals more than ready to see white workers as uniquely backward, Democratic strategists blaming peers who had not listened to their chatter regarding the white working class, and Republicans giddy at capturing a new constituency. In the aftermath of the election, Bernie Sanders tweeted, "I come from the white working class."[33] Biden's election postmortem emphasized the need for his party to "show enough respect" for the white working class and expressed a conviction that racism did not play any significant role in the election of Trump. Google Trends, which measures internet searches for specific terms, showed a sevenfold increase in searches for "white working class" after the election over a typical month before the election.[34]

The proliferation of "white working class" matured after Trump's election partly because it coincided with similar turns toward that phrase in what the political writer Pankaj Mishra has called the "white Anglosphere."[35] The British vote to leave the European Union in the Brexit referendum came months before Trump's victory. Amid complicated crosscurrents, the "leave" forces featured far-right nationalists who objected to the movement of migrants to England and who became the movement's public face. In Britain, there was a far-sturdier tradition of using "working class" by socialists and in popular culture. The writings of Lisa Tilley, Richard Seymour, and Robbie Shilliam offer some of the most illuminating reflections on UK appeals to the white working class. That the term echoes across the Anglosphere and beyond, in places where the electoral demographics of race so differ, underlines Seymour's point that white working-class analysis functions less to "leave anyone informed" as to political realities and more as a "cover story" that enables elites to at once bemoan racism and undertake new racist initiatives.[36]

Writers from academia in the United States added to the sense that the white working class was suddenly the key to everything. A spate of celebrated books, including J. D. Vance's *Hillbilly Elegy*, Nancy Isenberg's *White Trash*, and Arlie Russell Hochschild's *Strangers in Their Own Land*, appeared either just before or shortly after the 2016 vote, gaining notoriety in that context. Most were of course begun long before Trump's triumphs, showing again how the ground had been seeded for the swelling of interest in the white working class before he was taken seriously.[37] Further contributing to the rise of such discourse were splashy and weighty studies of the health crisis and particularly drug addiction in white working-class communities.[38]

If the legal scholar Joan C. Williams was not the first person to begin writing in response to Trump's 2016 election victory, she was at least tied for the top spot. Her work portrays broad swaths of Trump voters as alternately understandable and even noble but also as utterly beyond the experience of urban professionals. Williams's languages of class typify much of liberal discourse as they move jarringly from "white working" to "middle" class in describing white workers. Williams describes herself as working late into election night responding to a disaster. A bloggish article, properly rageful and admirably breezy, poured out. Two days after the election, the website of *Harvard Business Review*—get ready for several ironies—published the piece as "What So Many People Don't Get about the U.S. Working Class."[39] Hits and retweets encouraged a book, published by the journal's press a mere six months later.[40] The book, blurbed by Joe Biden, hovered on the edges of best-seller lists.[41]

Williams's book proved to be a not very serious one, but it remains potently symptomatic of where we are. Nowhere does this fact stand out more than in the book's slipperiness regarding the languages of race and class. She wanted, Williams remembered, to follow Greenberg's 1990s model by calling her aggrieved subjects the "middle class," in her case kicking the "clueless" professional-managerial elite out of that group in favor of genuine sons and daughters of toil, minus the poor. However, her publisher convinced her to substitute "working class" for "middle class."[42] The book version of Williams's research occasionally still uses "middle class" to describe her subject, and it offers definitions of "working class" as essentially middle income. The result is a "class" defined by an annual income of $41,005 to $131,962 (median: $75,144), and by its holding of values allegedly centered on family and independence. (K–12 teachers, professors, and indeed much of the professional-managerial class fall very largely in that income range, but they disappear as members of the working class and instead appear as its overbearing enemies.) At moments, Williams appears to want to talk about the whole working class, but her book is rightly titled *White Working Class*. So much does her work lean on that racially identified collective noun that Williams resorted to using the acronym WWC in the initial article as a space saver. In the book, as one reviewer puts it, "The 'white' modifier mostly disappears after the title page," but the whiteness of her subjects remains clear.[43]

The practices of designedly mixing up "middle class" and "white working class" are, as we have seen, long standing. Williams perhaps does a favor to debates on these matters with the outsized "WHITE" on her book's cover. But the potential costs are great, and the incoherence of her categories concerning both race and class is striking. At one point,

Williams hopes that restaurant owners will oppose Trump's border policies in order for them to better secure immigrant labor. Thus the restaurant *owners* are considered working class, and their racialized immigrant employees are somehow not.[44]

Both the original short article and the book began with a "native informant," Williams's father-in-law, credentialed as working class because he "grew up eating blood soup." Hostile to unions, which he considered "a bunch of jokers who take your money," the father-in-law counted as "a man before his time." He was a "blue-collar white man," Republican voter, and *Wall Street Journal* reader from the 1950s forward. Fair enough—there were such workers. But the jobs held by the father-in-law do not sound very blue collar. He might better be described instead as a serially failing entrepreneur who moonlighted in self-employment even as he held a salaried job. That job, as an inspector in a factory making museum-quality hygrometers, hardly fits the extravagance of the claims made for him as a precocious blue-collar outlier. In half-endorsing his disdain for unions, Williams finds that "starting in the 1970s, many blue-collar whites followed his example," a particularly unfeeling summary of what happened to the organizations representing working people and the vast amount of coercion and disinvestment that made it happen.[45]

White Working Class offers scant hints regarding what programmatic reforms can increase the power and organization of working people, or what would force elites to listen better to them. It addresses inequality, but of a sort based on supposed disparities in "paying attention" to groups who lack strategies to address mounting economic differences. Williams holds out hopes based almost purely on "identity politics," designed to flatter her subjects but not to redress their miseries. She plumps, as the sociologist Anthony Perrin has put it, for white workers to receive *"recognition* not redistribution." At one low point, Williams cautions that "[p]rogressives have lavished attention on the poor for over a century" and that must change.[46]

The initial inflated claims that white workers uniquely contributed to Trump's 2016 election proved unsustainable. Within days of the election, even before better data than early exit polls came in, such a view underwent sharp challenges. The lack of substantial movement of such workers toward Trump in relation to their votes for Mitt Romney in the 2012 election cast doubt on assertions that the new president had a special bond with white blue-collar workers.[47] As more sophisticated data emerged, other social facts came to seem more compelling than the association of white workers with Trump. One concerned the dearth of voting among the working poor and even the middle reaches of the working class. Those making less than $30,000 per year furnished 56 percent of the nation's nonvoters and just 28 percent of its voters, with those making between $30,000 and $75,000 less dramatically but still significantly underrepresented in the ranks of voters.[48] Even with the increased participation in 2020—at least six million more low-income voters than in 2016—low income continued to predict low turnout. About one voter in five made less than $50,000 in the year before the 2020 election. That same demographic furnished 43 percent of nonvoters.[49]

Instant analyses, and political polling generally, miss much by making the attainment of a high school diploma or less a convenient proxy for working-class membership. Twenty-two percent of the white electorate has high incomes and no college degree. They are, as Edsall writes, "rock-ribbed Republicans" who are counted as working-class conservatives but are often not actually working class. Conversely, one white voter in seven possesses a college degree but earns a low income. They are the "most loyal white Democratic constituency." Often poor, they get counted as "middle class."[50] On the other hand, polling recently commissioned by the AFL-CIO counts about 40 percent of the white non-college-educated electorate as Democratic or as leaning in that direction. Eighty percent of these white and working-class Democrats approve of Black Lives Matter, and 82 percent want no border wall.[51] Here is a demographic of white workers that is truly "forgotten."

Most importantly, among whites Trump won in 2016 not one particular income category but *all* income categories. The voting patterns of white workers were far more like those of whites in other class positions than like those of other groups of workers. Astonishingly, with his endorsement of sexual violence as a perk of being rich and male ringing in voters' ears, he carried white women's votes in 2016. To displace this broad white electoral consensus onto the white worker obscures reality.[52]

In the short run, popular attention to the white working class ebbed about as quickly as it flowed, although the term lurks in the playbooks of white nationalists in the Republican Party and in those of the center-right ranks of the Democrats. Among the latter group, considerable confusion reigns. Within a year of the 2016 election, Google Trends registered the same levels of popular disinterest in the term as had been typical during the decade before. Even Greenberg himself wrote that his party did not "have a 'white working-class problem'" but a "working-class problem." In 2017, he briefly argued for a strategy that would attack a system that only worked "for the rich, big corporations and cultural elites," but not "for average Americans."[53] Biden, the presidential candidate most situated in the center-right Democratic tradition and the language of class it has proposed and enforced, vaulted in the 2020 election cycle to leading-contender status based on hopes that the Macomb County working-class base of the party would support him against Trump.

OUR LONG MOMENT OF DANGER: THINKING OF CLASS BEYOND ELECTIONS

To close a book that brings history down so near the present with a final update seems a fool's errand; after all, it takes months for a book to appear, and the author cherishes hopes that it will be read decades hence. To scruple over narrating the last available development leaves the book only the slightest bit less dated. In this case it helps to recognize that these closing words conclude a very long history that reaches back at least to the 1930s and is unlikely to give way easily. That history, especially as it applies to electoral politics, has constrained and distorted our imaginations in specific ways for the last three decades. The obsession with saving the middle class shows slight signs of receding on its own, and the "white working class" rhetoric that has made an appearance as a distantly contending alternative regarding how politicians talk about class is itself unclear and retrograde. That we have been stuck so long suggests enduring problems with perspectives that advocate the salvation of the middle class within US politics and confuse understandings of class in the whole society.

Reactions to the 2020 election show that "white working class" lurks as a category of political analysis alongside louder overtures to the middle class. That election put in office, after all, a president for a good while identified with the position of paying sufficient attention to the white working class, within a long career centered on saving the middle class. Despite dissections of how premature and wrong analyses of the 2016 Trump victory that rested on the supposed backwardness of the "white working class" proved to be, the core of that analysis lingered and shaped responses to his somewhat-close defeat in 2020. Pundits still imagined a Trump base uniquely located among white workers misled by big business. Historian Kim Moody's trenchant analysis of voters and political donors in 2020 shows that such a portrait of the election describes neither the voter nor the donor base of Trump's support, neither of which are "white working class." But it persists. Philip Bump's *Washington Post* account used "no college" as a very dodgy proxy for "working class" in arguing that Trump merely named (and ultimately imperiled) a long electoral trend leading to white-working-class voting for Republicans, one predating and surviving his presidency.[54]

Reacting to the peak of rhetorical attention to the white working class after Trump's 2016 election, Anthony Perrin wrote: "The white working class was made, not found; deployed, not discovered."[55] To take aboard Perrin's insight requires that we regard ersatz languages of elections and class as malleable in the short run as well the long. If such discourse has receded in the recent past, we should delight in that fact. When the term is used, the accent will always fall on "white" and the mumbling on "working class." Curiously, we hear little about the needs of the Black working class. Greenberg's most recent book startlingly refers to the European immigrant working class of a century ago as the "real working class." Nor have appeals to the working class as a whole increased.[56]

Even as we rejoice in the decline of the targeting of supposed white working-class voters, we can hardly take comfort in renewed litanies to saving the middle class. The same liabilities that have so long applied to that strategy continue to do so. Moreover, in the decade just past, the overlap and lack of clarity that allows strategists to shuttle workers from the middle class to the white working class has only become clearer. That overlap emerged in a particularly stark way in a recent long piece by *Politico*'s Zack Stanton, a self-identified son of Macomb County. The article offered analysis of the 2020 election as a vindication of all things Stanley Greenberg, seeing him as an important thinker on class in the United States, after having been equally acute regarding South Africa. It posited that the 2020 Democratic victory rested on its success in attracting more affluent "Biden Republicans," briefly alienated by Trump's over-the-top white nationalism. Part of the way into the piece, Greenberg himself arrives to bask in the praise. The article becomes an interview, one at pains to point out how fragile the hold on the line-crossing Republicans remains. Greenberg adds that holding them will only be meaningful if Democrats also expand their share of "white working-class," or sometimes "middle-class," Reagan Democrats (more accurately, their children and grandchildren.) Crediting Biden as the man to do that job, Greenberg speaks with uncharacteristic specificity and boldness about demands: universal health care, wariness regarding trade deals, and childcare plus a child benefit payment. These are demands the Democrats remain at best slow to advance, but the more obvious problem is that suddenly the one white constituency placed at the center of progressive politics has become two: Reagan Democrats and Biden Republicans.[57]

At times, deployments of the labels "middle class," "white working class," and "blue-collar middle class" surely represent honest efforts to win an election; they may even contain the broken bits of grander hopes, or odd remembrances of that one inspirational working-class studies course taken in college. There is no need for harshness regarding how people use these discourses on Election Day. But in thinking about larger possibilities and local social movements, we do need to contest the ways in which such labels enforce constraints and spread illusions. In making the white voters in Macomb County—uplifted according to their worst impulses—the center of political life in America, politicians cause us to immobilize ourselves, especially as elections loom so large in how we consider political action. In their hardened forms, appeals to the (white) middle class and the *white* working class function as pedagogy, not sociology. They teach us what is impossible to demand and, in doing so, account not for the opinions of white workers in general, but specifically those of the white workers who are most reactionary.

It is of course good to listen to all workers and to think about the specific class-based miseries of those who see themselves a middle class. That is part of the job of ethnographers, reporters, politicians, union leaders, and even pollsters. To hail some workers as a "white working class," and to promise them respect and a sympathetic ear only on that specific basis, courts new rounds of calculated postponement of racial justice. To count them only as part of an inflated, undifferentiated middle class risks erasure of the profoundly working-class complaints that they have, on and off the job. To write them off as merely fooled by the middle-class label likewise misleads us.[58]

The emphasis on "winning back" the so-called white working class or the middle class exposes all of us to what journalist Eric Levitz has termed the "tyranny of the unwoke white swing voter," especially where immigration is concerned. Arlie Russell Hochschild's regrettable "cutting in line" analogy is in danger of becoming all that anyone remembers from her often perceptive *Strangers in Their Own*

Land. She offers it as an image shared by working-class white informants, whose dashed hopes for the American Dream seem stymied by line-jumping migrants rather than the chemical companies who dominate and scar the land where they live.[59] Hochschild herself constructed the "cutting in line" image by synthesizing many conversations and then gave it back to her informants, who, we are told, liked it. For a researcher to report these perceptions is apt, but without also challenging such views, we are left unable to speak to and listen to workers who are finding their ways to social and environmental justice and support for Indigenous rights.

Similarly, while recent writings by Greenberg and by Teixeira say many of the proper things regarding how a new and diverse United States beckons, their alternating currents of solicitude for the middle class or a white working class aim to limit debates on border control and other issues. The former ominously warns that all positive momentum will stall if Democrats are—his view—foolish enough to "rescue" the Republicans by "passing landmark comprehensive immigration reform ... that is viewed as ... comparable to the passage of the civil rights laws of the 1960s."[60] Arguing in the *Democratic Strategist* for "the diverse white working class" as the focus of the 2020 election campaigns, Teixeira offered a longer list of policy proposals that progressives must take off the table to win the mythical white working-class constituency: "How to make these gains? Hint: not by decriminalizing the border, not through Medicare for All that abolishes private health care plans; not by providing health coverage to undocumented immigrants and other similar—and similarly unpopular—ideas."[61]

This use of white working people, and at other moments of the (white) middle class, to preempt demands for justice and well-being cannot be turned on for the election and turned off after. We who believe in freedom have to dream better and fight harder than the discourses of saving the middle class or paying attention to the white working class allow. To hope for and organize toward openings for working-class forward motion, social movements will have to look for their poetry, and their clarity, beyond the social analysis offered by electoral politics. They must do so by listening to the many workers who identify with both the aspirations and the miseries of a middle class.

NOTES

CHAPTER 1: LANGUAGES OF CLASS AND THE EXHAUSTION OF POLITICAL IMAGINATION

1 Dylan Matthews, "What Is the Middle Class?," *Washington Post Wonkblog*, September 16, 2012, http://www.washingtonpost.com /blogs/wonkblog/wp/2012/09/16/what-is-the-middle-class/. The chapter's epigraph is from Jane McAlevey's *No Shortcuts: Organizing for Power in the New Gilded Age* (New York: Oxford University Press, 2016), xvii. The book's epigraph is from Orwell's *The Road to Wigan Pier* (New York: Harcourt, Brace & Company, 1938), 263–64.

2. Frank Parkin, *Marxism and Class Theory: A Bourgeois Critique* (New York: Columbia University Press, 1979) is useful for its connections of Marx, Weber, and Durkheim on this score; for Marx, see *Wage Labor and Capital*, (pamphlet, 1891, originally 1847).

3. C. Wright Mills, *White Collar: The American Middle Classes* (New York: Oxford University Press, 1956, originally 1951), title page and 351–52.

4. Richard V. Reeves, "America's Zip Code Inequality," *Brookings*, December 21, 2015. Reeves wrote as the director of the Future of the Middle Class Initiative. See also Amy Merrick, "Where the Middle Class Shops," *The New Yorker*, February 6, 2014.

5. Edward Andrew, "Class in Itself and Class against Capital: Karl Marx and His Classifiers," *Canadian Journal of Political Science / Revue Canadienne de Science Politique* 16 (September 1983), 577–84.

6. Erik Olin Wright, "Class Boundaries in Advanced Capitalist Societies," *New Left Review* 98 (July–August 1976), 3–41.

7. Anthony Ciluffo and Richard Fry, "An Early Look at the 2020 Electorate," Pew Research Center Social and Demographic Trends (January

30, 2019), https://pewresearch.org/social-trends/2019/01/30/an-early -look-at-the 2020-electorate-2/.

8. Lucy Madison, "Obama: I'm a Warrior for the Middle Class," *CBS News*, September 22, 2011, http://www.cbsnews.com/news/obama -im-a-warrior-for-the-middle-class/; Amie Parnes, "For 2012, White House Casts President Obama as Warrior for the Middle Class," *The Hill*, December 29, 2011, http://the hill.com/home news/administration 20195-white house-casts-obama-as-warrior -for-the-middle-class; Jon Ward, "President Obama Outpacing Mitt Romney in Mentions of 'Middle Class,'" *Huffington Post*, July 16, 2012, http://www.huffingtonpost.com/2012/07/16/obama-romney -middle-class_n_1677043.html.

9. Matthews, "What Is the Middle Class?"; "A Strong Middle Class Equals a Strong America," Middle Class Task Force website, January 30, 2009, http://www.whitehouse.gov/blog_post/Todaysevent; Kim Velsey, "How Many Houses Does Mitt Have?: A Helpful Guide to Romney's Landholdings," *Observer*, August 14, 2012, https:// observer.com/2012/08/how-many-houses-does-mitt-have-a-helpful -guide-to-romneys-landholdings/.

10. Lou Dobbs, *War on the Middle Class* (New York: Penguin, 2007); Stanley Greenberg and James Carville, *It's The Middle Class, Stupid* (New York: Plume, 2013).

11. Middle Class Task Force, "A Strong Middle Class"; Hope Yen, "What Does It Mean to Be 'Middle Class'?" *Christian Science Monitor*, July 18, 2012, http://www.csmonitor.com/USA/Latest-News-Wires/2012 /0718/What-does-it-mean-to-be-middle-class; David Rohde, "The American Working Class Is Shrinking," *Reuters* (US edition), January 13, 2012, http://blogs.reuters.com/david-rohde/2012/01/13 /white-house-the-american-middle-class-is-shrinking/.

12. Yen, "What Does It Mean to Be 'Middle Class'?"

13. Don Peck, "Can the Middle Class Be Saved?," *The Atlantic*, September, 2011, https://www.theatlantic.com/magazine/archive/2011/09 /can-the-middle-class-be-saved/308600/.

14. Harold Meyerson, "The First Post-Middle-Class Election," *American Prospect*, June 29, 2016, https://prospect.org/power/first-post-middle -class-election/; "Socioeconomic Class," Pew Charitable Trusts website, December 17, 2014, https://www.pewresearch.org/topics /socioeconomic-class/2014/.

15. Bernie Sanders, "The War on the Middle Class," *Boston Globe*, June 12, 2015, https://www.bostonglobe.com/opinion/2015/06/12/bernie -sanders-the-war-middle-class/hAJUTAjWgupBLx4zAMh7nN /story.html positioned the campaign; Sanders, *The Speech: On*

Corporate Greed and the Decline of Our Middle Class (New York: Nation Books, 2015).

16. CNN Wire, "Is $250,000 Middle Class? Hillary Clinton and Bernie Sanders Think So," reposted at *Fox 8*, February 18, 2016, https://myfox8.com/2016/02/18/is-250000-middle-class-hillary-clinton-and-bernie-sanders-think-so/.

17. See Sanders, *The Speech*; for 2020, Sanders seems hopeful that the odd sound bite "The middle class has a right to exist" might catch on. See Bernie Sanders, "The Middle Class Has a Right to Exist," *Daily Mail*, February 23, 2019, https://www.dailymail.co.uk/video/news/video-1279006/Bernie-Sanders-Middle-Class-right-exist.html.

18. "Hillary Clinton: Imperative to Bring Back a Healthy Middle Class," *Breaking CNBC*, March 4, 2016, https://www.cnbc.com/video/2016/03/04/hillary-clinton-imperative-to-bring-back-healthy-middle-class-.html; Kathleen Gray, "Bernie Sanders: Campaign Is about Survival of the Middle Class," *Detroit Free Press*, October 6, 2016, https://www.freep.com/story/news/politics/2016/10/06/bernie-sanders-election-survival-middle-class/91666238/; Amy Chozick, "Stress over Family Finances Propelled Hillary Clinton into Corporate World," *New York Times*, August 10, 2016, https://www.nytimes.com/2016/08/11/us/politics/hillary-clinton-money.html.

19. Tim Hains, "Trump TV Ad Highlights Middle Class Tax Cut Proposals," *RealClear Politics*, October 6, 2016, https://www.realclearpolitics.com/video/2016/10/06/trump_tv_ad_highlights_middle_class_tax_cut_plans.html; Dan Balz, "Charting Trump's Rise through the Decline of the Middle Class," *Washington Post*, December 12, 2015, https://www.washingtonpost.com/politics/charting-trumps-rise-in-the-decline-of-the-middleclass/2015/12/12/0f5df1d8-a037-11e5-8728-1af6af208198_story.html; Kevin Liptak, "With 2016 Speculation Mounting Biden Brings Populist Fire to Florida," *CNN Politics*, September 2, 2015, https://www.cnn.com/2015/09/02/politics/biden-florida-president-campaign/index.html; Elizabeth Warren, *This Fight Is Our Fight: The Battle to Save America's Middle Class* (New York: Metropolitan Books, 2017).

20. Marc Parry, "Can Robert Putnam Save the American Dream?," *Chronicle of Higher Education*, March 27, 2015, https://www.chronicle.com/article/Can-Robert-Putnam-Save-the/228443; Amanda Ripley, "Can Starbucks Save the Middle Class?," *The Atlantic*, May 2015, 60–72; Mandi Woodruff, "Why Women Just Might Save the Middle Class," *Wall Street Journal*, April 7, 2014, https://www.wsj.com/articles/the-middle-class-squeeze-1443194736. For Putnam and bowling, see

his *Bowling Alone: The Collapse and Revival of American Community* (New York: Simon & Schuster, 2000).

21. See Meagan Day, "Why We Need Free College for All—Even Rich People," *Jacobin*, July 10, 2019, https://jacobinmag.com/2019/07 /free-college-tuition-bernie-sanders-means-testing-universal-social -programs; and Sarah Sidoti, "Free College for Whom? The Emergent Barriers of Free Public College Policies," *Diverse Issues in Higher Education*, October 14, 2019, at https://www.diverseeducation.com /institutions/community-colleges/article/15105592/free-college-for -whom-the-emergent-barriers-of-free-public-college-policies.

22. For relatively sophisticated examples, see Nicholas Carnes and Noam Lupu, "It's Time to Bust the Myth: Most Trump Voters Were Not Working Class," *Washington Post*, June 5, 2017, https:// www.washingtonpost.com/news/monkey-cage/wp/2017/06/05 /its-time-to-bust-the-myth-most-trump-voters-were-not-working -class/?utm_term=.81b1b0800a69; and Kim Moody, "Who Put Trump in the White House?," *Against the Current* 186 (January– February 2017), https://solidarity-us.org/atc/186/p4859/.

23. Zach Stanton, "The Rise of the Biden Republicans," *Politico*, March 4, 2021, https://www.politico.com/news/magazine/2021/03/04/reagan -democrats-biden-republicans-politics-stan-greenberg-473330; Will Weissert, "Biden Republicans? Some in GOP Open to President's Agenda," *US News and World Report*, April 12, 2021.

24. Barbara Ehrenreich, *Fear of Falling: The Inner Life of the American Middle Class* (New York: Pantheon, 1989); Arlie Russell Hochschild, *Strangers in Their Own Land: Anger and Mourning on the American Right* (New York: New Press, 2016).

CHAPTER 2: THE PRETENSES OF A MIDDLE-CLASS UNITED STATES

1. Terry Hale et al., trans. and eds, *Four Dada Suicides: Selected Texts of Arthur Cravan, Jacques Rigaut, Julien Torma, and Jacques Vache* (London: Atlas Books, 1995), 165. The chapter's epigraph is from Bill Onasch, "No Middle Ground," *Labor Advocate*, January 1, 2012, http://www.kclabor.org/nomiddleground.htm.

2. Tami Luhby and Tiffany Baker, "What Is Middle Class Anyway?," *CNN Business*, December 1, 2016, https://money.cnn.com/infographic /economy/what-is-middle-class-anyway/index.html.

3. C. Wright Mills. *White Collar: The American Middle Classes* (New York: Oxford University Press, 1956, originally 1951), title page and 351–52.

4. Luhby and Baker, "What Is Middle Class Anyway?"; Nicolas Rapp and Matthew Heimer, "The Shrinking Middle Class: By the Numbers," *Fortune*, December 20, 2018, http://fortune.com/longform /shrinking-middle-class-math/; *Fortune* staff, "The Shrinking Middle Class," *Fortune*, December 20, 2018, http://fortune.com /longform/shrinking-middle-class/.

5. Pew Research Center, "The American Middle Class Is Losing Ground," Pew Research Center website, December 9, 2015, https://www .pewsocialtrends.org/2015/12/09/the-american-middle-class -is-losing-ground/; Jim Tankersley, "Why America's Middle Class Is Lost," *Washington Post*, December 12, 2014, https://www .washingtonpost.com/sf/business/2014/12/12/why-americas -middle-class-is-lost/?utm_term=.1d1b2d495b9c. For a generative account of the structural matters underpinning such decline, see Peter Temin, *The Vanishing Middle Class: Prejudice and Power in a Dual Economy* (Cambridge, MA: MIT Press, 2017).

6. *Fortune* staff, "The Shrinking Middle Class."

7. Michael Zweig, *The Working Class Majority: America's Best-Kept Secret* (Ithaca: ILR Press, 2012, originally 2000), esp. 2–36; see also "Working Definitions," *Class Matters*, http://classmatters.org /working_definitions2.php, distilling Metzgar's conclusions.

8. Zweig, *Working Class Majority*, vii and 23–45.

9. Barbara Ehrenreich and John Ehrenreich, *Death of a Yuppie Dream: The Rise and Fall of the Professional-Managerial Class* (New York: Rosa Luxemburg Stiftung, 2013), 2–11.

10. See, for example, Amer A'Lee Frost, "The Characterless Opportunism of the Managerial Class," *American Affairs*, November 20, 2019, https://americanaffairsjournal.org/2019/11/the-characterless -opportunism-of-the-managerial-class/; Catherine Liu, *Virtue Hoarders: The Case against the Professional Managerial Class* (Minneapolis: University of Minnesota Press, 2021); and Gabriel Winant, "Professional-Managerial Chasm," *n+1*, October 10, 2019.

11. Janelle Jones, "The Racial Wealth Gap," *Working Economics* (blog), Economic Policy Institute, February 13, 2017, https://www.epi.org /blog/the-racial-wealth-gap-how-african-americans-have-been -shortchanged-out-of-the-materials-to-build-wealth/.

12. Jerome P. Bjelopera, "White Collars and Blackface Race and Leisure among Clerical and Sales Workers in Early Twentieth-Century Philadelphia," *Pennsylvania Magazine of History and Biography* 126 (July

2002), 471–90; McKinsey and Company, *Race in the Workplace: The Black Experience in the US Private Sector*, February 21, 2021, https://www.mckinsey.com/featured-insights/diversity-and-inclusion/race-in-the-workplace-the-black-experience-in-the-us-private-sector. US Bureau of Labor Statistics, *Labor Force Statistics from the Current Population Survey (2020)*, https://www.bls.gov/cps/cpsaat11.htm.

13. *Fortune* staff, "The Shrinking Middle Class"; Nicolas Rapp and Matthew Heimer, "The Shrinking Middle Class: By the Numbers," *Fortune*, December 20, 2018, http://fortune.com/longform/shrinking-middle-class-math/.

14. Mills, *White Collar*, 294.

15. Rapp and Heimer, "The Shrinking Middle Class: By the Numbers."

16. Tami Luhby, "America's Middle Class: Poorer than You Think," *CNN Money*, August 5, 2014, https://money.cnn.com/2014/06/11/news/economy/middle-class-wealth/index.html. The data came from *Credit Suisse Global Wealth Databook*; see also David Leonhardt and Kevin Quealy, "The American Middle Class Is No Longer the World's Richest," *New York Times*, April 22, 2014, https://www.nytimes.com/2014/04/23/upshot/the-american-middle-class-is-no-longer-the-worlds-richest.html.

17. Harold Meyerson, "The First Post-Middle-Class Election," *American Prospect*, June 29, 2016, https://prospect.org/power/first-post-middle-class-election/; Kevin Phillips, *The Emerging Republican Majority* (Princeton: Princeton University Press, 2015, originally 1969).

18. Nicolas Lemann, "Survival of the Loudest," *New York Times*, July 12, 1992, https://www.nytimes.com/1992/07/12/opinion/survival-of-the-loudest.html; Alfonse D'Amato, "The Forgotten Middle Class," *Long Island Herald*, October 15, 2010, http://www.liherald.com/baldwin/baldwin/stories/The-forgotten-middle-class,28169?content_source=&category_id=&search_filter=&event_mode=&event_ts_from=&list_type=most_commented&order_by=&order_sort=&content_class=&sub_type=&town_id=.

19. Kevin Kruse, *White Flight: Atlanta and the Making of Modern Conservatism* (Princeton: Princeton University Press, 2005), 14–15, 51–54, 68, and 263; Robert O. Self, *American Babylon: Race and the Struggle for Postwar Oakland* (Princeton: Princeton University Press, 2003), 1–17, 120–25, and 256–327. On Wattenberg, see Lawrence R. Samuel, *The American Middle Class: A Cultural History* (New York: Routledge, 2014), 74.

20. Dave Boyer, "Obama Gets Poor Ranking on Mentions of 'Poverty'; More Abundance for 'Middle Class,'" *Washington Times*, July 8,

2013, http://www.washingtontimes.com/news/2013/jul/8/obama -gets-poor-ranking-on-mentions-of-poverty/?page=all.

21. Binyamin Appelbaum, "The Millions of Americans Donald Trump and Hillary Clinton Barely Mention: The Poor," *New York Times*, August 11, 2016, https://www.nytimes.com/2016/08/12/us/politics /trump-clinton-poverty.html; Domenico Montanaro, "Poll: Despite Record Turnout, 80 Million Americans Didn't Vote; Here's Why," *NPR*, December 15, 2020, https://www.npr.org/2020/12/15/945031391 /poll-despite-record-turnout-80-million-americans-didnt-vote-heres -why.

22. *"Politics* by Aristotle—Book Four," *Classical Wisdom Weekly* (undated), https://classicalwisdom.com/greek_books/politics-by-aristotle -book-iv/4/; Ayn Rand, "The Dead End," *Ayn Rand Newsletter* 1 (1971), http://aynrandlexicon.com/lexicon/middle_class.html.

23. Walt Whitman, *I Sit and I Look Out: Editorials from the Brooklyn Daily Times by Walt Whitman*, Emory Holloway and Vernolian Schwarz, eds. (New York: Columbia University Press, 1932), 132; Stuart Blumin, *The Emergence of the Middle Class: Social Experience in the American City, 1760–1900* (Cambridge, UK: Cambridge University Press, 1989), 1 and 245. For Crusoe, see Daniel Defoe, *The Life and Adventures of Robinson Crusoe* (London: Macmillan & Company, 1868, originally 1719), 3; B. C. Forbes, "Which Class Is Happiest?," *Forbes Quotes*, https://www.forbes.com/quotes/851/ pillages *Crusoe*.

24. Robert Wheeler, "Which Class Is Your Class?," *International Socialist Review* 12 (July 1911), 25–28; Jürgen Kocka, *White Collar Workers in America 1890–1940: A Social-Political History in International Perspective*, Manra Kealey, trans. (London and Beverly Hills: SAGE Publications, 1980), 7–9. Some socialist writings did of course appeal to possible alliances with the "middle classes," much as Marx had done and as German social democrats were doing. See the "Report of the Committee on Propaganda" in *Proceedings of the National Congress of the Socialist Party* (Chicago: The Socialist Party, 1910), 63–64. Thanks to Janine Giordano Drake for this reference.

25. Lynd and Lynd, *Middletown: A Study in Modern American Culture* (New York: Harcourt, Brace & World, 1956, originally 1929), 22, n.3, 23, and n.3 and 346.

26. Robert S. Lynd and Helen M. Lynd, *Middletown in Transition: A Study in Cultural Conflicts* (New York: Harcourt, Brace, & Company, 1937), 457–58 and 446–60 passim.

27. Werner Sombart, *Why Is There No Socialism in the United States?* (London: Macmillan, 1976, originally 1906); Sinclair Lewis, *Babbitt*

(New York: Harcourt, Brace, & Company, 1922); Erik Axel Karfeldt, "Presentation Speech," December 10, 1930, http://www.nobelprize .org/nobel_prizes/literature/laureates/1930/press.html.

28. George Fredrickson, *Racism: A Short History* (Princeton: Princeton University Press, 2002), 5; Christopher Vials, *Haunted by Hitler: Liberals, the Left, and the Fight against Fascism in the United States* (Amherst: University of Massachusetts Press, 2014), 70–71.

29. Stuart Blumin, *The Emergence of the Middle Class: Social Experience in the American City, 1760–1900* (Cambridge, UK: Cambridge University Press, 1989); Mary Ryan, *Cradle of the Middle Class: The Family in Oneida County, New York, 1790–1865* (Cambridge, UK: Cambridge University Press, 1983); Paul E. Johnson, *A Shopkeeper's Millennium: Society and Revivals in Rochester, New York, 1815–1837* (New York: Farrar, Straus, & Giroux, 2004, originally 1990); Richard Sennett, *Families against the City: Middle Class Homes of Industrial Chicago, 1872–1890* (Cambridge, MA: Harvard University Press, 1984); Jeanne Boydston, *Home and Work: Housework, Wages, and the Ideology of Labor in the Early Republic* (Oxford and New York: Oxford University Press, 1990); Sven Beckert, "Propertied of a Different Kind: Bourgeoisie and Lower Middle Classes in the Nineteenth Century United States," in *The Middling Sorts: Explorations in the History of the American Middle Class*, Burton Bledstein and Robert D. Johnston, eds. (New York: Routledge, 1993), 285–95; Gwendolyn Wright, *Moralism and the Model Home: Domestic Architecture and Cultural Conflict in Chicago, 1873–1913* (Chicago: University of Chicago Press, 1980). More globally, see Arno Mayer, "The Lower Middle Class as Historical Problem," *Journal of Modern History* 47 (September 1975).

30. Werner Sombart, *Why Is There No Socialism in the United States?* (London: Macmillan, 1976); Robert Wiebe, *The Search for Order, 1877–1920* (New York: Hill & Wang, 1967), 112.

31. Lynd and Lynd, *Middletown in Transition*, 446.

32. *Fortune* editors, "The People of the U.S.A.: A Self-Portrait," *Fortune*, February 21, 1940, 14, 20; Lewis Corey, *The Crisis of the Middle Class* (New York: Covici & Friede, 1935), 259 and 273.

33. *Fortune* editors, "The People of the U.S.A.," 14–20; Marina Moskowitz, "The Elephant in the Room: Culture, Cohesion, and Context in the American Middle Class," in *Considering Class: Essays on the Discourse of the American Dream*, Kevin Cahill and Lene Johannessen, eds. (Berlin: LIT Verlag, 2007), 13; George Horace Gallup and Saul Forbes Rae, *The Pulse of Democracy: The Public Opinion Poll and How It Works* (New York: Simon & Schuster, 1940), 169–71; on the

Fortune survey and construction of samples, see "Research Projects and Methods in Educational Sociology," *Journal of Educational Sociology* 14 (December 1940), 250–53.

34. Christopher Vials, ed., *American Literature in Transition, 1940–1950* (Cambridge, UK: Cambridge University Press, 2018), 5.

35. For Lynd and Bingham, see Moskowitz, "Elephant in the Room," 13–14; see also David Ramsey, "Middle Class Attitudes," *New Masses*, April 7, 1936, 39, and chapters 3 and 4 of this book.

36. *Fortune* editors, "The People of the U.S.A.," 20.

37. Andrew Grant, *Socialism and the Middle Classes* (New York: International Publishers, 1959, originally 1957), 7; Gallup and Rae, *Pulse of Democracy*, 169.

38. Louis Althusser, "Ideology and Ideological State Apparatuses," in *Lenin and Philosophy and Other Essays* (New York: Monthly Review Press, 1971), available at https://www.marxists.org/reference /archive/althusser/1970/ideology.htm; John Haer, "An Empirical Study of Social Class Awareness," *Survey* 36 (December 1957), 117–20; Richard Centers, *The Psychology of Social Classes* (Princeton: Princeton University Press, 1949), 77.

39. Eric Hoffer, "Sunday Thought," *San Francisco Examiner and Chronicle*, June 23, 1968; Hoffer, "The Middle Class Takes a Beating," *San Francisco Examiner and Chronicle*, September 24, 1968.

40. See American Federation of Teachers president Randi Weingarten, "My Labor Day Mention," email to her union's members, September 3, 2018; Bill Onasch, "No Middle Ground," *Labor Advocate Online*, January 1, 2012, http://www.kclabor.org/nomiddleground.htm.

41. A. Ricardo Lopez and Barbara Weinstein, eds. *The Making of the Middle Class: Toward a Transnational History* (Durham: Duke University Press, 2012), 7–9; Steve Knauss, "The Myth of the Global Middle Class," *Potemkin Review*, December, 2015, https:// www.tandfonline.com/doi/abs/10.1080/02255189.2019.1520692 ?tokenDomain=eprints&tokenAccess=RnyfYrhpdWwg7RYk5I Xe&forwardService=showFullText&doi=10.1080%2F02255189 .2019.1520692&doi=10.1080%2F02255189.2019.1520692& journalCode=rcjd20&; cf. Rohan Venkatararamakkrishan, "Almost Everyone in India Thinks They Are 'Middle Class' and Almost No One Actually Is," *Scroll.in*, September 21, 2015, https://scroll.in /article/740011/everyone-in-india-thinks-they-are-middle-class- and-almost-no-one-actually-is; Shawn Donnan and others, "Millions Are Tumbling Out of the Global Middle Class in Historic Setback," *Bloomberg Businessweek*, April 7, 2021, https://www .bloomberg.com/features/2021-emerging-markets-middle-class/;

Paul Mason, "Who Are the New Middle Classes around the World?" *The Guardian*, January 20, 2014, https://www.theguardian.com/commentisfree/2014/jan/20/new-middle-classes-world-poor.

42. For Turner, see his *The Frontier in American History* (New York: Henry Holt, 1920) at http://xroads.virginia.edu/~HYPER/TURNER/; Friedrich Engels, *The Condition of the Working Class in England* (n.p.: Panther Edition, 1969, originally in German in 1845 and in English, 1887), 6, available at https://www.marxists.org/archive/marx/works/download/pdf/condition-working-class-england.pdf.

43. For some of the debate and language among US Communists, see Mark Liberman, "The Third Life of American Exceptionalism," *Language Log*, February 23, 2012, https://languagelog.ldc.upenn.edu/nll/?p=3798; for Stalin and Lovestone, see Terrence McCoy, "How Stalin Gave Us American Exceptionalism," *The Atlantic*, March 15, 2012, https://www.theatlantic.com/politics/archive/2012/03/how-joseph-stalin-invented-american-exceptionalism/254534/.

44. Louis Hartz, *The Liberal Tradition in America* (New York: Harvest, 1991, originally 1955), 278, 51. On Hartz, see Rogers M. Smith, "Why No 'Liberalism' in the United States?," unpublished paper, 2006, http://digitalcommons.law.umaryland.edu/cgi/viewcontent.cgi?article=1001&context=schmooze_papers; on the *Fortune* survey and construction of samples, see "Research Projects and Methods in Educational Sociology," 250–53.

45. "US Millennials Feel More Working Class than Any Other Generation," *The Guardian*, March 15, 2016, https://www.theguardian.com/world/2016/mar/15/us-millennials-feel-more-working-class-than-any-other-generation; Frank Newport, "Fewer Americans Identify as Middle Class in Recent Years," *GALLUP*, April 28, 2015, https://www.schwartzreport.net/fewer-americans-identify-as-middle-class-in-recent-years/.

46. Burton Bledstein, *The Culture of Professionalism: The Middle Class and the Development of Higher Education in America* (New York: W. W. Norton & Company, 1976), 1; Loren Baritz, *The Good Life: The Meaning of Success for the American Middle Class* (New York: Knopf, 1989), xi.

47. For a competent if politically uncongenial account of Reagan's long connections to American exceptionalism and allied notions, see Annelise Anderson, "Ronald Reagan and American Exceptionalism," in *American Exceptionalism in a New Era*, Terrence McCoy, ed. (Stanford: Hoover Institution Press, 2017), 143–49.

48. Seymour Martin Lipset, *American Exceptionalism: A Double-Edged Sword* (New York: W. W. Norton & Company, 1996), 4, 252, and 51–59.

49. McCoy, "How Stalin Gave Us American Exceptionalism"; Newt Gingrich, *A Nation like No Other: Why American Exceptionalism Matters* (Washington, DC: Regnery Publishing, 2011).

50. Kelan Lyons, "Make the Middle Class Great Again," *Salt Lake City Weekly's Daily Feed*, April 18, 2019, https://www.cityweekly .net/BuzzBlog/archives/2019/04/18/make-the-middle-class-great -again; Jake Sullivan, "What Donald Trump and Dick Cheney Got Wrong about America," *The Atlantic*, January–February 2019, https:// www.theatlantic.com/magazine/archive/2019/01/yes-america -can-still-lead-the-world/576427/; Peter Beinart, "AOC's Generation Doesn't Presume America's Innocence," *The Atlantic*, June 21, 2019, https://www.theatlantic.com/ideas/archive/2019/06/aoc -isnt-interested-american-exceptionalism/592213/, and including the Obama quote.

51. Mills, *White Collar*; David Lockwood, *The Black-Coated Worker: A Study in Class Consciousness* (Fairlawn, NJ: Essential Books, 1958); Jürgen Kocka, *White Collar Workers in America 1890–1940: A Social-Political History in International Perspective*, Manra Kealey, trans. (London and Beverly Hills: SAGE Publications, 1980).

52. Ehrenreich and Ehrenreich, *Death of a Yuppie Dream*, 2–11; Barbara Ehrenreich, *Fear of Falling: The Inner Life of the Middle Class* (New York: Pantheon, 1989), 4–5.

53. Steve Fraser, *The Age of Acquiescence: The Life and Death of American Resistance to Organized Wealth and Power* (New York: Little, Brown & Company, 2015), 59.

54. For the World Bank data on this matter, see "Share of the Labor Force Employed in Agriculture, 2017, available at https://ourworldindata. org/grapher/share-of-the-labor-force-employed-in-agriculture; see also Alex Callinicos, "The 'New Middle Class' and Socialist Politics," *International Socialism* 2 (Summer 1983), esp. table 2, available at https://www.marxists.org/history/etol/writers/callinicos/1983/xx /newmc.html.

55. Mills, *White Collar*, xi–xii

56. G. William Domhoff, introduction to Richard Parker, *The Myth of the Middle Class: Notes on Affluence and Equality* (New York: Harper, 1972), x–xi.

57. Kocka, *White Collar Workers in America*, 86; see also Ruth Milkman's introduction to the second edition of Eli Chinoy, *Automobile Workers*

and the American Dream (Urbana and Chicago: University of Illinois Press, 1992), xii–xvii.

58. For the figures, which show a significant decline even in the recent past, see http://www.bls.gov/cps/cpsaat11.htm and http://www.careerbuildercommunications.com/pdf/cb-emsi_SelfEmployment2014.pdf; on failure rates see Chad Otar, "What Percentage of Small Businesses Fail?," *Forbes*, October 25, 2018, https://www.forbes.com/sites/forbesfinancecouncil/2018/10/25/what-percentage-of-small-businesses-fail-and-how-can-you-avoid-being-one-of-them/#5cf90be143b5.

59. Dan Margolies and Sam Zeff, "Thanks to Tax Cuts, Bill Self, Highest Paid State Employee, Owes Little in Kansas Income Taxes," *KCUR 89.3*, May 16, 2016, https://www.cbpp.org/research/state-budget-and-tax/kansas-provides-compelling-evidence-of-failure-of-supply-side-tax-cuts.

60. Saidiya Hartman, *Scenes of Subjection: Terror, Slavery, and Self-Making in Nineteenth-Century America* (New York: Oxford University Press, 1997), 115. For Marx see especially his *Wage Labor and Capital* (pamphlet, 1891, originally 1847).

61. Andrew Dilts, "From 'Entrepreneur of the Self' to 'Care of the Self': Neo-liberal Governmentality and Foucault's Ethics," *Foucault Studies* 12 (October 9, 2011), 130–46. On Kansas, see Michael Mazerov, "Kansas Provides Compelling Evidence of Failure of 'Supply Side' Tax Cuts," *Center on Budget and Policy Priorities*, January 22, 2018, https://www.cbpp.org/research/state-budget-and-tax/kansas-provides-compelling-evidence-of-failure-of-supply-side-tax-cuts; Thomas Shapiro, Tatjana Meschede, and Sam Osoro, "The Roots of the Widening Racial Wealth Gap," Institute on Assets and Social Policy, February 2020, at https://heller.brandeis.edu/iere/pdfs/racial-wealth-equity/racial-wealth-gap/roots-widening-racial-wealth-gap.pdf.

62. George Lipsitz, *The Possessive Investment in Whiteness: How White People Profit from Identity Politics* (Philadelphia: Temple University Press, 2006).

CHAPTER 3: HOW THE LEFT HAS LIVED WITH THE PROBLEM OF THE MIDDLE CLASS

1. "Labor Strategy and the DSLC: Resolution #32 DSA," August 2019, https://docs.google.com/document/d/1xulx3e-qz6qpJZ50oU61L-m3NnyfEaDzUw7coBo69ZE0/edit. The chapter's epigraph is as

quoted in C. Wright Mills, *White Collar: The American Middle Classes* (New York: Oxford University Press, 1956, originally 1951), xi.

2. Michael Zweig, *The Working Class Majority: America's Best-Kept Secret* (Ithaca: ILR Press 2000), 26–27; cf. Zweig's 2012 edition with same publisher at 24–27 for the very halting inclusion of some teachers and nurses as working class; "Resolution #32 DSA."

3. Eric Blanc, *Red State Revolt: The Teachers' Strike Wave and Working-Class Politics* (London and New York: Verso, 2019); cf. Michael Mochaidean, "Do All Organizing Roads Lead to Bernie?," *Black Rose / Rosa Negra*, February 28, 2019, http:blackrosefed.org/teacher-strikes-bernie-eric-blanc.

4. Andy Kroll, "How the Wisconsin Uprising Got Hijacked," *Mother Jones*, June 11, 2012, https://www.motherjones.com/politics/2012/06/how-wisconsin-uprising-got-hijacked/; Michael Yates, ed. *Wisconsin Uprising: Labor Fights Back* (New York: Monthly Review Press, 2012).

5. Nelson Lichtenstein, *The State of the Union: A Century of American Labor* (Princeton: Princeton University Press, 2002), 181 and 180–84.

6. Kathleen Elkins, "Most Young Americans Prefer Socialism to Capitalism, New Report Finds," *CNBC Make It*, August 14, 2018, https://www.cnbc.com/2018/08/14/fewer-than-half-of-young-americans-are-positive-about-;capitalism.html.

7. Friedrich Engels, "Preface to the 1888 English Edition" of Marx and Engels, *Manifesto of the Communist Party* (originally February 1848), 20, available at https://www.marxists.org/archive/marx/works/download/pdf/Manifesto.pdf.

8. Karl Marx, *The Civil War in France* (pamphlet, originally 1871), available at https://www.marxists.org/archive/marx/works/download/pdf/civil_war_france.pdf.

9. Karl Marx, *The Class Struggles in France, 1848–1850* (pamphlet, originally 1850), 32, available at https://www.marxists.org/archive/marx/works/download/pdf/Class_Struggles_in_France.pdf.

10. Marx as quoted in Béla Kun, "Marx and the Middle Classes," originally in *Pravda*, May 4, 1918, available at https://www.marxists.org/archive/kun-bela/1918/05/04.htm, which also contains the quotation from Kun himself.

11. Marx and Engels, *Manifesto of the Communist Party*.

12. E. P. Thompson, *The Making of the English Working Class* (New York: Pantheon, 1964), 9.

13. Marx, *Class Struggles in France*, 32.

14. George Orwell, *The Road to Wigan Pier* (New York: Harcourt, Brace & Company, 1938), 153–264; Barbara Ehrenreich, *Fear of Falling:*

The Inner Life of the Middle Class (New York: Pantheon, 1989); Arthur Miller, *Death of a Salesman* (New York: Viking Critical Library, 1967, originally 1949); Katherine Newman, *Falling from Grace: The Experience of Downward Mobility in the American Middle Class* (Berkeley: University of California Press, 1999).

15. Marx and Engels, *Manifesto of the Communist Party*.

16. Jürgen Kocka, *White Collar Workers in America 1890–1940: A Social-Political History in International Perspective*, Manra Kealey, trans. (London and Beverly Hills: SAGE Publications, 1980), 7 and 6–13 passim.

17. Kocka, *White Collar Workers*; Friedrich Engels, *The Condition of the Working Class in England* (n.p.: Panther Edition, 1969, originally in German in 1845 and in English, 1887), 32, available at https://www.marxists.org/archive/marx/works/download/pdf/condition-working-class-england.pdf.

18. Kun, "Marx and the Middle Classes."

19. Engels, *Condition of the Working Class*, 32.

20. Martin Nicolaus, "Proletariat and Middle Class in Marx: Hegelian Choreography and the Capitalist Dialectic," *Studies on the Left* 7 (1967), 41 ("theory") and 46 ("new middle class"), 45–46 ("constant increase") and 22–49.

21. For the wild reach of the category, see Nicolaus, "Proletariat and Middle Class in Marx," 42 and 49n45.

22. Andrew Grant, *Socialism and the Middle Classes* (New York: International Publishers, 1959, originally 1957), 65; Karl Marx, *Capital: A Critique of Political Economy*, volume 3, *The Process of Capitalist Production as a Whole* (Chicago: Charles H. Kerr & Company, 1909), 354 and 350–56 passim. On one Marxological point I think Nicolaus may err: that is in holding that Marx did not regard clerks as workers. Cf. Nicolaus, "Proletariat and Middle Class in Marx," 49n40, though perhaps the point more worth insisting on is that Marx did not so carefully mount a "theory of the middle class" that he spoke consistently on this central matter.

23. Val Burris, "The Discovery of the New Middle Classes," in *The New Middle Classes: Life-Styles, Status Claims, and Political Orientations*, Arthur Vidich, ed. (New York: New York University Press, 1995), esp. 24–32. See also Vidich's introduction to the volume at 9–10. On monthly salaries, see Kocka, *White Collar Workers in America*, 85.

24. Burris, "Discovery of the New Middle Classes," 29 ("single organization"); Emil Lederer and Jacob Marschak, "The New Middle Class," in Vidich, ed. *The New Middle Classes*, 56 and 55–86; "Emil Lederer,

1882–1939," *History of Economic Thought* website, https://www. hetwebsite.net/het/profiles/lederer.htm.

25. Siegfried Kracauer, *The Salaried Masses: Duty and Distraction in Weimar Germany* (London and New York: Verso, 1998, originally 1930), 88–112. For "rumblings," see Vidich's introduction to Vidich, *New Middle Classes*, 2. See also John Abromeit, "Siegfried Kracauer and the Early Frankfurt School's Analysis of Fascism as Right-Wing Populism" (unpublished paper, in the possession of its author at Buffalo State University).

26. Leon Trotsky, *Whither France?* (London: New Park, 1974, originally 1936), available at https://www.marxists.org/archive/trotsky/1936 /whitherfrance/ch00.htm.

27. Daniel Guérin, *Fascism and Big Business* (New York: Pathfinder, 1973, originally in French 1939), 53–84.

28. Erich Fromm, *Escape from Freedom* (New York: Rinehart, 1941), 221.

29. Fromm, *Escape from Freedom*, 212 and 123–239; Mark P. Worrell, *Dialectic of Solidarity: Labor, Antisemitism, and the Frankfurt School* (Chicago: Haymarket Books, 2008), esp. xi–16 and 249–50; most useful on the 1929 studies is John Abromeit, *Max Horkheimer and the Foundations of the Frankfurt School* (Cambridge, UK: Cambridge University Press, 2013), 211–26. On relations of white- and blue-collar workers in that time and place, see Hans Speier, *German White-Collar Workers and the Rise of Hitler* (New Haven: Yale University Press, 1986), esp. 55–68.

30. Paul Buhle, *A Dreamer's Paradise Lost: Louis C. Fraina / Lewis Corey (1892–1953) and the Decline of Radicalism in the United States* (Atlantic Highlands, NJ: Humanities Press, 1995), esp. 128–38 ("write" on 134); Robert S. Lynd and Helen M. Lynd, *Middletown in Transition: A Study in Cultural Conflicts* (New York: Harcourt, Brace & Company, 1937), 457; Lewis Corey, *The Crisis of the Middle Class* (New York: Covici & Friede, 1935), 151, 171, 283, 112–70, and 278–309 passim.

31. C. Wright Mills, *New Men of Power: America's Labor Leaders* (Urbana: University of Illinois Press, 2001, originally 1948), 24 and 274–80; Kocka, *White Collar Workers*, 223–250; Steven Rosswurm, ed. *The CIO's Left-Led Unions* (New Brunswick, NJ: Rutgers University Press, 1992), esp. 2–4 and 143–46. The special issue of *New Masses* appeared in April 1936.

32. Cf. Mills, *White Collar*, 63–64 with Corey, *Crisis of the Middle Class*, 274.

33. Daniel Geary, *Radical Ambition: C. Wright Mills, the Left, and American Social Thought* (Berkeley: University of California Press, 2009),

113–14 and 125 ("disillusioned"); Mills privately on the "setup" is as quoted in Robert D. Johnston, *The Radical Middle Class: Populist Democracy and the Question of Capitalism* (Princeton: Princeton University Press, 2003), 4.

34. Corey, *Crisis of the Middle Class*, 275; Anna Roboton, "Most Americans Are Hourly Workers," *CBS News*, February 17, 2017, https://www.cbsnews.com/news/most-americans-are-hourly-workers/.

35. See also Harry Braverman, *Labor and Monopoly Capital* (New York: Monthly Review Press, 1998, originally 1974), 319, 239, and 296–318 passim; Evelyn Nakano Glenn and Roslyn Feldberg, "Proletarianizing Clerical Work: Technology and Organizational Control in the Office," in *Case Studies in the Labor Process*, Andrew Zimbalist, ed. (New York: Monthly Review Press, 1979), 51–72.

36. Newman, *Falling from Grace,* esp. 143–73 and 202–28; Ehrenreich, *Fear of Falling.*

37. Richard Sennett and Jonathan Cobb, *The Hidden Injuries of Class* (New York: Knopf, 1972), 185; a summary of the debates is found, amid sad-to-reread attacks on feminism, based on the loosest of links with the "new middle class," in Alex Callinicos, "The 'New Middle Class' and Socialist Politics," *International Socialism* 2 (Summer 1983), available at https://www.marxists.org/history/etol/writers/callinicos/1983/xx/newmc.html#n20.

38. Erik Olin Wright, "Class Boundaries in Advanced Capitalist Societies," *New Left Review* 98 (July–August 1976), 26 and 3–41; for oversimplifications of Wright, see Vivek Chibber, "Erik Olin Wright (1947–2019)," *Jacobin*, January 24, 2019, https://www.jacobinmag.com/2019/01/erik-olin-wright-obituary-class-marxism; see also Peter Meiksins, "Beyond the Boundary Question," *New Left Review* 157 (May–June 1986), https://newleftreview.org/issues/I157/articles/peter-meiksins-beyond-the-boundary-question; and Hua Hsu, "Sandra Oh's Masterful Performance of Empathy in *The Chair*," *The New Yorker*, August 23, 2021, 62–65.

CHAPTER 4: FALLING, MISERY, AND THE IMPOSSIBILITIES OF MIDDLE-CLASS LIFE

1. Seth Prins et al., "Anxious? Depressed? You Might Be Suffering from Capitalism: Contradictory Class Locations and the Prevalence of Depression and Anxiety in the United States," *Sociology of Health and Illness* 37 (November 2015), https://www.ncbi.nlm.nih.gov/pmc/articles/PMC4609238/#R80; Herbert Marcuse, *One-Dimensional*

Man (Boston: Beacon Press; 1991, originally 1964), xlv–xlvi. The epigraph is from Germaine Greer, *The Female Eunuch* (New York: Bantam Books, 1972), 213.

2.   As quoted in Daniel Geary, *Radical Ambition: C. Wright Mills, the Left, and American Social Thought* (Berkeley: University of California Press, 2009), 114.

3.   Nikil Saval, *Cubed: A Secret History of the Workplace* (New York: Doubleday, 2014), 242 ("lost"), 210–20, and 242–44 passim; Dwight Garner, "The Office Space We Love to Hate," *New York Times*, April 24, 2014, https://www.nytimes.com/2014/04/25/books/nikil-savals -cubed-tells-the-history-of-the-modern-workplace.html.

4.   Herman Melville, *Bartleby, the Scrivener* (Brooklyn: Melville House, 2004, originally 1853), 6–15 and 59–60.

5.   Arthur Miller, *Death of a Salesman* (New York: Viking Critical Library, 1967, originally 1949), 62–63, 73, and 108–9.

6.   C. Wright Mills, *White Collar: The American Middle Classes* (New York: Oxford University Press, 1956, originally 1951), 175–76.

7.   Emily Crane, "California's Hidden Homeless," *Daily Mail*, December 26, 2017, https://www.dailymail.co.uk/news/article-5212977 /Californias-middle-class-homeless-living-parking-lots.html; Donna Freydkin, "When Homelessness Reaches Middle-Class Families," *Today*, January 18, 2018, https://www.today.com/news /when-homelessness-reaches-middle-class-working-families -t121406; Mary Jordan and Kevin Sullivan, "'I'm Going to Work until I Die': More Older People Travel the Country in Search of Seasonal Jobs," *Washington Post*, September 30, 2017, http://www .chicagotribune.com/business/ct-elderly-workers-20170929-story. html.

8.   Jim Hightower, "The Highly Educated Working Poor: Adjunct Professors," *Nation of Change*, February 5, 2014, https:// hightowerlowdown.org/podcast/the-highly-educated-working-poor -adjunct-professors/; Alastair Gee, "Facing Poverty, Academics Turn to Sex Work and Sleeping in Cars," *The Guardian*, September 28, 2017, https://www.theguardian.com/us-news/2017/sep/28/adjunct -professors-homeless-sex-work-academia-poverty.

9.   Alexandria Heisel, "You Cannot Eat a House: The Hunger Secrets in the Middle Class," *Hunger and Health*, September 8, 2017, https:// hungerandhealth.feedingamerica.org/2017/09/cannot-eat-house -hunger-secrets-middle-class/; Tracie McMillan, "The New Face of Hunger," *National Geographic Magazine*, July 16, 2014, https://www .nationalgeographic.com/foodfeatures/hunger/; Ashley A. Smith, "Discrepancies in Estimates on Food Insecurity," *Inside Higher Ed*,

April 30, 2019, https://www.insidehighered.com/news/2019/04/30
/new-research-finds-discrepancies-estimates-food-insecurity
-among-college-students.

10. Neal Gabler, "The Secret Shame of Middle Class Americans,"
    The Atlantic, May 2016, https://www.theatlantic.com/magazine
    /archive/2016/05/my-secret-shame/476415/.

11. Richard V. Reeves, Katherine Guyot, and Eleanor Krause, "Defining
    the Middle Class: Cash, Credentials, or Culture?," *Brookings*, May
    18, 2018, https://www.brookings.edu/research/defining-the-middle
    -class-cash-credentials-or-culture/. See also Allstate Newsroom,
    "New Poll Shows Middle Class to Be More Anxious than Aspirational,"
    Allstate Newsroom, April 25, 2013, https://www.allstatenewsroom
    .com/news/new-poll-middle-class-more-anxious-than-aspirational/.

12. Terry Eagleton, *After Theory* (New York: Basic Books, 2003), 28;
    Mills, *White Collar*, 237.

13. For elaboration, see David Roediger, "Jaw Breakers, Spuds Mac-
    Kenzie, and Fordism," and "Waiting to Inhale," both in Roediger,
    History against Misery (Chicago: Charles H. Kerr, 2006), 3–5 and
    6–8.

14. Juliet Schor, *The Overworked American: The Unexpected Decline of
    Leisure* (New York: Basic Books, 1993) esp. 108 and 119 ("work and
    spend"). See also 31 and 157–59, and Schor, *The Overspent Amer-
    ican: Upscaling, Downshifting and the New Consumer* (New York:
    Harper Perennial, 1998), esp. 19, 108, and 113–28.

15. Juliet Schor, "What's Driving Consumption?" *Boston Review* 24,
    Summer 1999, 4–9; cf. Adam Tooze, "The Global Climate Ledger,"
    Dissent (Winter 2021), available at https://www.dissentmagazine
    .org/article/the-global-climate-ledger.

16. Steven Watts, *Self-Help Messiah: Dale Carnegie and Success in Mod-
    ern America* (New York: Other Press, 2013), esp. 189–91; "Dale
    Carnegie, Author, Is Dead," *New York Times*, November 2, 1955.

17. From "Car Jamming" on The Clash's album *Combat Rock* (1982).

18. Mills, *White Collar*, 176.

19. Dale Carnegie, *How to Win Friends and Influence People* (New York:
    Simon & Schuster, 1937), 18.

20. Carnegie as quoted in Watts, *Self-Help Messiah*, 64; Sinclair Lewis,
    as quoted in Marshall Fishwick, *Great Awakenings: Popular Religion
    and Popular Culture* (New York: Routledge, 2011), 48.

21. Andrew Dilts, "From 'Entrepreneur of the Self' to 'Care of the Self':
    Neo-liberal Governmentality and Foucault's Ethics," *Foucault Stud-
    ies* 12 (October 2011), 131 and 130–46 passim.

22. Carnegie, as quoted in Reinhard Bendix, *Work and Authority in Industry: Ideologies of Management in the Course of Industrialization* (New York: Harper Torchbooks, 1956), 303; for Hollywood, see Carnegie, *How to Win Friends and Influence People*, 101, 104, and 234.

23. Ingrid F. Smyer, *Relationship within* (Bloomington, IN: Balboa Press, 2013), 66; Watts, *Self-Help Messiah*, 13, 189; Carnegie, *How to Win Friends*, 101, 104, and 234.

24. Irving D. Tressler, *How to Lose Friends and Alienate People: A Burlesque* (New York: Stackpole Sons, 1937), 34; William Saroyan, "The Dale Carnegie Friend," in his collection *The Trouble with Tigers* (New York: Harcourt, Brace, & Company, 1938), 229–30.

25. Bendix, *Work and Authority in Industry*, 303 and 304.

26. Greil Marcus, introduction to Constance Rourke, *American Humor: A Study of the National Character* (New York: New York Review of Books, 2004, originally 1931), xiv.

27. Melville, *Bartleby, the Scrivener*, 15–16; Thomas Augst, *A Clerk's Tale: Young Men and Moral Life in Nineteenth Century America* (Chicago: University of Chicago Press, 2003), esp. 13–14 and 215–31.

28. Bendix, *Work and Authority in Industry*, 301–13; Edgar Cabanas and Eva Illouz, *Manufacturing Happy Citizens: How the Science and Industry of Happiness Control Our Lives* (Cambridge, UK: Polity Press, 2019), 86–89. See also Harry Braverman, *Labor and Monopoly Capital* (New York: Monthly Review Press, 1998, originally 1974), 60–61.

29. Richard Edwards, *Contested Terrain: The Transformation of the Workplace in the Twentieth Century* (New York: Basic Books, 1979), 134–43.

30. Richard Sennett, "Office Max," *New York Times*, June 13, 2014, https://www.nytimes.com/2014/06/15/books/review/cubed-by -nikil-saval.html; Cabanas and Illouz, *Manufacturing Happy Citizens*, 91 and 82–110 passim; William Davies, *The Happiness Industry: How Government and Big Business Sold Us Well-Being* (London and New York: Verso, 2015), 114–15 (on lack of enthusiasm) and 105–37 passim.

31. Braverman, *Labor and Monopoly Capital*, 239 ("factory-like") and 203–47 passim.

32. Margery Davies, "Woman's Place Is at the Typewriter: The Feminization of the Clerical Labor Force," *Radical America* 8 (July–August 1974), 7 and 1–28.

33. Geary, *Radical Ambition*, 128–29; Evelyn Nakano Glenn and Roslyn Feldberg, "Proletarianizing Clerical Work: Technology and Organizational Control in the Office," in *Case Studies in the Labor*

Process, Andrew Zimbalist, ed. (New York: Monthly Review Press, 1979), 66 and 51–72 passim.

34. Susan Porter Benson, *Counter Cultures: Saleswomen, Managers, and Customers in American Department Stores* (Urbana: University of Illinois Press, 1986).

35. Mills, *White Collar*, xi and 198–204 ("white-collar girls"); Richard Sennett, "Middle Class Families and Urban Violence: The Experience of a Chicago Community in the Nneteenth Century," in *Nineteenth Century Cities: Essays in the New Urban History*, Stephan Thernstrom and Richard Sennett, eds. (New Haven: Yale University Press, 1969), 387 and 386–420 passim; Christopher Morley, *Kitty Foyle* (Philadelphia: J. B. Lippincott Company, 1939).

36. Booth Tarkington, *Alice Adams* (Bloomington: Indiana University Press, 2003, originally 1921), 15; James T. Farrell, *$1000 a Week and Other Stories* (New York: Vanguard Press, 1942), 135–43.

37. Stephen Meyer III, *The Five-Dollar Day: Labor Management and Social Control in the Ford Motor Company, 1908–1921* (Albany: State University of New York Press, 1981).

38. David Roediger and Philip Foner, *Our Own Time: A History of American Labor and the Working Day* (London and New York: Verso Books, 1990), esp. 101–277; Christopher Hermann, "Neoliberalism and the End of Shorter Work Hours," *Socialist Project E-Bulletin* 590 (January 25, 2012), http://socialistproject.ca/bullet/590.php; David Kestenbaum, "Keynes Says We'd Be Working 15-Hour Weeks: Why Was He So Wrong?" *NPR*, August 13, 2015, https://www.npr .org/2015/08/13/432122637/keynes-predicted-we-would-be-working -15-hour-weeks-why-was-he-so-wrong.

39. Schor, *Overworked American*, esp. 17–41; Roediger and Foner, *Our Own Time,* esp. 257–77.

40. Schor, *Overworked American*, 17.

41. Schor, *Overworked American*, 8, 11, 13, 17 ("squeeze"), 36, and 83–106 (on the household); Jonathan Clary, *24/7: Late Capitalism and the Ends of Sleep* (London and New York: Verso, 2013), 58–59.

42. Kayleena Makortoff, "Goldman Sachs Junior Banker Speaks Out over 18-Hour Shifts and Low Pay," *The Guardian*, March 24, 2021, https://www.theguardian.com/business/2021/mar/24/goldman -sachs-junior-bankers-rebel-over-18-hour-shifts-and-low-pay; Abigail Johnson Hess, "Coronavirus Highlights the Inequality of Who Can—and Can't—Work from Home," *CNBC Make It*, March 4, 2020, https://www.cnbc.com/2020/03/04/coronavirus-highlights-who -can-and-cant-work-from-home.html; Joan Williams and Heather Boushey, "The Poor, the Professionals, and the Missing Middle,"

Center for American Progress, January 25, 2010, https://www.americanprogress.org/issues/economy/reports/2010/01/25/7194/the-three-faces-of-work-family-conflict/, tables 2 and 3.

43. Elaine Tyler May, *Homeward Bound: American Families in the Cold War Era* (New York: Basic Books, 2008), 8, 9–11, and 155–66; Betty Friedan, *The Feminine Mystique* (New York: W. W. Norton, 2013, originally 1963).

44. Schor, *Overworked American,* 150–52; Brigid Schulte, *Overwhelmed: Work, Love, and Play When No One Has the Time* (New York: Farrar, Straus, & Giroux, 2014); Karine Moe and Dianna Shandy, *Glass Ceilings and 100-Hour Couples: What the Opt-Out Phenomenon Can Teach Us about Work and Family* (Athens, GA: University of Georgia Press, 2010), esp. 35–44.

45. Elizabeth Warren and Amelia Warren Tyagi, *The Two-Income Trap: Why Middle-Class Mothers and Fathers Are Going Broke* (New York: Basic Books, 2004).

46. Schor, *Overworked American,* 31; G. E. Miller, "The US Is the Most Overworked Developed Nation in the World?," *20-Something Finance,* January 2, 2018, https://20somethingfinance.com/american-hours-worked-productivity-vacation/.

47. Mills, *White Collar,* 237 and 258; Maurie Backman, "Here's How Many Hours the American Works," *Motley Fool,* December 17, 2017, https://www.fool.com/careers/2017/12/17/heres-how-many-hours-the-average-american-works-pe.aspx; Williams and Boushey, "The Poor, the Professionals, and the Missing Middle"; on workaholism, see Barbara Killinger, *Workaholics: The Respectable Addicts* (Buffalo: Firefly Books, 1997).

48. American Time Use Survey, "Charts by Topic: Household Activities," *Bureau of Labor Statistics,* undated (2015 data), https://www.bls.gov/tus/charts/household.htm; Bloomberg, "The Economic Reason Why Men Should Do More Housework," *Fortune,* August 1, 2017, https://fortune.com/2017/08/01/women-men-housework-gender-divide-equality/.

49. Schor, *Overspent American,* title page and 68–76.

50. "Opioids in the Workplace," Centers for Disease Control and Prevention / National Institute for Occupational Safety and Health, undated (2017 data), https://www.cdc.gov/niosh/topics/opioids/data.html; Miriam Boeri, *Women on Ice: Methamphetamine Use among Suburban Women* (New Brunswick: Rutgers University Press, 2013), 1 ("perfect drug"), and 3–53; Chelsea Summers, "'Procrasturbation' Is the Last Refuge of the Over-burdened, Under-pleasured Worker," *Vice,* May 26, 2015, https://www.vice.com/en_us/article/nn9vgb/

procrasturbation-is-the-last-refuge-of-the-over-burdened-under-pleasured-worker.

51. Schor, *Overspent American*, 7, 15, and 108 (figures on "needs" and dissatisfactions) and 6–16 passim. Cf. Juliet Schor, "What's Driving Consumption?," *Boston Review* 24 (Summer 1999), 4–9, for broaching of the ecological implications of the fact that 35 percent aspired to quickly be in top 6 percent income bracket and 84 percent in top 18 percent, with only 15 percent satisfied to live a "comfortable life." For Warren, see Teresa A. Sullivan, Elizabeth Warren, and Jay Lawrence Westbrook, *The Fragile Middle Class: Americans in Debt* (New Haven: Yale University Press, 2000), 3 and 6.

52. Karl Marx, *Economic and Philosophical Manuscripts of 1844*, available at https://www.marxists.org/archive/marx/works/1844/manuscripts/needs.htm.

53. Lendol Calder, *Financing the American Dream: A Cultural History of Consumer Credit* (Princeton: Princeton University Press, 1999), 56 ("ethic") and 45–75.

54. Louis Hyman, *Borrow: The American Way of Debt* (New York: Vintage, 2012), 17 ("BC") and 18–40. On character, see Calder, *Financing the American Dream*, 157–203.

55. Jerome Bjelopera, *City of Clerks: Office and Sales Workers in Philadelphia, 1870–1929* (Urbana: University of Illinois Press, 2005), 27 and 40; Sharon Hartman Strom, *Beyond the Typewriter: Gender, Class, and the Origins of Modern American Office Work, 1900–1930* (Urbana: University of Illinois Press, 1992), 35–47, 70, 72–73, and 236–51.

56. Martin Sklar, "On the Proletarian Revolution and the End of Political-Economic Society," *Radical America*, May–June 1969, 1–41.

57. Calder, *Financing the American Dream*, 201.

58. Hyman, *Borrow*, 57–58 and 261 (on character and on Post); Calder, *Financing the American Dream*, 58–68, 20–29.

59. Winifred Wandersee, *Women's Work and Family Values, 1920–1940* (Cambridge, MA: Harvard University Press, 1981), 59–60 and 70–76.

60. David Riesman, as quoted in Calder, *Financing the American Dream*, 11; John Kenneth Galbraith, *The Affluent Society* (Boston: Houghton Mifflin, 1998, originally 1958), 14.

61. Daniel J. Clark, *Disruption in Detroit: Autoworkers and the Elusive Postwar Boom* (Urbana: University of Illinois Press, 2018), 38, 81, 86, 150, 167–78, and 209.

62. Schor, *Overspent American*, 72; "Total Household Debt Climbs for Twentieth Straight Quarter as Mortgage Debt and Originations

Rise," Federal Reserve Bank of New York, August 13, 2019, https://www.newyorkfed.org/newsevents/news/research/2019/20190813; "Household Debt and Credit Report, Q2 2019," Center for Microeconomic Data, Federal Reserve Bank of New York, https://www.newyorkfed.org/microeconomics/hhdc.html.

63. Alex Morrow, "Americans Haven't Had This Much Credit Card Debt since the Eve of the Fiscal Crisis," *Business Insider*, December 16, 2016, https://www.businessinsider.com/american-credit-card-debt-nearing-all-time-highs-2016-12; "Total Household Debt Climbs"; Board of Governors of the Federal Reserve System, "Total Consumer Credit Outstanding," Wikipedia Commons, 2011, https://upload.wikimedia.org/wikipedia/commons/1/13/Chart_---_Total-US-Consumer-Credit-Outstanding-1945-2011.png.

64. Alexandre Tanzi, "US Student Loan Delinquencies Hit Record," *Bloomberg Businessweek*, February 22, 2019, https://www.bloomberg.com/news/articles/2019-02-22/u-s-student-loan-delinquencies-hit-record; Benjamin Landy, "Graph: Why Student Loan Delinquency Is Still So High," *The Century Foundation*, August 27, 2013, https://tcf.org/content/commentary/graph-why-student-loan-delinquency-is-still-so-high/; Elizabeth Warren and Amelia Warren Tyagi, *The Two-Income Trap: Why Middle-Class Mothers and Fathers Are Going Broke* (New York: Basic Books, 2004), 40–46.

65. Paul Buchheit, "The New American Exceptionalism," *Inequality.org*, October 22, 2015, https://inequality.org/research/2015-wealth-data/.

66. Maurizio Lazzaroto, *The Making of Indebted Man* (Los Angeles: Semiotexte, 2011), 20, 37, 65–83 ("confidence"), 112 ("learning" and "debt economy"), 113–14; Jay Hancock and Elizabeth Lucas, "'UVA Has Ruined Us': Health System Sues Thousands of Patients, Seizing Paychecks and Putting Liens on Their Homes," *Washington Post*, September 9, 2019, https://www.washingtonpost.com/health/uva-has-ruined-us-health-system-sues-thousands-of-patients-seizing-paychecks-and-putting-liens-on-homes/2019/09/09/5eb23306-c807-11e9-be05-f76ac4ec618c_story.html.

67. Michael Staub, *The Mismeasure of Minds: Debating Race and Intelligence between Brown and The Bell Curve* (Chapel Hill: University of North Carolina Press, 2018); Staub, "Controlling Ourselves: Emotional Intelligence, the Marshmallow Test, and the Inheritance of Race," *American Studies* 55:1 (2016), 60 (for the mug) and 59–80; see also Jessica McCrory Calarco, "Why Rich Kids Are So Good at the Marshmallow Test," *The Atlantic*, June 1, 2018, https://www.theatlantic.com/family/archive/2018/06/marshmallow-test/561779/.

CHAPTER 5: MIDDLE-CLASS VOTES

1. Harry Schenawolf, "Artisans Were the Middle-Class Muscle behind the American Revolution," *Revolutionary War Journal*, January 10, 2019, https://www.revolutionarywarjournal.com/colonial-artisan-mechanicks-middle-class-muscle-behind-the-american-revolution/.

2. Neil Davidson, *How Revolutionary Were the Bourgeois Revolutions?* (Chicago: Haymarket Books, 2012), esp. 55–62, Gerald Horne, *The Counter-Revolution of 1776: Slave Resistance and the Origins of the United States of America* (New York: New York University Press, 2014); Jesse Lemisch, "Jack Tar in the Streets: Merchant Seamen in the Politics of Revolutionary America," *William and Mary Quarterly* 25 (July 1968), 371–407; Barrington Moore, *The Social Origins of Dictatorship and Democracy* (Boston: Beacon Press, 1966).

3. David Brion Davis, *Slavery and Human Progress* (New York: Oxford University Press, 1984) esp. 15 and 254; Thomas L. Haskell, "Capitalism and the Origins of Humanitarian Sensibility," *American Historical Review* 90 (April 1985), 350; Betty Fladeland, *Abolitionists and Working-Class Problems in the Age of Industrialization* (London: Macmillan, 1984), esp. vii–xiv; David Roediger, *Seizing Freedom: Slave Emancipation and Liberty for All* (London and New York: Verso, 2015), 25–146.

4. Joan Hoff Wilson, *Herbert Hoover: Forgotten Progressive* (Long Grove, IL: Waveland Press, 1992, originally 1975), esp. 10–12; Elizabeth Esch, *The Color Line and the Assembly Line: Managing Race in the Ford Empire* (Oakland: University of California Press, 2018), 76–77; Gabriel Kolko, *The Triumph of American Conservatism: A Reinterpretation of American History, 1900–1916* (New York: Free Press, 1977); Michael McGerr, *A Fierce Discontent: The Progressive Movement in America, 1870–1920* (New York: Oxford University Press, 2003).

5. Jesse Walker, "Hooded Progressivism: The Secret Reformist History of the Ku Klux Klan," *Reason*, December 2, 2005, https://reason.com/2005/12/02/hooded-progressivism/; Robert Wiebe, *The Search for Order, 1877–1920* (New York: Hill & Wang, 1967); John Howard Keiser, "John Fitzpatrick and Progressive Unionism, 1915–1925," unpublished PhD diss., Northwestern University, 1965.

6. Robert Allen with Pamela P. Allen, *Reluctant Reformers: Racism and Social Reform Movements in the United States* (Washington, DC: Howard University Press, 1983, originally 1974); David Roediger, *Working toward Whiteness: How America's Immigrants Became White* (New York: Basic Books, 2005), 64–72 and 143.

7. Nancy Yang, "Then and Now: What Does It Mean to Be 'Progressive?'" *MPR News*, February 12, 2016.

8. Dylan Rodríguez, *White Reconstruction: Domestic Warfare and the Logics of Genocide* (New York: Fordham University Press, 2021), 113 ("louder" and "unions") and 107–34; Kevin Phillips, *The Emerging Republican Majority* (Princeton: Princeton University Press, 2015, originally 1969); Ian Haney-López, *Dog Whistle Politics: How Coded Racial Appeals Have Reinvented Racism and Wrecked the Middle Class* (New York: Oxford University Press, 2015); David R. Roediger, *How Race Survived US History from Settlement and Slavery to the Obama Phenomenon* (London and New York: Verso, 2008), esp. 200–2.

9. Linda Gordon, "How Welfare Became a Dirty Word," *Journal of Comparative Social Welfare* 14 (1998), 13 and 1–14 passim. See also Jill Quadagno, *The Color of Welfare: How Racism Undermined the War on Poverty* (New York: Oxford University Press, 1996).

10. Mike Davis, *Prisoners of the American Dream: Politics and Economy in the History of the US Working Class* (London and New York: Verso, 2000, originally 1986), esp. 157–255; David Harvey, *A Brief History of Neoliberalism* (New York: Oxford University Press, 2005), 7–9.

11. Harvey, *Brief History*; see also Barry Bluestone, Bennett Harrison, and Lawrence Baker, *Corporate Flight: The Causes and Consequences of Economic Dislocation* (Washington, DC: Progressive Alliance, 1981); Davis, *Prisoners*, 157–300; Andrew Elrod, "The Specter of Inflation," *Boston Review*, August 19, 2021.

12. Immanuel Wallerstein, *World-Systems Analysis: An Introduction* (Durham: Duke University Press, 2004).

13. Kim Moody, "Workers of the World: Growth, Change, and Rebellion," *New Politics* 70 (Winter 2021), available at https://newpol.org/issue_post/workers-of-the-world-%E2%80%A8growth-change-and-rebellion/.

14. Joe Burns, *Reviving the Strike* (Brooklyn: Ig Publishing, 2011), chapter 1; Aaron Brenner, Robert Brenner, and Cal Winslow, eds., *Rebel Rank and File: Labor Militancy and Revolt from Below during the Long 1970s* (London and New York: Verso, 2010).

15. Philip Rubio, *Undelivered: From the Great Postal Strike of 1970 to the Manufactured Crisis of the US Postal Service* (Chapel Hill: University of North Carolina Press, 2020), chapters 2–5; Joseph A. McCartin, *Collision Course: Ronald Reagan, the Air Traffic Controllers and the Strike That Changed America* (New York: Oxford University Press, 2013).

16. James O'Connor, *The Fiscal Crisis of the State* (New York: Routledge, 2017, originally 1973); Ruth Wilson Gilmore, *Golden Gulag: Prisons, Surplus, Crisis and Opposition in Globalizing California* (Berkeley:

University of California Press, 2007), 5–180 and 245; Roediger, *How Race Survived*, 203–7; Alan Wolfe, *America's Impasse: The Rise and Fall of the Politics of Growth* (New York: Pantheon, 1981).

17. "About the Founders," Democracy Corps website, http://www.democracycorps.com/the-founders/.

18. Noah Davis, "Why Are You So Smart, Stan Greenberg?," *Pacific Standard*, June 13, 2013, https://psmag.com/news/why-are-you-so-smart-stan-greenberg-61117. The main oral histories are "Stanley Greenberg (2005), Pollster," January 27, 2005, https://millercenter.org/the-presidency/presidential-oral-histories/stanley-greenberg-oral-history-2005-pollster; and "Stanley Greenberg (2007), Pollster," October 11, 2007, https://millercenter.org/the-presidency/presidential-oral-historiesstanley-greenberg-oral-history-2007-pollster.

19. "Stanley Greenberg (2005)."

20. "Stanley Greenberg (2005)."

21. "Stanley Greenberg (2005)"; Rotenstein, "Silver Spring, Maryland Has Whitewashed Its Past," *History News Network*, October 15, 2016, https://historynewsnetwork.org/article/163914. Thanks especially to the great historian John Bracey for discussions of race, neighborhood, and schools in Washington, DC, in the 1950s and early '60s.

22. "Stanley Greenberg (2005)."

23. Erik Olin Wright, "Class Boundaries in Advanced Capitalist Societies," *New Left Review* 98 (July–August 1976), 26 and 3–41. For Wright the contradiction is not simply that the father moved from entrepreneurship to waged and salaried labor or that he was in a skilled professional job without a college degree. The engineer's bossed but necessarily somewhat autonomous job itself contained contradictions for Wright.

24. "Stanley Greenberg (2005)."

25. "Stanley Greenberg (2005)"; Davis, "Why Are You So Smart, Stan Greenberg?"

26. "Stanley Greenberg (2005)"; Stanley Greenberg, "Unlearning the Lessons of *Hillbilly Elegy*," *American Prospect Longform* (January 8, 2019), https://prospect.org/article/unlearning-lessons-hillbilly-elegy.

27. James Q. Wilson, "A Life in the Public Interest," *Wall Street Journal*, September 21, 2009; Wilson, *The Amateur Democrat: Club Politics in Three Cities* (Chicago: University of Chicago Press, 1962); Greenberg, "Unlearning the Lessons"; "Stanley Greenberg (2005)"; Jim Crumer, "Banfield's Back," *Harvard Crimson*, August 1, 1975.

28. James Q. Wilson and George L. Kelling, "Broken Windows: The Police and Neighborhood Safety," *The Atlantic*, March 1982, https://www.theatlantic.com/magazine/archive/1982/03/broken-windows/304465/; Roediger, *How Race Survived*, 200–2; Wilson and Herrnstein, *Crime and Human Nature: The Definitive Study of the Causes of Crime* (New York: Simon & Schuster, 1985). For reception, see Robert A. Beauregard, *Voices of Decline: The Postwar Fate of U.S. Cities* (New York: Routledge, 2002), 159–76. See also William Muraskin's rollicking review essay "The Moral Basis of a Backward Sociologist: Edward Banfield, the Italians, and the Italian-Americans," *American Journal of Sociology* 74 (May 1974), 1484–96.

29. Banfield as quoted in Chaim Isaac Waxman, *The Stigma of Poverty: A Critique of Poverty Theories and Policies* (New York: Pergamon Press, 1983), 13; Stanley Greenberg, *Politics and Poverty: Modernization and Response in Five Poor Neighborhoods* (New York: John Wiley & Sons, 1974), esp. 75–103.

30. Greenberg, "Unlearning the Lessons"; Greenberg, "From Crisis to Working Majority," *American Prospect*, Fall 1991, https://prospect.org/article/crisis-working-majority; Greenberg, *Politics and Poverty*, 49 ("resignation"). It is of course not the case that Appalachian migrants were incapable of political organization. See, for example, Kathy Kahn, *Hillbilly Women: Struggle and Survival in Southern Appalachia* (New York: Avon, 1973); Amy Sonnie and James Tracy, *Hillbilly Nationalists, Urban Race Rebels and Black Power: Community Organizing in Radical Times* (New York: Melville House, 2011).

31. "Stanley Greenberg (2005)"; Greenberg, *Politics and Poverty*, esp. 169–70, including the Alinsky quotation.

32. The exception is that Greenberg did establish differences, very loosely based on political economy, among Black neighborhoods in Chicago and Detroit. See Greenberg, *Politics and Poverty*, 75–76 for the quote and esp. 53–72.

33. All the quotes come from Greenberg, "Unlearning the Lessons," save the passage ending in "collective political urge" and "politics of resignation," which are from Greenberg, *Politics and Poverty*, 75–76 and 49, respectively.

34. Greenberg, *Politics and Poverty*, 2 ("bizarre forms"), 3 ("liberal political man"), 75–103 ("lower class"), 108–9, and 195–200.

35. Greenberg, *Politics and Poverty*, 206–7.

36. Greenberg, *Politics and Poverty*, 206–29, at 226 ("limits, "cabals," and "trivial"), 228 ("demanding"), and 229.

37. Emphasis on "the left wing of the possible" is most associated with the work of the far leftist turned reformist socialist Democrat

Michael Harrington, especially through the 1960s, '70s, and '80s. During that time, as journalist Victor Navasky wrote, Harrington's fuller goal became to discover "the left wing of the possible within the Democratic Party." See Navasky, "The Left Wing of the Possible," *New York Times*, May 28, 2000. On violence, see Greenberg, *Politics and Poverty*, esp. 13–14, 63–77, 106–16, 160–72, and 202–11.

38. "Stanley Greenberg (2005)"; Greenberg, *Dispatches from the War Room: In the Trenches with Five Extraordinary Leaders* (New York: St. Martin's Press, 2009), 118–19.

39. "Stanley Greenberg (2005)"; for the context, see Julius Getman, *Restoring the Power of Unions: It Takes a Movement* (New Haven: Yale University Press, 2010); Zach Schwartz-Weinstein, "On Bill and Hillary's First Date in 1971, They Crossed a Picket Line," *In These Times*, February 9, 2016, http://inthesetimes.com/working/entry/18841/hillary_rodham_bill_clinton_and_the_1971_yale_strike.

40. Stanley Greenberg, *Race and State in Capitalist Development: Comparative Perspectives* (New Haven: Yale University Press, 1980), ix–x, 73–74, 115, and 116–18.

41. "Stanley Greenberg (2005)"; Greenberg, *Dispatches*, 19; Robert T. McFadden, "Giamatti, Scholar and Baseball Chief, Dies at 51," *New York Times*, October 2, 1989, https://www.nytimes.com/1989/09/02/obituaries/giamatti-scholar-and-baseball-chief-dies-at-51.html.

42. "Stanley Greenberg (2005)."

43. Stanley Greenberg, *Legitimating the Illegitimate: State, Markets, and Resistance in South Africa* (Berkeley: University of California, 1987), 201; Greenberg, *Dispatches from the War Room*, 16, 115, and 447.

44. "Stanley Greenberg (2005)."

45. Greenberg, *Dispatches*; Stanley B. Greenberg, *Middle Class Dreams: The New American Majority* (New York: Times Books, 1996, originally 1995); Chris Hegedus and D. A. Pennebaker, dirs., *The War Room* (London: October Films, 1993).

46. "Reagan Democrat," *Oxford Dictionaries* (accessed March 25, 2019), https://en.oxforddictionaries.com/definition/us/reagan_democrat; Michael Rogin, "Politics, Emotion, and the Wallace Vote," *British Journal of Sociology*, 20 (March, 1969): 27–49; Pete Hamill, "The Revolt of the White Lower Middle Class," *New York*, April 14, 1969, http://nymag.com/news/features/46801/; see also Joseph Kraft, "The Revolt of the Lower Middle Class," *San Francisco Examiner*, June 15, 1968.

47. David Riddle, "Race and Reaction in Warren, Michigan, 1971 to 1974: 'Bradley v. Milliken' and the Cross-District Busing Controversy," *Michigan Historical Review* 26 (Fall 2000), 1–49.

48. Zack Stanton, "The Bellwether County That Explains Eminem and Kid Rock," *Politico Magazine*, October 11, 2017, https://www.politico.com/magazine/story/2017/10/11/eminem-kid-rock-macomb-county-politics-215700; John Judis to David Roediger, email, December 10, 2019 (on the 1980 stories).

49. On prior focus groups on the Republican side, see "Stanley Greenberg (2005)"; John Judis, "Exposing the Opposition in 2016 May Be the Best Strategy," *The Democratic Strategist*, June 5, 2015, https://thedemocraticstrategist.org/2015/06/exposing_the_opposition_in_201/.

50. Greenberg, *Middle Class Dreams*, 26, 27, 19, and 23–54 passim; "Macomb Voters Turn from Dems," *Detroit Free Press*, October 6, 1985.

51. See Tiya Alicia Miles, *The Dawn of Detroit: A Chronicle of Slavery and Freedom in the City of the Straits* (New York: New Press, 2017), 74–79, 102–3, 132, and 298n96 on the Macombs, Detroit, and Macomb County.

52. Greenberg, *Middle Class Dreams*, 322n27 for the 45 percent figures. See also 23–54 passim.

53. "Hannity vs. Limbaugh Attack Mastermind," *Fox News*, March 26, 2009, https://www.foxnews.com/story/hannity-vs-limbaugh-attack-mastermind; Greenberg, *Dispatches from the War Room*, 19 ("venomous"); Greenberg, *Middle Class Dreams*, 32–34 ("listening to Macomb"), 39, and 40–42.

54. Nancy L. Cohen. *Delirium: How the Sexual Counterrevolution Is Polarizing America* (Berkeley: Counterpoint, 2012), 92 ("short"); Greenberg, *Middle Class Dreams*, 29.

55. Christopher Hitchens, *No One Left to Lie To: The Triangulations of William Jefferson Clinton* (London and New York: Verso, 1991), 17–18; Cohen, *Delirium*, 92 and 93–100; Greenberg, *Middle Class Dreams*, 325–26n14 and 44–49. For Reagan and masculinity in the focus groups, see also "Stanley Greenberg Oral History (2007)"; Stanley B. Greenberg, *The Two Americas: Our Current Political Deadlock and How to Break It* (New York: Thomas Dunne Books, 1984), 235–37; see Richard David Riddle, "The Rise of the Reagan Democrat in Warren, Michigan, 1964–1984," PhD dissertation, Wayne State University, 1998, 251–80.

56. Rogin, "Politics, Emotion, and the Wallace Vote," 27–49; Riddle, "Rise of the Reagan Democrat," 290 and 315–16; Lucy Geismer, *Don't Blame Us: Suburban Liberals and the Transformation of the Democratic Party* (Princeton: Princeton University Press, 2015).

57. Cohen, *Delirium*, 93 ("McGoverniks") is also excellent at establish-
ing the point that unionized autoworkers were not in fact among
the most reactionary people in the United States. For some of the
possible logic of the union leaders, see Daniel Galvin, "Resilience
in the Rust Belt: Michigan Democrats and the UAW," Institute for
Policy Research, Northwestern University, December 2012, https://
www.ipr.northwestern.edu/publications/docs/workingpapers/2013/
IPR-WP-13-04.pdf.

58. Riddle, "Rise of the Reagan Democrat," 104–79, 251–65, 288, 293–
94, and 300–14; Cf. The Analysis Group [Greenberg], *Recapturing
Democratic Majorities: Housewives and Their Men* (New Haven: The
Analysis Group, 1985), 16, 17–18 (for some expressed opposition
to arms spending in the focus groups), 58; Greenberg, *Report on
Democratic Defectors, Prepared for the Michigan House Democratic
Campaign* (New Haven: The Analysis Group, 1985), 31–32. On the
real but limited cross-racial class politics in plants, especially in the
'70s, see Riddle, "Rise of the Reagan Democrat," 251–89.

59. "Stanley Greenberg (2005)"; Stanley Greenberg, "The Mythology
of Centrism," *American Prospect*, September–October 1997, https://
prospect.org/article/mythology-centrism.

60. "Stanley Greenberg (2005)." For Greenberg's continuing sense that
the Rainbow Coalition forces prevented his ideas from gaining
a serious hearing, see the interview with him included in Zach
Stanton, "The Rise of the Biden Republicans," *Politico*, March 4,
2021 at https://www.politico.com/news/magazine/2021/03/04/rea-
gan-democrats-biden-republicans-politics-stan-greenberg-473330.

61. Stanley Greenberg, "Reconstructing a Democratic Vision,"
American Prospect, Spring 1990, https://prospect.org/article/
reconstructing-democratic-vision.

62. Stanley Greenberg, "From Crisis to Working Majority," *American
Prospect*, Fall 1991, https://prospect.org/article/crisis-working-ma-
jority. See also AAIHS editors, "Rethinking H. Rap Brown and
Black Power," *Black Perspectives*, September 29, 2018, https://www.
aaihs.org/rethinking-h-rap-brown-and-black-power/.

63. Greenberg, *Report on Democratic Defectors*, 3 ("vulnerability"), 17
("victims"), 18–31 passim; The Analysis Group [Greenberg], *Recapturing Democratic Majorities*, 3 and 6 ("middle class poor").

64. Greenberg, *Report on Democratic Defectors*, 27 ("Republicans are
management"), 29 ("John Wayne"), and 38–47; The Analysis Group
[Greenberg], *Recapturing Democratic Majorities*, 36 and 38. On
earlier militancy, which however coincided with conservative turns
politically, see Riddle, "Rise of the Reagan Democrat," 251–94.

65. Greenberg, *Dispatches*, 116 and, for an unhappy ending to that romance, 12–32 and chapter 4 below; Greenberg, "Popularizing Progressive Politics," in *The New Majority: Toward a Popular Progressive Politics*, Greenberg and Theda Skocpol, eds. (New Haven: Yale University Press, 1997), 279–98. Harold Meyerson, "Wither the Democrats," *American Prospect*, March–April 1996, https://prospect.org/article/wither-democrats. Unions, then in the midst of a brief period of reform, are still more strikingly absent from Greenberg's 2004 study *The Two Americas* than even from the union-supported *Middle Class Dreams*.

66. "Bill Clinton Presidential Campaign Announcement," *C-SPAN*, October 3, 1991, https://www.c-span.org/video/?21803-1/governor-bill-clinton-d-ar-presidential-campaign-announcement; Hitchens, *No One Left to Lie To*, 33–34; Ishmael Reed, *Airing Dirty Laundry* (Reading, MA: Addison Wesley, 1993), 35; "Stanley Greenberg (2007)."

67. See David Roediger, "White Workers, New Democrats, and Affirmative Action," in Wahneema Lubiano, ed., *The House That Race Built* (New York: Random House, 1997), 48–65; Roediger, "The Racial Crisis of American Liberalism," *New Left Review* 196 (November–December, 1992), 114–19, for cries in the wilderness at the time.

68. See the 2018 data from Open Secrets at https://www.opensecrets.org/expends/vendor.php?year=2018&vendor=Greenberg+Quinlan+Rosner+Research; "Stanley Greenberg (2005)"; Scott Beaulieu, "Senator Blumenthal Is One of 10 Richest in Congress" *NBC Connecticut*, August 23, 2011, https://www.nbcconnecticut.com/news/local/Sen-Blumenthal-is-One-of-the-Ten-Richest-in-Congress-128244983.html.

69. Ryan Lizza, "The Gatekeeper: Rahm Emanuel on the Job," *The New Yorker*, February 21, 2009, https://www.newyorker.com/magazine/2009/03/02/the-gatekeeper; Owen Thomas, "Rahn Emanuel Bunked for Free in Pollster's Apartment," *Gawker*, February 5, 2009, https://gawker.com/5147456/rahm-emanuel-bunked-for-free-in-pollsters-basement.

70. Aimee Levitt, "Dick Durbin and Monsanto: An Unholy Alliance that Will Put an End to Agricultural Freedom?," *Riverfront Times*, August 31, 2010, https://www.riverfronttimes.com/foodblog/2010/08/31/dick-durbin-and-monsanto-an-unholy-alliance-that-will-put-an-end-to-agricultural-freedom.

71. Thomas J. McCormick, *America's Half-Century: United States Foreign Policy in the Cold War and After* (Baltimore: Johns Hopkins University Press, 199), esp. 12–16.

72. Ron Brownstein, "The American Operatives Behind Mandela's Presidential Campaign," *The Atlantic*, December 12, 2013, https://www.theatlantic.com/politics/archive/2013/12/the-american-campaign-operatives-behind-mandelas-presidential-campaign/439116/.

73. Dennis W. Johnson, *Democracy for Hire: A History of American Political Consulting* (New York: Oxford University Press, 2017), 385; Roger Cohen, "Haider the Rightist Is Firing Up Vienna's Election with Slurs," *New York Times*, March 12, 2001, https://www.nytimes.com/2001/03/12/world/haider-the-rightist-is-firing-up-vienna-s-election-with-slurs.html.

74. "About the Founders"; Shmuel Rosner, "Bibi's Blunders," *The New Republic*, December 23, 2008, https://newrepublic.com/article/63860/bibis-blunders.

75. Greenberg, *Dispatches*, 347.

76. "Our Mission," The Israel Project, https://www.theisraelproject.org/mission; Sudhir Muralidhar, "The Making of El Presidente," *American Prospect*, March 17, 2006, https://prospect.org/article/making-el-presidente. For an incredibly defensive account of the Bolivian election, the failed presidency of Gonzalo Sánchez de Lozado, the film, and the questionable notion that "elites" supported Evo Morales and were behind criticisms of the "pollster-consultant industrial complex," see Greenberg, *Dispatches*, 392 and 348–91.

77. Justin Delacour, "Spinning 'Lies, Damn Lies, and Statistics' in Venezuela," *Venezuela Analysis*, July 31, 2004, https://venezuelanalysis.com/analysis/608; Tom Hayden, "Obama vs. Clinton on Honduras?," *Huffington Post*, May 26, 2011, https://www.huffpost.com/entry/obama-vs-clinton-on-hondu_b_231168.

78. Melissa Levin, "Little Stan Greenberg Is Dead," *Africa Is a Country*, August 5, 2013, https://africasacountry.com/2013/08/little-stan-greenberg-is-dead; Levin and Greenberg together wrote over sixty radio scripts for the ANC's successful presidential campaign in 1999. See Greenberg, *Dispatches*, 175–76.

79. John Judis, "Exposing the Opposition in 2016 May Be the Best Strategy," *The Democratic Strategist*, June 5, 2015, https://thedemocraticstrategist.org/2015/06/exposing_the_opposition_in_201/.

80. Thomas B. Edsall,"How Immigration Foiled Hillary," *New York Times*, October 5, 2017, https://www.nytimes.com/2017/10/05/opinion/clinton-trump-immigration.html; Greenberg and Nancy Zdunkewizc, "Macomb County in the Age of Trump," *Democracy Corps*, March 9, 2017, https://democracycorps.com/macomb-county/macomb-county-in-the-age-of-trump/.

AFTERWORD: DOUBLY STUCK

1. Francis Fukayama, "Francis Fukayama on the End of American Hegemony," *The Economist*, August 18, 2021 and Fukayama, *The End of History and the Last Man* (New York: Free Press, 1992). The chapter's epigraph is from Lisa Tilley, "The Making of the 'White Working Class': Where Fascist Resurgence Meets Leftist White Anxiety," *Wildcat Dispatches*, November 28, 2016, http://wildcatdispatches.org/2016/11/28/lisa-tilley-the-making -of-the-white-working-class-where-fascist-resurgence-meets-leftist-white-anxiety.

2. See Thomas McCormick, *America's Half-Century: US Foreign Policy in the Cold War and After* (Baltimore: Johns Hopkins University Press, 1995), 1–16, on the broad history of hegemony.

3. Ashley Smith, "Imperialist Keynesianism: Biden's Program for Rehabilitating US Capitalism," *Tempest*, May 18, 2021, available at http://europe-solidaire.org/spip.php?article58544.

4. Vishwas Satgar, ed., *BRICS and the New American Imperialism: Global Rivalry and Resistance* (Johannesburg: Wits University Press, 2021) esp. 1–28 and 76–104.

5. Toni Morrison, *Playing in the Dark: Whiteness and the Literary Imagination* (Cambridge, MA: Harvard University Press, 1992), 47–50; "Make America Great Again," *Wikipedia*, https://en.wikipedia.org/ wiki/Make_America_Great_Again; "Chippewa Falls Say Goodbye to Its Most Famous Citizen" *Chippewa Herald-Telegram*, October 30, 1967.

6. Anthony Scaramucci, *Trump, the Blue-Collar President* (New York and Nashville: Center Street, 2018), 16–17.

7. James Traub, "Biden's 'Foreign Policy for the Middle Class' Is a Revolution," *Foreign Policy*, March 17, 2021; the initiative dovetails with the Carnegie Endowment for International Peace's Task Force on US Foreign Policy for the Middle Class. For "Main Street" see Abigail Bellows, "An Anti-Corruption Agenda for the Middle Class," Carnegie Endowment for International Peace website, July 22, 2021, https:// carnegieendowment.org/2021/07/22/anti-corruption-agenda-for-middle-class-pub-84996; Smith, "Imperialist Keynesianism."

8. For the speeches of Killer Mike and Sanders, see "Solidarity with Amazon Workers," March 26, 2021, Bernie Sanders official Facebook page, https://www.facebook.com/berniesanders/videos /3132988826803454; on the Alabama organizing campaign, see Jane MacAlevey, "Blowout in Bessemer," *The Nation*, April 9, 2021,

at https://www.thenation.com/article/activism/bessemer-alabama
-amazon-union/.

9. Bernie Sanders, *The Speech: A Historic Filibuster on Corporate Greed and the Decline of Our Middle Class* (New York: PublicAffairs, 2011). For the October 2, 2018 press release by Sanders on Amazon minimum wage policy, see https://www.sanders.senate.gov/press-releases/sanders-statement-on-amazon-15-minimum-wage/.

10. Arthur Delaney, "Who Calls Joe Biden 'Middle Class Joe'?," *HuffPost*, March 7, 2019, https://www.huffpost.com/entry/joe-biden-middle-class_n_5c8032d8e4b06ff26ba55799; Ben Schreckinger, "Biden, Inc.," *Politico*, August 2, 2019.

11. Katherine Igoe, "Where Did Joe Biden's Nickname, 'Amtrak Joe,' Come from?," *Marie Claire*, May 4, 2020.

12. Joan Walsh, "Last Night Was Joe Biden's Moment, May there Be Many More," *The Nation*, April 29, 2021, https://www.thenation.com/article/politics/biden-american-jobs-families-plan/.

13. Don Peck, "Can the Middle Class Be Saved?" *The Atlantic*, September, 2011, https://www.theatlantic.com/magazine/archive/2011/09/can-the-middle-class-be-saved/308600/.

14. Harold Meyerson, "The First Post-Middle-Class Election," *American Prospect*, June 29, 2016, https://prospect.org/power/first-post-middle-class-election/; Hope Yen, "What Does It Mean to Be 'Middle Class'?," *Christian Science Monitor*, July 18, 2012, http://www.csmonitor.com/USA/Latest-News-Wires/2012/0718/What-does-it-mean-to-be-middle-class; see also "Socioeconomic Class," Pew Charitable Trusts Fact Tank, December 17, 2014, https://www.pewresearch.org/topics/socioeconomic-class/2014/.

15. "A Strong Middle Class Equals a Strong America," Middle Class Task Force website, January 30, 2009, http://www.whitehouse.gov/blog_post/Todaysevent; Yen, "What Does It Mean to Be 'Middle Class'?"; David Rohde, "The American Working Class Is Shrinking," *Reuters* (US edition), January 13, 2012, http://blogs.reuters.com/david-rohde/2012/01/13/white-house-the-american-middle-class-is-shrinking/; Meyerson, "First Post-Middle-Class Election."

16. Drew Desilver, "Amazon Vote Comes amid Recent Uptick in US Unionization Rate," Pew Research Centers Fact Tank, March 29, 2021, https://www.pewresearch.org/fact-tank/2021/03/29/amazon-vote-comes-amid-recent-uptick-in-u-s-unionization-rate/; Wade Rathke, "The Unanswered Question about the Future of US Labor Unions," *Working-Class Perspectives*, September 6, 2021. For a hopeful but sober perspective of the differences between the 1970s and now see "Labor Day on the Picket Line," September 5, 2021, https://www.

tempestmag.org/2021/09/labor-day-on-the-picket-line/. See also Kim Moody, "Upticks, Waves, and Social Upsurge: The Strikes of 2021 in Context," *Spectre*, November 15, 2021, https://spectrejournal.com/upticks-waves-and-social-upsurge/.

17. For strike figures see Heidi Schierholz and Margaret Poydock, "Continued Surge in Strike Activity Signals Worker Dissatisfaction with Wage Growth," *Economic Policy Institute*, February 11, 2020, epi.org.

18. See, for example, Josh Mound, "What Democrats Must Do?" *Jacobin*, September 30, 2017, https://jacobinmag.com/2017/09/democratic-party-2016-election-working-class.

19. Aaron Brenner, Robert Brenner, and Cal Winslow, eds. *Rebel Rank and File: Labor Militancy and Revolt from Below during the Long 1970s* (London and New York: Verso, 2010); Michael Omi and Howard Winant, *Racial Formation in the United States* (New York: Routledge, 2015), 109–32 and 185–270.

20. On Metzger's career, see Steven Atkins, *Encyclopedia of Right-Wing Extremism in Modern America* (Santa Barbara: ABC-CLIO, 2011), 55–58; and Chip Berlet, "What Is the Third Position?," *Public Research Associates*, December 19, 2016, https://www.politicalresearch.org/2016/12/19/what-third-position.

21. "Bill Clinton Presidential Campaign Announcement," *C-SPAN*, October 3, 1991, https://www.c-span.org/video/?21803-1/governor-bill-clinton-d-ar-presidential-campaign-announcement; Thomas Byrne Edsall and Mary Edsall, "Race," *The Atlantic*, May 1991, https://www.theatlantic.com/past/docs/politics/race/edsall.htm; Edsall and Edsall, *Chain Reaction: The Impact of Race, Rights, and Taxes on American Politics* (New York: W. W. Norton, 1992). For Greenberg, see his *Middle Class Dreams: The New American Majority* (New York: Times Books, 1996, originally 1995), 12 and 92 for the book's two uses of "white working class," (as adjective and noun) and chapter 5 above.

22. For useful commentary on uses of "middle class," "working class,"and their variants see Christopher Cimaglio, "Contested Majority: The Representation of the White Working Class in US Politics from the 1930s to the 1990s," 2018, Publicly Accessible Penn Dissertation 3006, https://repository.upenn.edu/edissertations/3006, 300–305, an account capturing how such languages of class were at once imprecise and less than serious, but nevertheless shifted in important ways over time.

23. Ruy Teixeira and Joel Townsley Rogers, *America's Forgotten Majority: Why the White Working Class Still Matters* (New York: Basic Books, 2001). Cf. Andrew Levison, *The White Working Class Today:*

Who They Are, How They Think, and What Progressives Can Do to Regain Their Support (n.p.: Democratic Strategist Press, 2013).

24. Ed Pilkington, "Obama Angers Midwest Voters with Guns and Religion Remark," *The Guardian*, April 14, 2008, https://www.theguardian.com/world/2008/apr/14/barackobama.uselections2008.

25. Thomas B. Edsall, "The Persistence of Racial Resentment," *New York Times*, reposted at *Portside*, February 10, 2013, https://portside.org/2013-02-10/persistence-racial-resentment; cf. Edsall, "How Democrats Can Compete for the White Working Class," *New York Times*, March 11, 2014. See also Ruy Teixiera, "The White Working Class: The Group that Will Likely Decide Obama's Fate," *The New Republic*, June 20, 2011, https://newrepublic.com/article/90241/obama-election-2012-working-class-kerry; see also Lucy Madison, "Obama: I'm a Warrior for the Middle Class," *CBS News*, September 22, 2011, http://www.cbsnews.com/news/obama-im-a-warrior-for-the-middle-class/. A CBS News report recently put working-class whites at about 40 percent of the US population; see Aimee Picchi, "America's White Working Class Is the Smallest It Has Ever Been," *CBS News*, September 26, 2019, https://www.cbsnews.com/news/americas-white-working-class-is-the-smallest-its-ever-been/; John Hudak, "A Reality Check on 2016's Economically Marginalized," *Brookings*, November 16, 2016, https://www.brookings.edu/blog/fixgov/2016/11/16/economic-marginalization-reality-check/.

26. Andrew Levison, "Democrats Have a White Working Class Problem—and Not Just in the South," *The New Republic*, August 6, 2014, https://newrepublic.com/article/118960/democrats-white-working-class-problem-isnt-just-south.

27. Stanley Greenberg, "Why the White Working Class Matters," *Washington Monthly*, June–August 2014, https://washingtonmonthly.com/magazine/junejulyaug-2014/why-the-white-working-class-matters/; *The American Prospect* and the White Working Class Roundtable, *Democrats and the White Working Class* (Lexington, KY.: Democratic Strategist Press, 2017), front matter; The Democratic Strategist and *Washington Monthly*, *The Second Roundtable on the White Working Class*, https://thedemocraticstrategist.org/the-white-working-class-roundtables/.

28. Susan Glasser, "The Democratic Civil War Is Getting Nasty, Even If No One Is Paying Attention," *The New Yorker*, November 1, 2017, https://www.newyorker.com/news/news-desk/the-democratic-civil-war-is-getting-nasty-even-if-no-one-is-paying-attention.

29. Katie Reilly, "Read Hillary Clinton's 'Basket of Deplorables' Remarks about Donald Trump Supporters," *Time*, September 10, 2016,

https://time.com/4486502/hillary-clinton-basket-of-deplorables
-transcript/. The remark applied to "half" of Trump supporters
and did not specify which ones by class. The Trump campaign's
response, aware that her speech came at an LGBT for Hillary gala,
branded the comment as an attack on "ordinary Americans."

30. Connor Martin as quoted in Sam Harnett, "What We Talk about when
We Talk about the 'White Working Class,'" *KQED News: The California
Report*, November 7, 2017, https://www.kqed.org/news/11620388
/what-we-talk-about-when-we-talk-about-the-white-working-class.

31. Walter D. Burnham, "Breitbart, Steve Bannon, and Trump against
the World," *USApp – American Politics and Policy Blog*, October
2016, http://eprints.lse.ac.uk/68401/.

32. Ken Stern, "Exclusive: Steve Bannon, Trump's New C.E.O., Hints
at His Master Plan," *Vanity Fair*, August 17, 2016," https://www.
vanityfair.com/news/2016/08/breitbart-stephen-bannon-donald
-trump-master-plan; Michael Stumo, "Steve Bannon Sees
Transatlantic Working-Class Revolt," Coalition for a Prosperous
America website, November 14, 2017, https://prosperousamerica
.org/steve-bannon-sees-transatlantic-working-class-revolt-against
-post-war-order/; Ryan Lizza, "Steve Bannon's Vision for the
Trump Coalition after Election Day," *The New Yorker*, October 16,
2016, https://www.newyorker.com/news/news-desk/steve-bannons
-vision-for-the-trump-coalition-after-election-day.

33. Nicolas Carnes and Noam Lupu, "It's Time to Bust the Myth: Most
Trump Voters Were Not Working Class," *Washington Post*, June 5, 2017,
https://www.washingtonpost.com/news/monkey-cage/wp/2017
/06/05/its-time-to-bust-the-myth-most-trump-voters-were-not
-working-class/ includes the *Times* material and much more.
For Sanders' November 14, 2016, tweet, see https://twitter.com
/berniesanders/status/798192678785716224?lang=en. See also
Anthony Perrin, "The Invention of the 'White Working Class,"
Public Books, January 30, 2018, https://www.publicbooks.org/the
-invention-of-the-white-working-class/.

34. John T. Bennett, "Biden: Democrats Must Show 'Respect' for
Working-Class Whites," *Roll Call*, December 8, 2016, https://www
.rollcall.com/politics/democrats-must-show-respect-working-class
-whites. The Google Trends searches were done on September 29,
2019.

35. Pankaj Mishra, "The Religion of Whiteness Becomes a Suicide Cult,"
New York Times, August 30, 2018.

36. Tilley, "Making of the 'White Working Class'"; Richard Seymour,
"What's the Matter with the 'White Working Class'?," *Salvage*,

February 2, 2017, http://salvage.zone/online-exclusive/whats-the-matter-with-the-white-working-class/; Robbie Shilliam, *Race and the Undeserving Poor* (Newcastle-on-Tyne: Agenda Publishing, 2018), 135–64. For an empirical standpoint, though not an analytical one, see Justin Gest, *The New Minority: White Working Class Politics in an Age of Immigration and Inequality* (Oxford and New York: Oxford University Press, 2016). More broadly still, see Mark Bergfeld's astute "The Perils of 'the White Working Class': Analysing the New Discussion on Class," *Global Labour Journal* (January 2019), https://mulpress.mcmaster.ca/globallabour/article/view/3868.

37. For review essays on this literature, see Perrin, "Invention of the 'White Working Class,'" and Bergfeld, "Perils of 'the White Working Class.'"

38. Anne Case and Angus Deaton, "Mortality and Morbidity in the 21st Century," *Brookings Papers on Economic Activity*, Spring 2017, https://www.brookings.edu/wp-content/uploads/2017/08/casetext-sp17bpea.pdf; cf. Jonathan M. Metzl, *Dying of Whiteness: How the Politics of Racial Resentment Is Killing America's Heartland* (New York: Basic Books, 2019).

39. Joan C. Williams, "What So Many People Don't Get about the US Working Class," *Harvard Business Review*, November 10, 2016, https://www.google.com/search?q=joan+williams+harvard+business+review&rlz=1C1GCEA_enUS791US803&oq=joan++williams+harvard+business&aqs=chrome.1.69i57j0.29361j0j4&sourceid=chrome&ie=UTF-8.

40. Joan C. Williams, *White Working Class: Overcoming Class Cluelessness in America* (Cambridge: Harvard Business Review Press, 2017).

41. Biden's endorsement is found on the book's Amazon webpage at https://www.amazon.com/White-Working-Class-Overcoming-Cluelessness/dp/1633693783.

42. Williams, *White Working Class*, 9–10; for a fuller critique of the book, see David Roediger, "Who's Afraid of the White Working Class," *Los Angeles Review of Books*, May 17, 2017, https://lareviewofbooks.org/article/whos-afraid-of-the-white-working-class-on-joan-c-williamss-white-working-class-overcoming-class-cluelessness-in-america/.

43. Perrin, "Invention of the 'White Working Class."

44. Williams, *White Working Class*, 115.

45. Williams, *White Working Class*, 1 ("soup"), 3 ("jokers" and "followed").

46. Williams, *White Working Class*, 13; Perrin, "Invention of the 'White Working Class,'" for "recognition."

47. Hudak, "Reality Check"; Thomas Edsall, "The 2016 Exit Polls Led Us to Misinterpret the 2016 Election," *New York Times*, March 29, 2018.

48. "An Examination of the 2016 election, Based on Validated Voters," *Pew Research Center*, August 8, 2018, https://www.people-press.org/2018/08/09/an-examination-of-the-2016-electorate-based-on-validated-voters/.

49. Sarah Anderson and Margot Rathke, "After Boosting Low-Income Voter Turnout, Poor Peoples' Campaign Mobilizes for Covid Relief," *Inequality.org*, November 9, 2020, https://inequality.org/great-divide/poor-peoples-campaign-voter-turnout/; Domenico Montanaro, "Poll: Despite record Turnout, 80 Million Americans Didn't Vote; Here's Why," *NPR*, December 15, 2020, https://www.npr.org/2020/12/15/945031391/poll-despite-record-turnout-80-million-americans-didnt-vote-heres-why.

50. Thomas B. Edsall, "We Aren't Seeing White Support for Trump for What It Is," *New York Times*, August 28, 2019.

51. Eric Levitz, "The Tyranny of the Unwoke White Swing Voter," *New York Intelligencer*, June 26, 2019, http://nymag.com/intelligencer/2019/06/the-tyranny-of-the-unwoke-white-swing-voter.html; Thomas B. Edsall, "There Are Really Two Distinct White Working Classes," *New York Times*, June 26, 2019.

52. Carnes and Lupu, "It's Time to Bust the Myth"; Aamna Mohdin, "American Women Voted Overwhelmingly for Clinton, Except the White Ones," *Quora*, November 8, 2016, https://qz.com/833003/election-2016-all-women-voted-overwhelmingly-for-clinton-except-the-white-ones/. Even the statistics on white health and morbidity came in for revision in, for example, Malcolm Harris, "The Death of the White Working Class Has Been Grossly Exaggerated," *Pacific Standard*, June 14, 2017, https://psmag.com/news/the-death-of-the-white-working-class-has-been-greatly-exaggerated.

53. Ronald Brownstein, "The Democratic Debate over Winning Back Trump's Base," *The Atlantic*, May 2, 2019, https://www.theatlantic.com/politics/archive/2019/05/joe-bidens-bid-white-working-class-vote/588613/; Stanley Greenberg, "The Democrats' 'Working Class Problem,'" *American Prospect*, June 1, 2017, https://prospect.org/labor/democrats-working-class-problem/; cf. Stanley Greenberg, *R.I.P. G.O.P.: How the New America Is Dooming the Republicans* (New York: Thomas Dunne Books, 2019).

54. Kim Moody, "Analyzing the 2020 Election: Who Paid? Who Benefits?," *Against the Current*, 211 (March–April, 2021), https://againstthecurrent.org/atc211/analyzing-the-2020-election-who

-paid-who-benefits/; Philip Bump, "Republicans May Be Drawing the Trump/White-Working-Class Arrow Backwards," *Washington Post*, March 31, 2021, https://www.washingtonpost.com/politics /2021/03/31/republicans-may-be-drawing-trumpwhite-working -class-arrow-backwards/. See also Joan Williams, "How Biden Won Back (Enough of) the White Working Class," *Harvard Business Review*, November 10, 2020, https://hbr.org/2020/11/how -biden-won-back-enough-of-the-white-working-class.

55.   Perrin, "Invention of the 'White Working Class."

56.   Malaika Jabali, "Joe Biden Is Not a Blue-Collar Candidate," *Jacobin*, May 2, 2019, https://www.jacobinmag.com/2019/05/joe-biden -presidential-primary-working-class; Greenberg, *R.I.P. G.O.P.*, 199 and 200–4.

57.   Zach Stanton, "The Rise of the Biden Republicans," *Politico*, March 4, 2021, https://www.politico.com/news/magazine/2021/03/04/reagan -democrats-biden-republicans-politics-stan-greenberg-473330. See also Will Weissert, "Biden Republicans? Some in GOP Open to President's Agenda," *US News and World Report*, April 12, 2021, https://www.usnews.com/news/politics/articles/2021-04-12 /biden-republicans-some-in-gop-open-to-presidents-agenda.

58.   Doyle McManus, "Democrats' Hunt for the White Working-Class Male Voter," *Los Angeles Times*, April 18, 2015, https://www.latimes .com/nation/la-oe-0419-mcmanus-whites-20150419-column.html.

59.   Arlie Russell Hochschild, *Strangers in Their Own Land: Anger and Mourning on the American Right* (New York: New Press, 2018), esp. 135–45. Hochschild seems not to use "white working class" as a noun, and rarely as an adjective, but the paperback edition's back cover makes the "white working class" the book's subject.

60.   Greenberg, *R.I.P. G.O.P.*, 268 and 265–69 passim.

61.   Ruy Teixeira, "The Diverse White Working Class," *The Democratic Strategist*, July 9, 2019, https://thedemocraticstrategist.org/2019/07 /teixeira-the-diverse-white-working-class/.

INDEX

DAVID ROEDIGER teaches in American studies, history, and African and African American Studies at the University of Kansas. His recent books include *How Race Survived United States History* and *Class, Race, and Marxism.*

ABOUT THE HAYMARKET BOOKS

Haymarket Books is a radical, independent, nonprofit book publisher based in Chicago.

Our mission is to publish books that contribute to struggles for social and economic justice. We strive to make our books a vibrant and organic part of social movements and the education and development of a critical, engaged, international left.

We take inspiration and courage from our namesakes, the Haymarket martyrs, who gave their lives fighting for a better world. Their 1886 struggle for the eight-hour day—which gave us May Day, the international workers' holiday—reminds workers around the world that ordinary people can organize and struggle for their own liberation. These struggles continue today across the globe—struggles against oppression, exploitation, poverty, and war.

Since our founding in 2001, Haymarket Books has published more than five hundred titles. Radically independent, we seek to drive a wedge into the risk-averse world of corporate book publishing. Our authors include Noam Chomsky, Arundhati Roy, Rebecca Solnit, Angela Y. Davis, Howard Zinn, Amy Goodman, Wallace Shawn, Mike Davis, Winona LaDuke, Ilan Pappé, Richard Wolff, Dave Zirin, Keeanga-Yamahtta Taylor, Nick Turse, Dahr Jamail, David Barsamian, Elizabeth Laird, Amira Hass, Mark Steel, Avi Lewis, Naomi Klein, and Neil Davidson. We are also the trade publishers of the acclaimed Historical Materialism Book Series and of Dispatch Books.